Theory of Social Choice on Networks

T0305744

Classical social choice theory relies heavily on the assumption that all individuals have fixed preference orderings. This highly original book presents a new theory of social preferences that explicitly accounts for important social phenomena such as coordination, compromise, negotiation, and altruism. Drawing on network theory, it extends classical social choice theory by constructing a framework that allows for dynamic preferences that are modulated by the situation-dependent social influence that they exert on each other. In this way the book shows how members of a social network may modulate their preferences to account for social context. This important expansion of social choice theory will be of interest to readers in a wide variety of disciplines, including economists and political scientists concerned with choice theory as well computer scientists and engineers working on network theory.

WYNN C. STIRLING is Professor of Electrical and Computer Engineering, as well as Dean of Graduate Studies at Brigham Young University. He is the author of *Satisficing Games and Decision Making* (Cambridge University Press, 2003) and *Theory of Conditional Games* (Cambridge University Press, 2012). He is also the co-author of *Mathematical Methods and Algorithms for Signal Processing* (2000) with Todd Moon.

Theory of Social Choice on Networks

Preference, Aggregation, and Coordination

WYNN C. STIRLING
Brigham Young University, Utah

CAMBRIDGE
UNIVERSITY PRESS

CAMBRIDGE
UNIVERSITY PRESS

University Printing House, Cambridge CB2 8BS, United Kingdom

Cambridge University Press is part of the University of Cambridge.

It furthers the University's mission by disseminating knowledge in the pursuit of education, learning, and research at the highest international levels of excellence.

www.cambridge.org
Information on this title: www.cambridge.org/9781107165168

First published 2016

A catalogue record for this publication is available from the British Library.

Library of Congress Cataloging-in-Publication Data
Names: Stirling, Wynn C., author.
Title: Theory of social choice on networks : preference, aggregation, and coordination / Wynn C. Stirling.
Description: Cambridge, United Kingdom : Cambridge University Press, 2016. | Includes bibliographical references and index.
Identifiers: LCCN 2016012075 | ISBN 9781107165168 (Hardback)
Subjects: LCSH: Social choice–Mathematical models. | System theory–Social aspects–Mathematical models. | System analysis–Mathematical models. | BISAC: BUSINESS & ECONOMICS / Economics / Microeconomics.
Classification: LCC HB846.8 .S75 2016 | DDC 003/.72–dc23
LC record available at https://lccn.loc.gov/2016012075

ISBN 978-1-107-16516-8 Hardback

To my eternal companion Patti
who, for me, is the epitome of socialis,
Latin for "companionship."

Contents

List of Figures		*page* x
List of Tables		xii
Preface and Acknowledgments		xv
Introduction		xix
1	Preference	1
	1.1 Categorical Preferences	5
	1.2 Reactive vis-à-vis Responsive Models	10
	1.3 Influence Networks	17
	1.3.1 Conditional Preferences	17
	1.3.2 Social Models	24
	1.4 Related Research	29
	1.5 Summary	31
2	Aggregation	32
	2.1 Classical Aggregation	33
	2.2 Coordinated Aggregation	37
	2.3 Social Coherence	39
	2.3.1 Democratic Social Choice	40
	2.3.2 An Order Isomorphism	44
	2.3.3 Operational Democracy	45
	2.4 Epistemology vis-à-vis Praxeology	51
	2.5 Coherent Aggregation	57
	2.5.1 Bayesian Networks	58
	2.5.2 The Aggregation Theorem	59
	2.6 Solution Concepts	62
	2.7 Reframing	69
	2.8 Summary	71

3   Deliberation   74
    3.1   Dynamic Influence Models   75
    3.2   Closed-Loop Collaboration   82
    3.3   Non-Simple Cycles   89
          3.3.1   Graphs with Sub-Cycles   89
          3.3.2   Embedded Cycles   91
    3.4   Summary   95

4   Coordination   96
    4.1   Coordination Concepts   96
    4.2   A Mathematical Characterization of Coordination   98
          4.2.1   Entropy   102
          4.2.2   Mutual Information   106
    4.3   Coordinatability for Networks   108
    4.4   Summary   113

5   Randomization   115
    5.1   Social Choice with Stochastic Agents   116
    5.2   Social Choice with Randomized Preferences   122
          5.2.1   Expected Utility   123
          5.2.2   Expected Utility on Networks   124
    5.3   Summary   131

6   Satisficing   133
    6.1   Solution Concepts   133
    6.2   A Change in Perspective   137
          6.2.1   Error Avoidance   138
          6.2.2   Failure Avoidance   142
    6.3   The Neo-Satisficing Model   145
          6.3.1   Single-Agent Satisficing   145
          6.3.2   Multiple Selves   148
          6.3.3   Satisficing Social Choice   151
    6.4   Satisficing Coordinatability   156
    6.5   Summary   157

Appendix A   Dutch Book Theorem   158
Appendix B   Bayesian Networks   163
Appendix C   Probability Concepts   169

Appendix D   Markov Convergence Theorem   174
Appendix E   Entropy and Mutual Information   178

Bibliography   186
List of Authors   196

Index   199

Figures

1.1   The Three Stooges Network with Ordinal Linkages.   *page* 22
1.2   The Three Stooges Tree Diagram.   25
2.1   The Three-Stooges Network with Utility Linkages.   63
2.2   An Alternate Framing of the Three-Stooges
      Network with Mo Taking the Lead.   70
2.3   An Alternate Framing of the Three-Stooges
      Network with Curly Taking the Lead.   71
3.1   The Three Stooges Dinner Party with Cyclic Preferences.   75
3.2   The Three Stooges dinner party viewed as a
      dynamic network.   76
3.3   A Simple k-Cycle.   77
3.4   An Equivalent Dynamic Network.   77
3.5   A k-Cycle Expressed in Terms of Transition Linkages.   79
3.6   A Converged k-Cycle.   82
3.7   Influence Cycles for Meeting Scheduling Example.   85
3.8   A Four-Agent Directed Cyclic Graph with a Sub-Cycle.   90
3.9   A Directed Graph with an Embedded Root Cycle.   92
3.10 The Steady-State Equivalent Graph.   92
3.11 A Non-Root Cyclic Graph.   93
3.12 The Equivalent Steady-State Graph with Parent.   94
3.13 A Graph with an Embedded 4-Cycle.   94
3.14 A Steady-State Embedded 4-Cycle Graph.   95
4.1   A Communications Channel.   100
4.2   The Conditional Probability Model for a Binary
      Transmission Channel.   100
4.3   A Two-Agent Network.   102
4.4   The Conditional Utility Model for a Two Agent,
      Two Alternative Coordination Scenario.   102
4.5   The Range of the Subordination Function.   103
4.6   The Entropy Function for $N = 2$.   104

4.7 Mutual Information for the Three Stooges for
   $\alpha = \beta = \gamma \in (0, 1/2)$. 109
4.8 The Coordination Index for the Three Stooges for
   $\alpha = \beta = \gamma \in (0, 1/2)$. 113
5.1 Transitions between Stochastic and Deterministic
   Individuals. 116
5.2 A Stochastic Network. 119
5.3 The Three Stooges Network with Stochastic Agents. 121
5.4 *Ex post* Expected Utilities for the Randomized
   Three Stooges Dinner Party 131
6.1 Dispositional Regions: G = Gratification,
   A = Ambivalence, D = Dubiety, R = Repulsion 150
6.2 A Two-Agent, Four-Atom Network. 151
6.3 The Satisficing Model for the Three Stooges. 156
A.1 Geometrical Illustration of Obtuse θ. 159
A.2 Convex Hull of Belief Vectors that Satisfy the
   Probability Axioms. 161
A.3 Convex Hull with Beliefs that Conform to
   Probability Axioms. 162
B.1 Vertex Connections for Bayesian Networks 164

Tables

1.1 The Number of Stooges Whose Preferences
   are Honored.   *page* 26
2.1 Coordination Function for the Three Stooges
   Dinner Party.   65
2.2 The Coordination Function for Edwin the Egoist.   67
2.3 The Coordination Function for Edwin the Altruist.   68
3.1 The Condorcet Cyclic Preference Paradox.   85
5.1 Maximum Expected Coordination Function for
   Three Stooges.   131
6.1 Optimization vis à vis Satisficing.   143

The only mental tool by means of which a very finite piece of reasoning can cover a myriad cases is called "abstraction" ... The purpose of abstraction is *not* to be vague, but to create a new semantic level in which one can be absolutely precise.

— Edsger Dijkstra
The Humble Programmer, ACM Turing Lecture, 1972

At root, mathematics is the name we give to the collection of all possible patterns and interrelationships ... The essence of mathematics lies in the relationships between quantities and qualities.

— John D. Barrow
Impossibility (Oxford University Press, 1998)

Preface and Acknowledgments

Network theory provides a powerful and expressive framework for the analysis and synthesis of collectives whose members exert social influence on each other. When such a collective is engaged in a social choice, all social relationships that could influence the decision must be taken into consideration. This book advances social choice theory by introducing extended concepts of preference, aggregation, deliberation, and coordination that enable the group to incorporate social influence relationships into a comprehensive social model from which a coordinated social choice can be deduced.

Historically, social choice theory has focused mainly on the study of human behavior and has principally fallen under the purview of the social sciences. Increasingly, however, computer science has applied social choice theory to the design and synthesis of artificial societies such as multiagent systems and networks. A principle motivation for this book is to present a view of the theory that is applicable to both cultures.

Although both the social science and computer science disciplines rely on abstract mathematical models, they use them differently. Social science uses social models primarily as *analysis* tools to understand, predict, explain, or recommend behavior for human society. Such models may provide useful insights regarding social behavior, but they are not causal – they do not dictate behavior. They are idealized approximations whose validity hinges on assumptions regarding human social behavior. Computer science and engineering, however, use social models as *synthesis* tools to design and construct artificial social systems populated by autonomous agents who are designed to function in ways that are compatible with human behavior. In this sense, the models are causal, since they generate the behavior of the members of the society as they interact.

The difference between analysis and synthesis is that with analysis, models are used to reduce reality *to* an abstraction, while synthesis uses models to create a reality *from* an abstraction. The difference between these two applications is important. With analysis, psychological or sociological attributes such as cooperation and altruism, or even such overtly antisocial attributes as conflict and avarice, can be ascribed to individuals as a function of the solution concept, even if such attributes are not formally part of the mathematical model. But when synthesizing an artificial society, such attributes must be explicitly incorporated into the mathematical model or they will not exist.

This book fits at the intersection of social science and computer science. It provides an interface between game theory, social choice theory, and welfare economics on the one hand, and artificial intelligence, multiagent systems, and distributed control theory on the other. It advances social choice theory for both analysis and synthesis applications. It is intended to reach an interdisciplinary audience comprising academics, practitioners, and students of general decision theory from the social science, management science, control engineering, computer science, and biological science disciplines. They will find the material covered in this book to be quite different from the standard treatments of social choice theory, but with the hope of fostering renewed interest in the fundamental assumptions that underlie the theory and its applicability to complex social networks. In addition, since this book touches on such philosophical issues as epistemology and rationality, it should be of interest to philosophers and other students of rational choice theory.

This work is truly an interdisciplinary study; it is a merging of concepts from social science, engineering/computer science, and philosophy. As is the case with many interdisciplinary efforts, it asks readers from all disciplines to tolerate the sometimes awkward attempts to bridge the gap between them. In particular, I ask for the forbearance of social scientists who may consider the treatment of traditional social choice theory as limited. My intent is *not* to criticize a theory that has proven to be of great value. Rather, it is to add to the overall discussion – to supplement, not supplant. Thus, I apologize in advance for any inaccurate representations of social choice theory.

One may indeed wonder how a person trained in electrical engineering with a specialization in optimal control theory would develop an interest in social choice theory. In fact, this book is in many ways the unintended consequence of a rather unconventional intellectual journey. It began with an engineering question: What are reasonable principles that would govern the design of a collective of autonomous distributed agents who are designed to behave in accord with human notions of rational behavior? The conventional notions of optimization theory do not easily extend to distributed systems, and constrained optimization solutions, such as Nash equilibria, place the accent on defensive behavior and do not foster cooperation (e.g., the Prisoner's Dilemma and other mixed-motive scenarios). Of course, there are many ways to generalize the notion of optimization, such as seeking Pareto efficient solutions to multi-attribute decision problems, but at the end of the day, such approaches rely on some notion of maximization, which is an intrinsically individualized concept. The hypothesis governing the development in this book, however, is that when dealing with multiagent decision making in contexts where individuals exert social influence on each other, it is often more relevant to evaluate behavior according to concepts that are intrinsically social. In that regard, a fundamental attribute of such a collective is its ability to coordinate. Etymologically, coordination comes from the Latin *co* (together) + *ordinare* (to regulate). The Oxford English Dictionary defines *to coordinate* as

to place or arrange (things) in proper position relative to each other and to the system of which they form parts; to bring into proper combined order as parts of a whole

(Murray et al., 1991). Thus, from a group perspective, the ability of a collective to arrange itself according to some systematic notion of group-level behavior is a more relevant concept than for each individual to pursue a solution that is best for the self according to a measure of individual material benefit, but may not be good for the group or even for the self when viewed from a social perspective.

Placing emphasis on coordination, rather than focusing exclusively on optimization, requires more than a change in perspective. It requires an expanded concept of individually rational behavior and an enhanced mechanism by which individuals may express their preferences in terms of both material and social interests. The pursuit of these goals led to my book *Theory of Conditional Games* (Stirling, 2012). This present work extends that approach to social choice problems where explicit social influence exists among the members of the collective, and where social behavior is characterized in terms of systematic group-level behavior that emerges as a result of shared interests.

Many colleagues have contributed to the ideas contained in this work. Of particular note are three of my former graduate students – Darryl Morrell, Michael Goodrich, and Matthew Nokleby – whose creativity and enthusiasm have sustained me many times, and whose ideas are integral to the development of this theory. I have also greatly benefited from my collaborations with Richard Frost, Harold Miller, Todd Moon, Dennis Packard, Teppo Felin, and Luca Tummolini. The research environment and support offered by Brigham Young University and, in particular, by my colleagues in the Electrical and Computer Engineering Department who have graciously tolerated my unorthodox research agenda, are greatly appreciated. My greatest debt, however is to my wife Patti, whose love has sustained and nourished me for nearly five decades. Her special insights and wisdom contribute an intangible, but nevertheless essential, element to this enterprise.

Introduction

If we want to start new things rather than trying to elaborate and improve
old ones, then we cannot escape reflecting on our basic conceptions.

— Hans Primas
Chemistry, Quantum Mechanics, and Reductionism
(Springer-Verlag, 1981)

A social choice arises when a collective of autonomous individuals
must choose one and only one element from a set of distinct and
mutually exclusive alternatives. The most widely established way
to frame this issue is to assume that each individual comes to the
social engagement with a fixed linear preference ordering over the
set of alternatives that accounts for all issues deemed to be relevant
to the individual's welfare. Given this profile of *ex ante* preference
orderings, the social choice problem reduces, essentially, to defining
an appropriate aggregation mechanism that produces a rational social
choice.

A social influence network comprises a collective whose members
are able to influence each other through some direct means of
communication or control. When faced with a social choice, the
members of such a network may each have preferences over the
set of alternatives in terms of individual welfare, but they are also
subject to the social influence that others exert on them. As the
individuals interact, this influence propagates through the collective,
creating a complex social structure as the end result of a deliberative
process by which individuals incorporate the influence of others into
their own preferences. In such an environment, a set of *ex ante*
preference orderings expressed in terms of individual welfare is not
a complete manifestation of the social structure and may even obscure
the true nature of the society. This is the nub of the issue. A true
characterization of the society requires a comprehensive social model
defined in terms of social influence relationships as well as individual

welfare, from which a coordinated social choice that incorporates all of the social influence can be deduced.

This book undertakes the task of developing such a model. Unlike many treatments of social choice theory, however, the point of departure is not Arrow's impossibility theorem. Arrow's fundamental hypothesis is that all members of a society come to a social engagement with fully formed preference orderings from which all issues regarding aggregation and the existence of social welfare functions and social choice functions stem. The approach taken by this work, however, is to move upstream to get closer to the headwaters of the way preferences are formed when individuals are subjected to social influence. The focus is on the structure of the social linkages between individuals, that is, on the mechanisms by which influence is transmitted and incorporated, rather than on psychological or sociological motivations for behavior. The distinctive features of this approach are as follows.

- Networks are expressed as directed graphs whose vertices are individuals and whose edges constitute the medium by which social influence is propagated between individuals.
- The individual preference framework is extended to enable members of the network to modulate their preferences in response to the social influence that others exert on them.
- The concept of aggregation is expanded to generate a comprehensive social model that provides a compete characterization of the complex social structure that emerges as influence propagates through the network and social relationships are formed. A coordinated social choice that takes full account of all social relationships can then be deduced from the social model.
- A social deliberation process is developed that enables dialogue among the members of the network in order to pursue a compromise social choice.
- A formal mathematical theory is established to quantify the intrinsic ability of a network to produce coordinated behavior.
- The model is extended to incorporate stochastic agents into a network and to accommodate social choice scenarios where individuals possess randomized preferences.
- The concept of neo-satisficing is applied to social choice theory in order to provide a flexible framework within which groups can develop meaningful negotiation protocols.

All of these features are entirely consistent with conventional social choice theory, which becomes a special case of this more general approach.

Chapter Synopses

Preference Chapter 1 extends the notion of individually rational behavior whereby the members of an influence network expand their interests beyond their own narrowly construed individual welfare in order to incorporate the influence of others into their own rationality. Such a network is expressed as a graph whose vertices are the individuals and whose edges transmit the social influence (using common graph-theoretic terminology) from parent to child. Influence is conveyed as the antecedent of a hypothetical proposition regarding the preferences of the parents, and the consequent is the resulting *conditional preference ordering* for the child given the hypothesized preferences, termed *conjectures*, for the parents. These hypothetical propositions thus serve as the mechanism by which individuals modulate their preferences in response to the social influence that is exerted on them.

Aggregation The propagation of social influence throughout a network raises the possibility that some form of systematic behavior may emerge as a result of nascent social relationships that are thus formed. To the extent that the interests of the individuals are shared through the social linkages, the collective may possess an ability to coordinate in the sense that individual behaviors generate some form of rational behavior for the group. Chapter 2 develops a generalized concept of aggregation that combines the conditional preferences to create a social model that characterizes such emergent behavior. Key features of this model are that a) it is endogenous, in the sense that it is a function of, and only of, the conditional preferences; b) it is comprehensive, in that it captures all of the social relationships that emerge as the individuals interact; and c) it is socially coherent in the sense that no individual can either unilaterally subvert coordinated behavior or is the victim of categorical subjugation. By appealing to the Dutch book theorem and Bayesian network theory, it is established that these conditions can be met if, and only if, the conditional preferences are combined according to the syntax of probability theory.

Deliberation The presence of social influence, coupled with the ability of individuals to modulate their preferences in response, renders it possible for individuals to engage in dialogue. This ability addresses one of the criticisms leveled against social choice theory by advocates of deliberative democracy, who argue that constraining individuals to fixed preferences prohibits any form of deliberation. Chapter 3 extends the basic model structure developed in Chapter 2 to account for influence cycles, which enables individuals to engage in back-and-forth discussions and thereby modify their preferences. The presence of influence cycles, however, introduces the possibility of unstable behavior, where individual preferences continually oscillate. This chapter establishes necessary and sufficient conditions to ensure that cyclic conditional preferences converge to stable preferences. The key mathematical basis for this extension is the Markov convergence theorem.

Coordination The presence of social influence generates an ability for the network to coordinate its behavior *as a function of the social structure*. Chapter 4 introduces a mathematically precise concept of coordination that arises due to the social influence relationships that exist among the members of the network. The key theoretical result, based on Shannon information theory, is the development of a coordinatability index that provides a measure of the intrinsic ability of the network to coordinate as a result of social influence.

Randomization Chapter 5 deals with social choice in the presence of uncertainty. Two manifestations of stochastic social choice are developed. One involves the incorporation of stochastic agents into the network as fully integrated members of the society, and the other involves situations where the agents employ mixed strategies and generate the expected utility of the social choice.

Satisficing Chapter 6 presents a reformulation of social choice in terms of neo-satisficing theory as originally developed in Stirling (2003). Classical concepts of decision making, including social choice theory, are developed according to a concept of rational behavior based on inter-alternative preference comparisons, which are designed to identify optimal solutions. Optimization, however, is an intrinsically individual-based concept. For members of a group to comply with this form of rational behavior, they must seek a constrained optimal solution (e.g., a Nash equilibrium). The accent falls on defensive behavior, where others are viewed more as constraints than as partners. Neo-satisficing, however, employs a concept of rational behavior based on intra-alternative comparisons, which is designed to identify solutions that are "good enough." This more flexible concept of rational behavior easily accommodates the design of negotiation protocols that lead to compromise solutions (what is best for me may not be best for you, but there may be a compromise that is good enough for both of us).

Appendices Since this book employs several mathematical concepts that are not normally encountered in conventional treatments of social choice theory, several appendices has been included that provide additional detail and proofs in order to make this book as self-contained as possible. Appendix A provides a proof of the Dutch book theorem; Appendix B establishes important features of Bayesian networks; Appendix C summarizes key concepts of measure theory and probability theory; Appendix D provides a proof of the Markov convergence theorem; and Appendix E summarizes key features of Shannon information theory.

1 | *Preference*

This is called practice, but remember to first set forth the theory.

— Leonardo da Vinci
Codex Madrid I

Ever since Galileo rolled balls down an inclined plane and realized that he could use mathematics to describe that motion, mathematical models have been central to the understanding of natural phenomena – physical, biological, and social.[1] Such models are abstract representations of real phenomena that help us understand how, but not necessarily why, the phenomena occur. Social science uses mathematical models as mechanisms for the study of selected features of human social behavior. A complex social problem is defined and factors that are deemed to be relevant are encoded into mathematical expressions, while those factors considered to be irrelevant are ignored. Such models can be used to conduct systematic investigations, test theories, simulate behavior, and evaluate performance. They can also be used to design and synthesize artificial social systems that are intended to function in ways that are compatible with human social behavior.

Since the days of Condorcet, the problem of how a collective of autonomous individuals should choose from a set of distinct and mutually exclusive alternatives has been subjected to intense mathematical modeling. There are two basic ways to address this question. Either the rationale for making the choice is a direct attribute of the collective viewed as single entity, or it is derived from the desires of the individuals by some process of aggregation. To comply with democratic principles, social choice theory has adopted the latter approach, and focuses first on the individual.

---

[1] "The great book of nature is written in the mathematical language, ... without whose help it is impossible to comprehend a single word of it" (Galilei, 1623, sect. 6).

The classical way to construct a social choice model is to make only minimal assumptions about the behavior of the individuals and then investigate what can be deduced about the behavior of the collective. The behavioral assumption generally used to define a social choice model is the doctrine of individual rationality: The members of a collective are primarily (some might argue exclusively) motivated by self-interest. Philosophers may argue about the veracity of such a claim; nevertheless, individual rationality continues to be at the core of much of decision theory. Tversky and Kahneman explain why individual rationality is so dominant.

The assumption of [individual] rationality has a favored position in economics. It is accorded all of the methodological privileges of a self-evident truth, a reasonable idealization, a tautology, and a null hypothesis. Each of these interpretations either puts the hypothesis of rational action beyond question or places the burden of proof squarely on any alternative analysis of belief and choice. The advantage of the rational model is compounded because no other theory of judgment and decision can ever match it in scope, power, and simplicity.

   Furthermore, the assumption of rationality is protected by a formidable set of defenses in the form of bolstering assumptions that restrict the significance of any observed violation of the model. In particular, it is commonly assumed that substantial violations of the standard model are (i) restricted to insignificant choice problems, (ii) quickly eliminated by learning, or (iii) irrelevant to economics because of the corrective function of market forces (Tversky and Kahenman, 1986, p. 89).

As a general concept, individual rationality may admit several definitions, but when used as a mathematical model, it must be given a precise operational definition in terms of some mathematically expressible concept. The simplest possible concept of self-interested behavior is that an individual prefers more to less, and manifests that preference in the form of comparative evaluations between alternatives.[2] Such binary comparisons are ordinal; they do not require specifications of intensity. They are also relative; there need be no fixed standard of performance against which the alternatives are evaluated.

---

[2] "Among the classical economists, such as Smith and Ricardo, rationality had the limited meaning of preferring more to less" (Arrow, 1986, p. 204).

To ensure that minimal properties of consistency are maintained, the comparison model is usually assumed to be reflexive, antisymmetric, transitive, and complete, that is, it is a *linear ordering*, denoted by the symbol $\succsim$. For any two alternatives a and a', the expression $a \succsim a'$ means that one either strictly prefers a to a' ($a \succ a'$) or is indifferent ($a \sim a'$).[3] This bare bones model is stripped of all irrelevant considerations and contextual issues. It is a model for the most elementary notion of individual rationality.

This book expands beyond the narrow confines of this classical model. It keeps some meat on the bone by not completely removing all context from an individual's preference model. It develops an expanded operational definition of individual rationality that is designed to characterize the behavior of societies where its members are interconnected by explicit social linkages. Such a collective is a *network* if it can be expressed by a graph whose vertices represent the individual members and whose edges represent the connecting linkages. In this study we focus on networks with linkages that enable the individuals to influence each other. A special case of a network is a graph with no edges – a trivial network. Since there are no explicit influence linkages, each individual is confined to consideration of its own welfare as expressed through its linear preference ordering. This egocentric structure severely limits an individual's ability to expand its sphere of interest beyond its own narrowly construed concerns.

Applying social choice theory in a nontrivial network environment suggests the need for a critical examination of the way individual preferences are expressed. Is a linear order the only mathematically precise way to express the concept of individually rational behavior? In other words, does adherence to the doctrine of individual rationality automatically imply that members of a collective care about and (at least ostensibly), only about, their own narrow self-interest without regard for the welfare of others? Or does individual rationality allow space for individuals to incorporate the interests of others into their own interests? And if the latter posit is allowed, how can such an

---

[3] Some social choice theorists deny that transitivity applies to indifference, and therefore focus on strict partial orders. Such distinctions, however, are not central to the topics of this treatment, and will not be pursued.

expanded notion of individual rationality be expressed operationally in an individual's preference model? Once that question is answered, the next one emerges: Can these more complex expressions of individual preference be used to define an operational notion of rational social behavior?

These are the questions that must be considered when applying social choice theory to nontrivial networks. Indeed, it is in this more structured social context that social choice theory has extended beyond the confines of social science, its traditional purview. Social models are increasingly being applied in the computer science and engineering disciplines as a means of designing and synthesizing artificial social systems. (Genesereth et al., 1986; Weiss, 1999; Parsons and Wooldridge, 2002; Russell and Norvig, 2003; Goyal, 2007; Nisan et al., 2007; Shamma, 2007; Vlassis, 2007; Jackson, 2008; Shoham and Leyton-Brown, 2009; Easley and Kleinberg, 2010). Although the social science and computer science and engineering domains are distinct, the models and mathematical techniques they use have much in common. Social science disciplines use models primarily for analysis; that is, to explain, predict, justify, and recommend human behavior. In this context, the models are idealized approximations of reality, but they are not causal. Computer science and engineering disciplines use models for synthesis; that is, to design and construct artificial entities whose behavior is governed by the models. In this context, the models are used to control behavior – they are causal. Put another way, the difference between analysis and synthesis applications is that the former uses models to reduce a reality to an abstraction, while the latter uses them to create a reality from an abstraction. This distinction is important. With analysis, simulated decisions induced by a model can be interpreted as socially motivated without actually endowing the individuals with any specific social attributes or with the ability to act situationally. Social context can then be overlaid on the mathematical model through the solution concept, that is, by the concept of aggregation that is applied. Such expressions of social behavior are exogenous – arising from some source other than the model. With synthesis, however, social attributes must be explicitly incorporated into the model and the agents must possess the ability to respond dynamically to specific social situations. Such expressions of social behavior are endogenous – arising from the model.

1.1 Categorical Preferences

In this field, there are many conflicts and many dilemmas.

— Amartya Sen
Collective Choice and Social Welfare (North-Holland, 1979)

Given an alternative set $\mathcal{A}$ and a collective $\{X_1, \ldots, X_n\}$ of individuals, classical social choice theory is based on the assumption that each X_i possesses a linear ordering over $\mathcal{A}$, denoted $\succsim_i$. A theoretically ideal approach would be to identify a *social welfare function*, an aggregation process by which an arbitrary preference profile $\{\succsim_1, \ldots, \succsim_n\}$ would generate a linear *social order* over $\mathcal{A}$, denoted $\succsim_s$, for the collective. Perhaps the first to recognize the inherent difficulties of such a pursuit was Condorcet (1785) who showed that non-transitivity can arise with social preference orderings, even though individual orderings are transitive. Subsequently, Arrow (1951) showed that such dilemmas are impossible to eliminate without violating a set of arguably desirable and reasonable properties.[4] Without doubt, the most heavily studied issue of social choice theory is how to respond to this conundrum.

As astutely noted by Shubik (1982, p. 11), "A model is defined by its boundaries." A natural way to deal with boundary problems is to minimize the effect that un-modeled phenomena have on the model. One way to do this is simply to eliminate the need for a concept of social rationality and argue that, although it must be conceded that groups indeed do make decisions, ascribing rational behavior to a group is nothing more than an anthropomorphic trap. According to Shubik (1982, p. 124):

It may be meaningful, in a given setting, to say that a group 'chooses' or 'decides' something. It is rather less likely to be meaningful to say that the group 'wants' or 'prefers' something.

---

[4] These properties are *monotonicity*, the property that if the rank of an alternative changes for one individual, then the social rank of that alternative changes in the same direction or remains unchanged; *independence of irrelevant alternatives*, the property that if some alternatives are deleted from $\mathcal{A}$, then the social ranking of the remaining alternatives does not depend on the individual rankings of the deleted alternatives; *unanimity*, the property that if one alternative is ranked higher than another by all individuals, then the social ordering also preserves that ordering; and *non-dictatorship*, the property that the ranking of no single individual unilaterally induces the social ranking.

Elster (1986, p. 3) appeals to the principle of methodological individualism to assert that "there do not exist collective desires or collective beliefs. A family may, after some discussion, decide on a way of spending its income, but the decision is not based on 'its' goals and 'its' beliefs, since there are no such things." Another approach is to argue, as does Arrow (1974, p. 17), that

A truly rational discussion of collective action in general or in specific contexts is necessarily complex, and what is even worse, it is necessarily incomplete and unresolved.

Luce and Raiffa (1957, p. 196) simply concede that adequately characterizing social rationality may be beyond the scope of individual rationality: "it may be too much to ask that any sociology be derived from the single assumption of individual rationality."

As a result of these positions, it may be tempting to conclude that individual rationality and social rationality cannot coexist. But that is not the content of the impossibility theorem, which states only that a particular model of expressing individual preference ordering is not compatible with the same preference ordering model for society. Limitations of the *model*, however, do not imply limitations of the *concept*. There is no obvious logical or intrinsic contradiction between individually rational behavior and socially rational behavior. On the contrary, there is much empirical evidence that they can and do coexist. And if in the *practice* of making social choices the two concepts can be compatible, it would seem to be important also to establish their compatibility in *theory*.

The validity of using the binary relation $\succsim$ to express individual preferences rests on the assumption that each individual's preference ordering is fixed, immutable, and acontextual – it is *categorical*. Furthermore, it is *static* and cannot adapt to a dynamic social environment as the members of the collective interact. All individuals are assumed to come to the decision problem with their preferences already defined *ex ante*, and they are impervious to making any changes for any reason. This is a strong assumption, but it is one that traditional social choice theory makes without apology. As Arrow (1951, p. 17) puts it, "It is assumed that each individual in the community has a definite ordering of all conceivable social states, in terms of their desirability to him. ... It is simply assumed that the individual orders all social states by whatever standards he deems relevant." Friedman (1962, p. 13) even argues that one does not need to know how the preferences are formed to arrive at a solution: "The economist has little to say about the formation of wants; this is the province of the psychologist. The economist's task is to trace the consequences of any given set of wants." Johnson (1998, p. 4) also justifies reliance on this assumption: "In social choice theory, as in the broader field of rational choice, individual goals are typically taken as 'givens,' part of the data provided by a study of a particular situation. This is a practical decision, based in large part on the need to keep research projets manageable." The consequence of this practice, however, is that any history or explanation regarding the origin or justification of individual preferences is considered to be irrelevant to the decision-making process.

Since Arrow's pioneering work, many developments, extensions, and refinements have been introduced to account for social issues such as fairness, justice, welfare, resource allocation, coalition formation, etc. Also, the interdisciplinary field of computational social choice is becoming increasingly important as an interface of social science and computer science. Notwithstanding these developments, the underlying categorical preference ordering mechanism has remained unchanged. It has not, however, remained unchallenged. Sen notably threw down the gauntlet long ago:

A person is given *one* preference ordering, and as and when the need arises this is supposed to reflect his interests, represent his welfare, summarize his idea of what should be done, and describe his actual choices and behavior. Can one preference ordering do all these things? A person thus described may be "rational" in the limited sense of revealing no inconsistencies in his choice behavior, but if he has no use for these distinctions between quite different concepts, he must be a bit of a fool. The *purely* economic man is indeed close to being a social moron. Economic theory has been much preoccupied with this rational fool decked in the glory of his *one* all-purpose ordering. To make room for the different concepts related to his behavior **we need a more elaborate structure** [italic emphasis in original, bold emphasis added] (Sen, 1977, pp. 335–336).

Sober and Wilson add to this concern by arguing that pure selfishness as an explanation of human behavior, and which is the assumption (at least implicitly) upon which reliance on categorical preferences is based, has yet to be conclusively established.

Psychological egoism is hard to disprove, but it also is hard to prove. Even if a purely selfish explanation can be imagined for every act of helping, this doesn't mean that egoism is correct. After all, human behavior also is consistent with the contrary hypothesis—that some of our ultimate goals are altruistic. Psychologists have been working on this problem for decades and philosophers for centuries. The result, we believe, is an impasse—the problem of psychological egoism and altruism remains unsolved (Sober and Wilson, 1998, pp. 2–3).

Regardless of its structure, a preference model is simply an abstract mathematical characterization of social behavior and, as Friedman (1962, p. 13) observes: "The legitimacy of any justification for this abstraction must rest ultimately, in this case as with any other abstraction, on the light that is shed and the power to predict that is yielded by the abstraction." Since the introduction of social choice as a formal theory, much of the modeling light has been focused by the lens of narrow self-interest as expressed with categorical preference orderings. But as is true in optics, the wider the lens, the sharper can be the focus. Expanding the lens of individual rationality beyond myopic self-interest may permit greater focus, or precision, for modeling social behavior.[5] Shubik (1982, p. 1) put it this way: "The usefulness of mathematical methods – game theory or not – depends upon precision in model, and in economics as elsewhere, precise modeling implies a careful and critical selectivity." Arrow further amplified the need for careful and critical selectivity with regard to the appropriateness of relying models that are restricted to narrow self-interest.

Rationality in application is not merely a property of the individual. Its useful and powerful implications derive from the conjunction of individual rationality and other basic concepts of neoclassical theory – equilibrium, competition, and completeness of markets. ... When these assumptions fail, the very concept of rationality becomes threatened, because perceptions of others and, in particular, their rationality become part of one's own rationality (Arrow, 1986, p. 203).

Individually rational behavior does not prohibit an individual from incorporating the interests of others into its own self-interest – in fact, it can require it.

---

[5] An individual's interests are myopic if it does not take into consideration all of the material and social consequences of its choice.

Classical social choice theory is, and has been, a successful tool for the analysis of society. It is settled theory. But being settled makes it a candidate for an observation by Dewey (1938, p. 8, 9): "In scientific inquiry, the criterion of what is taken to be settled, or to be knowledge, is being *so* settled that it is available as a resource in further inquiry [emphasis in original]." A fundamental issue that deserves further inquiry is how to define a preference model structure for an expanded concept of individual rationality that allows the incorporation of the rationality of others as part of one's own rationality. In particular, an expanded model should enable the accommodation of such social concepts as coordination, cooperation, compromise, and altruism. Accounting for such concepts, however, requires the individual to define its preferences according to specific situations. The preference relations must be context dependent, allowing the individual to change its preference ordering in response to given situations. Categorical preferences simply do not provide that flexibility. The only way complex social behavior can emerge from the association of a group of individuals is if social relationships among the individuals are explicitly modeled.

Simply put, a categorical preference model is too blunt an instrument to provide the precision necessary to characterize the behavior of individuals in a network. Any new instrument must extend precision in two ways. First, it must provide an explicit mechanism by which influence can be exerted between individuals. Second, it must accommodate an expanded concept of individually rational behavior that extends beyond narrow and myopic self-interest and incorporates the interests of others as part of ones own interest. A model of individually rational behavior in a complex social context must be true to the Latin root for *social*, namely *socialis* (meaning "of companionship" or "of allies"). Companions and allies do not operate in social vacuums; they operate in context.

Arrow's impossibility theorem is simply the mathematical confirmation of a fundamental truth; namely, a group of asocial individuals cannot generate a society with complex attributes. Nevertheless, many approaches have been offered to modify or bypass Arrow's theorem, while retaining the categorical preference model structure. These approaches include restricting the domain, limiting the number of alternatives, relaxing the independence of irrelevant alternatives assumption, and substituting social choice for social

preference. Another approach is to overlay the model with a veneer
of psychological features such as the reputation of being "nice" that
is employed by Axelrod (1984) to describe the behavior of individuals
in the context of repeated play of the Prisoner's Dilemma game. Such
features, however, are not part of the mathematical model; they only
affect the solution concept that is either imposed on the individuals
or is learned as a result of experience or as the end result of social
evolution. Although such approaches may achieve limited success
in an analysis context, there is no way to overlay the model with
psychological features or other assumptions or constraints that are
not part of the model in a synthesis context, where the goal is to
design and construct artificially intelligent decision-making societies
such as multiagent systems and distributed control systems that must
function autonomously.

1.2 Reactive vis-à-vis Responsive Models

Homans (1961) offers three criteria for behavior to qualify as *social*.
First, an individual's actions must elicit some form of reward or
punishment as a result of behavior by another individual. Second,
behavior toward another individual must result in reward or punishment from that individual, not just a third party. Third, the behavior
must be actual behavior, not just a norm of behavior. A natural way
to categorize societies is to order them according to the sophistication
of their social relationships.

Social Framework I – Anarchies: Perhaps the least structured social
framework is an anarchy, comprising individuals who are constrained
by no sense of order or purpose for the society, each is a law unto itself
with no controlling rules or principles to give order. Individuals may
or may not have preferences, and even if they do, their preferences
may or may not govern their behavior.

Social Framework II – Collectives: Evaluating alternatives by means
of categorical preference orderings is consistent with a particular
economic theory termed the *price system* (Hayek, 1945; Friedman,
1962). Prices constitute the information that guides both users and
providers of products as they make decisions regarding the various
transactions they undertake. Prices are attached to all products, which
can be bought and sold, thereby creating an efficient and standardized

way of functioning. One of the consequences of expressing material benefit by means of a common medium of exchange is that it frees individuals to focus their attention on, and only on, their own interests, since the social effects of their behavior are automatically regulated by the price system. If an individual changes the price of some product in the interest of its own welfare, that signal will propagate through the society and others will respond by adjusting their demand for the product in the interest of their individual welfare. This group-level automatic regulation mechanism makes it possible for considerations of rational behavior to be restricted to individual interests, and thus feeds naturally into the view that individuals are justified in uninhibitedly pursuing their selfish interests. As Arrow (1974, p. 21) observes, "It makes a virtue out of selfishness."

The inhabitants of a society that is governed by the price system are of the species *homo economicus*. It is the realm wherein conventional game theory and social choice theory are designed to operate. The critical feature of such an environment is that individuals behave *reactively*. In the game-theoretic context, they make their choices as a reaction to the possible choices others can make, and in a social choice environment, they simply react to their own pre-conceived preferences. Comparisons are made with categorical preference orderings and behavior is governed by self-interest.

Definition 1.1 A *collective social framework* comprises a set of individuals $\{X_1, \ldots, X_n\}$, a finite set of alternatives $\mathcal{A}$ and a preference profile $\{\succsim_1, \ldots, \succsim_n\}$ over $\mathcal{A}$. □

Aggregation in a collective framework requires combining individual preference orderings to form a social choice. Goodin (1986, pp. 86–87) argues, however, that aggregation is more complex than is generally assumed. "Formal models of collective choice tend to represent it as some mechanical process of aggregating individual preferences. This badly understates the true complexity of the process. Whereas these models usually take preferences as given, ... the social decision machinery changes them in the process of aggregating them." Unfortunately, if the preference orderings are taken as givens, then there is no way to change them in the process of aggregation. This reveals a fundamental limitation of classical aggregation approaches. Shubik further accentuates this issue and implies that it is time to move past the classical approaches.

Economic man, operations research man and the game theory player were all gross simplifications. They were invented for conceptual simplicity and computational convenience in models loaded with implicit or explicit assumptions of symmetry, continuity, and fungibility in order to allow us (especially in a pre-computer world) to utilize the methods of calculus and analysis. Reality was placed on a bed of Procrustes to enable us to utilize the mathematical techniques available (Shubik, 2001, p. 4).

Social Framework III – Networks: Few would dispute that the price system framework is a valuable characterization of behavior that fits economic scenarios where markets clear and competition dominates behavior. But it is also subject to important constraints. It assumes that all notions of value can be expressed through a common medium of exchange. While this claim may be valid with regard to material benefit, extending it to social benefit, psychological benefit, and moral benefit is problematic. As Arrow (1974, p. 22) observes, "it [the price system] cannot be made the complete arbiter of social life."

Without an explicit linking mechanism between individuals to express social relationships, the only way to introduce social influence into the framework is to augment the categorical preferences with parameters that account for social features such as fairness, reciprocity, altruism, and so forth. Such an approach is designed to simulate social concerns by fostering behavior consistent with having social relationships, but not actually having them. An example of this approach is provided by Fehr and Schmidt:

We model fairness as self-centered inequity aversion. Inequity aversion means that people resist inequitable outcomes; i.e., they are willing to give up some material payoff to move in the direction of more equitable outcomes. Inequity aversion is self-centered if people do not care per se about inequity that exists among other people but are only interested in the fairness of their own material payoff relative to the payoff of others (Fehr and Schmidt, 1999, p. 819).

According to this view, possessing a notion of fairness does not imply that the individual has any real concern for the welfare of others. The individual acts in a seemingly unselfish manner simply because it dislikes inequitable outcomes – the effect on others is irrelevant. However, this logic results in a paradox: such an individual has purely selfish reasons for acting unselfishly. Although perhaps necessary to retain allegiance to a strict interpretation of individual rationality, simply relabeling fairness as "self-centered inequity aversion" is little more than a Procrustean-motivated semantic manoeuver designed to recast the inherently social attribute of fairness as an asocial individual attribute. This approach only simulates equitable treatment of others; it does not express genuine situation-dependent concern for others. At the end of the day it merely replaces one static (i.e., situation invariant) preference ordering with another static ordering.

Once notions such as fairness are recognized as legitimate social attributes, it is both natural and appropriate to enlarge the concept of individual rationality to incorporate the interests of others into one's own rational behavior. Doing so, however, requires a preference ordering structure that can account for the social, as well as the material, consequences of the choices. To meet this demand it will be necessary to create, as suggested by Sen (1977), a "more elaborate structure" for preference specification that is capable of dealing with social relationships dynamically; that is, with situation-dependent social relationships.

In addition to accommodating material benefit, this expanded structure must allow individuals to express *social benefit*; that is, benefit derived from acting in accord with social attributes such as fairness, reciprocity, loyalty, cooperation, and altruism, or even with such overtly antisocial attributes as conflict, vindictiveness, revenge, and betrayal. A social benefit, however, cannot be expressed as a material payoff or other tangible or easily quantifiable reard. Rather, it is an intention to behave in ways that depend on context-dependent situations – in other words, to act *responsively*. This behavior is consistent with Arrow's (1986) recognition that the "perceptions of others and, in particular, their rationality become part of one's own rationality."

Once the preferences of an individual are influenceable by the preferences of others, that individual is endowed with an expanded notion of self-interest that includes social as well as material benefit. This expansion thus moves beyond the assumptions imposed by the price system framework and renders inadequate the conventional notions of narrowly construed self-interest and categorical preference orderings. An individual with such an expanded view of individual welfare will have an appreciation for social benefit as well as material benefit to the extent that it is potentially willing to exchange the latter for the former in some situations. However, if an individual possesses such aspirations, that propensity must be explicitly incorporated into its preference model, as emphasized by Elster.

Once we have constructed a normative theory of rational choice, we may go on to employ it for explanatory purposes. We may ask, that is, whether a given action was performed *because* it was rational. To show that it was, it is not sufficient to show that the action was rational, since people are sometimes lead by accident or coincidence to do what is in fact best for them. We must show, in addition, that the action arose in the proper way, through a proper kind of connection to desires, beliefs, and evidence (Elster, 1986, p. 2, emphasis in original).

Sen offers two concepts of connections that would motivate individuals to account for social, as well as material benefit. Drawing on terminology introduced by Edgeworth (1881), he introduces the concepts of *commitment* and *sympathy*. "One way of defining a commitment is in terms of a person choosing an act that he believes will yield a lower level of personal welfare to him than an alternative that is also available to him" (Sen, 1977, p. 327). Sympathy obtains when "the concern for others directly affects one's own welfare" (Sen, 1977, pp. 326). A preference is based on a commitment if the individual exerts a constraint on itself without any anticipation of benefit to itself. A commitment could be for social reasons such as altruism or malevolence, or for other social reasons such as adopting the self-imposed constraint of inequity aversion. A preference is based on sympathy if the individual's welfare is affected by the welfare of others. Sympathy can also be either positive or negative (in which case Sen suggests that "antipathy" could be used, but instead he chooses to expand the meaning of sympathy to include negative influence relationships.)

To illustrate Sen's concepts, suppose Peter is given a cake (his favorite desert) and may share half of it with Paul or keep it all for himself. Once Peter determines his preference ordering, however, he cannot change it because it is categorical. Consider the following three scenarios. Let S denote sharing, and N denote not sharing.

Selfishness: $N \succ S$. Peter prefers not to share the cake because he wants only to maximize his own happiness and he does not give a fig about Paul's welfare.

Commitment: $S \succ N$. Peter prefers to share the cake because he is committed to avoiding inequity, but he does not really give a fig about Paul's welfare.

Sympathy: $S \succ N$. Peter prefers to share the cake because it pleases him to make Paul happy.

Based purely on selfishness, the categorical ordering $N \succ S$ is consistent with narrow self-interest, where Peter seeks to, and only to, maximize his own welfare without regard to the effect doing so has on Paul. Consequently, no influence exists between the two individuals, resulting in the trivial network

$$\boxed{\text{Paul}} \qquad \boxed{\text{Peter}} \, . \qquad\qquad (1.1)$$

But if either commitment or sympathy were to influence Peter, then he would be inclined to reverse his ordering, yielding $S \succ N$. However, unless the reason for this reversal were established by the model to be consistent with his desires and beliefs, then the only explanation for such a reversal is that Peter's behavior would be irrational. He would simply be making a mistake.

Although the commitment and sympathy scenarios yield the same result, there is a significant social difference between them. With the commitment scenario, coming into the possession of a cake while Paul is in the neighborhood simply triggers Peter's inequity aversion reflex, and he reacts by choosing to share. But Peter has a potential problem. His choice to share because of his self-imposed constraint pretends that there is no social context. Peter can get away with that illusion if Paul's response does not contradict Peter's implicit assumption that choosing to share means that sharing is actually accomplished. But if Paul refuses the offer, then Peter is left in an untenable situation – he cannot share the cake and he cannot keep it all for himself without violating his commitment to inequity aversion.

Under the sympathy scenario, coming into the possession of a cake while Paul is in the neighborhood triggers Peter's desire to make Paul happy, and he reacts by choosing to share. Peter's preference to share is based on the assumption that sharing will please Paul, thereby providing Peter that social benefit as well as maintaining some material benefit for himself. This choice is based on Peter's *ex ante* assumption that receiving the gift will make Paul happy. But it also leaves open a potential problem for Peter: If receiving the gift makes Paul so unhappy that he throws it away, then Peter would be denied the anticipated positive social benefit and would have needlessly sacrificed considerable material benefit.

With either the commitment or sympathy scenarios, a categorical ordering does not account for the social context that underlies its creation. All Peter can do is react to the *ex ante* assumed context, and that reaction may be inappropriate if the consequence of the choice does not comport with the premise that motivated the preference ordering. The only way to resolve this issue is to let the context influence the preference ordering. An obvious way to do this is for Peter to possess two preference orderings, one for each of Paul's possible preferences.

Accept: If Paul were to prefer to accept the offer to share, then Peter could respond with $S \succ N$, which would comport with both scenarios. If Peter's preference were based on inequity aversion, then he would fulfill that commitment. If the preference were based on sympathy, then Peter would achieve the desired material and social benefit.

Reject: If Paul were to prefer to reject the offer to share, then Peter's response of $N \succ S$ comports with both scenarios. With the commitment scenario, Paul's preference would absolve Peter of his self-imposed constraint, because he can avoid inequity only if there is an opportunity to act equitably. Since it is given that there is no such opportunity, Peter may prefer not to share without violating his commitment. If Paul were to prefer to reject the offer to share under the sympathy scenario, Peter's willingness to sacrifice some of his own material benefit to make Paul happy would go unrealized. Thus, Peter could prefer to keep the cake all to himself and at the same time enjoy the social benefit of at least honoring Paul's feelings by not contributing to his unhappiness.

Since Paul's preferences can influence Peter's preferences, an influence relationship exists between them that can be expressed graphically as

$$\boxed{Paul} \longrightarrow \boxed{Peter} ,\qquad (1.2)$$

a nontrivial network.

If all members of a collective possess categorical preferences, then all individuals view others as competitors who serve to constrain the own welfare. They behave reactively, and the accent falls on competitive and defensive behavior. But if individuals are able to incorporate the interests of others into expressions of their own interests, they may act responsively, and the accent falls on coordinated and synergistic behavior. To put it another way, the behavior of a reactive individual is passive – it is controlled by the possible actions of others, but a responsive individual takes active control of its behavior by adapting to the interests of others.

The networks represented by (1.1) and (1.2) correspond to two very different environments. The assumption governing (1.1) is that there is no social influence between Peter and Paul and that Peter's preferences are based on narrow self-interest. The assumption governing (1.2), however, is that there is some mechanism for expressing social influence between Peter and Paul and that Paul's preferences exert influence on Peter's preferences.

1.3 Influence Networks

The mind which entrusts itself to the operation of symbols acquires an intellectual tool of boundless power, but its use makes the mind liable to perils the range of which seems also unlimited.

Michael Polanyi
Personal Knowledge (University of Chicago Press, 1958)

1.3.1 Conditional Preferences

In the social choice context, an influence network comprises a collective of individuals, denoted $\{X_1, \ldots, X_n\}$, who are linked together by some means of communication or control that enables them to exert social influence on each other, and who must make a collective decision over a finite set $\mathcal{A} = \{z_1, \ldots, z_N\}$ of alternatives. The process of conveying influence from one individual to another is termed *propagation*. To be clear, propagation is not the *creation* of influence; it is the transmission and reception of influence. It must also be emphasized that influence is neutral. It can be either positive, in the sense of representing cooperative intentions, or it can be negative, in the sense of representing conflictive intentions.

Definition 1.2 The *graph* of a network comprises a set of *vertices* comprising the individuals X_i, $i = 1, \ldots, n$, and a set of *edges*, also termed *linkages*, that serve as the medium by which influence is propagated between individuals. An edge is *directed* (denoted with the arrow symbol "$\to$") if the linkage is unidirectional: $X_j \to X_i$ means that X_j directly influences X_i. A *path* from X_j to X_i is a sequence of directed edges from X_j to X_i, denoted $X_j \mapsto X_i$. A path is a *cycle*, or *closed path*, if $X_j \mapsto X_j$. A graph is said to be a *directed acyclic graph*, or DAG, if all edges are directed and there are no cycles. $\qquad\square$

Definition 1.3 A *conjecture* for X_i, denoted $a_i \in \mathcal{A}$, is an alternative that is hypothetically viewed, either by or in behalf of X_i, as the one that is intended, and is denoted by the expression $X_i \vDash a_i$. The n-fold Cartesian product set $\mathcal{A}^n = \mathcal{A} \times \cdots \times \mathcal{A}$ comprises the set of *conjecture profiles* of the form $\mathbf{a} = (a_1,\ldots,a_n) \in \mathcal{A}^n$, where $X_i \vDash a_i, i = 1,\ldots,n$. $\qquad\square$

[**Notational convention.** The symbol a_i is used to denote the particular element of $\mathcal{A}$ that is associated with X_i as a conjecture. Thus, the expression $a_i \in \mathcal{A}$ refers to the particular $z_k \in \mathcal{A}$ such that $a_i = z_k$, where z_k is the kth element of $\mathcal{A}$.]

Definition 1.4 The *parent* set for X_i, denoted pa $(X_i) = \{X_j : X_j \to X_i\}$, is the subset of individuals that directly influence X_i. If X_i has $p_i > 0$ parents, then pa $(X_i) = \{X_{i_1},\ldots,X_{i_{p_i}}\}$, where $X_{i_k} \to X_i$, $i = 1,\ldots,p_i$. For notational convenience, let pa $(i) = \{i_1,\ldots,i_{p_i}\}$ denote the indices corresponding to the elements of pa (X_i). Also, let $\mathbf{a}_i = \{a_{i_1},\ldots,a_{i_{p_i}} : X_{i_k} \vDash a_{i_k}, k = 1,\ldots,p_i\}$ denote a *conditioning conjecture* for the parents of X_i. The subset of all individuals who are directly influenced by X_i is termed the *child set* of X_i, denoted ch $(X_i) = \{X_j : X_i \to X_j\}$. The *descendants* of X_i, denoted de $(X_i) = \{X_j : X_i \mapsto X_j\}$ is the subset of all individuals that are elements of any path emanating from X_i. $\qquad\square$

Definition 1.5 Given a parent set pa (X_i) and a conditioning conjecture $\mathbf{a}_i$, A *conditional preference ordering* is a linear preference relation over $\mathcal{A}$, denoted $\succsim_{i|\mathrm{pa}(i)}$, such that

$$a_i \succsim_{i|\mathrm{pa}(i)} a_i' \,|\mathbf{a}_i \tag{1.3}$$

means that X_i prefers conjecture a_i to a_i' or is indifferent, given that pa $(X_i) = \{X_{i_1},\ldots,X_{i_{p_i}}\} \vDash \mathbf{a}_i = (a_{i_1},\ldots,a_{i_{p_i}})$. The conditioning symbol "|" separates the conditioned entity on the left from the conditioning entity on the right.[6] If $p_i = 0$, then $\succsim_{i|pa(i)} = \succsim_i$, a categorical preference ordering for X_i. □

It is important to distinguish between the relations $\succsim_i$ and $\succsim_{i|pa(i)}$. The relation "$\cdot \succsim_i \cdot$" is a bivariate comparison that generates a set of ordered pairs $\{(a_i, a_i') \in \mathcal{A} \times \mathcal{A}\}$ for X_i. The relation "$\cdot \succsim_{i|pa(i)} \cdot | \cdot$" is a conditional bivariate comparison that generates a family of sets of conditionally ordered pairs, namely,

$$\{(a_i, a_i') \in \mathcal{A} \times \mathcal{A} : pa(X_i) \vDash a_i, \forall a_i \in \mathcal{A}^{p_i}\}. \tag{1.4}$$

Thus, each conditioning conjecture a_i generates a different conditional ordering for X_i.

A conditional ordering involves a special logical structure, namely, that the ordering is a consequent of a hypothetical proposition whose antecedent is an assertion attributed to the conditioning entity, whereas the categorical ordering involves no such structure. Once the antecedent is given, the conditional ordering relation $\succsim_{i|pa(i)}$ is a linear ordering, and thus is reflexive, antisymmetric, transitive, and complete. However, there is a significant operational difference between $\succsim_i$ and $\succsim_{i|pa(i)}$. The former provides sufficient information for the individual to take action, whereas the latter is used to define situational, or context dependent, relationships, and taking action requires the appropriate context to be actualized.[7] To reiterate, a

---

[6] This notation is similar to the concept of probabilistic conditioning, $P(A|B)$, the probability that A is realized given that B is realized.

[7] The notion of conditional preference used here employs a syntax similar to the well-known concept of state-dependent preferences (cf. Karni and Schmeidler (1981); Karni et al. (1983); Karni (1985); Drèze (1987)), where the decision maker's preferences are modulated by the state of nature. The two notions, however, have different semantics. State dependence yields a preference ordering corresponding to a particular state of nature, where a state, as defined by Arrow (1971, p. 45), is "a description of the world so complete that, if true and known, the consequences of every action would be known." The state of nature is an assumption imposed on the decision maker that constrains the preferences to a particular environment. The concept of conditional preferences used herein, however, deals with an individual's ability to modulate its preferences to account for the varying preferences of other individuals who are participants in the multiagent decision dynamics. Rather than constraining the model to a particular environment, the intent of such preferences is to extend the model to a more complex social environment. Conventional state-dependent preferences are used to account for the presence of uncertainty, while the conditional preferences are used herein to extend beyond narrow self-interest and accommodate a complex social structure.

conjecture is not an action—it is a hypothetical intention. It is the antecedent of a hypothetical proposition of the form "if p then q," meaning that if the antecedent p were actualized, then the consequent q would be actualized. Thus, with the statement "$a_i \succsim_{i|\mathrm{pa}(i)} a_i' \,|\, \mathbf{a}_i$," the antecedent is the statement "$\mathbf{a}_i$ is a conjecture for $\mathrm{pa}(X_i)$," and the consequent is the statement "$a_i \succsim_i a_i'$." If the consequent were to be separated from the antecedent, then it could be erroneously be interpreted as the unconditional statement "X_i prefers a_i to a_i'," which would enable taking action. But when attached to the antecedent, it is simply part of the hypothetical proposition "$a_i \succsim_{i|\mathrm{pa}(i)} a_i' \,|\, \mathbf{a}_i$" which enables action only if the antecedent is actualized.

Definition 1.6 A *conditional preference profile* is a family of conditional preference orderings corresponding to all possible conditioning conjectures of $\{X_1, \ldots, X_n\}$, denoted $\{\mathfrak{P}_1, \ldots, \mathfrak{P}_n\}$, where

$$\mathfrak{P}_i = \{\succsim_{i|\mathrm{pa}(i)} \ \forall \, \mathbf{a}_i \in \mathcal{A}^{p_i}\}, \tag{1.5}$$

with $\mathbf{a}_i = (a_{i_1}, \ldots, a_{i_{p_i}})$, the conditioning conjecture for $\mathrm{pa}(X_i)$. If $\mathrm{pa}(X_i) = \varnothing$, then $\mathfrak{P}_i = \{\succsim_i\}$.   □

Definition 1.7 A *network social framework* comprises a set of individuals $\{X_1, \ldots, X_n\}$, a set of alternatives $\mathcal{A}$, and a conditional preference profile $\{\mathfrak{P}_1, \ldots, \mathfrak{P}_n\}$.   □

Developers of social models have faithfully adhered to Occam's razor and have resisted the introduction of complicating factors that are not deemed essential. When characterizing an influence network, however, it is imperative also to consider what some have termed Einstein's razor: "It can scarcely be denied that the supreme goal of all theory is to make the irreducible basic elements as simple and as few as possible without having to surrender the adequate representation of a single datum of experience" (Einstein, 1934, p. 165).[8] Seemingly, everyone can agree with the first part of this dictum to keep things simple. But it is the latter injunction, not to surrender adequate representation, that is perhaps more difficult to accommodate. The introduction of social influence unavoidably increases the complexity of the society. Research (cf. Castellano et al. (2009); Christakis and

---

[8] This quote has sometimes been reworded into such variants as "Everything should be made as simple as possible, but not simpler."

Fowler (2009)) has established, however, that social networks typically possess topologies such as hierarchical, community, and other sparse influence structures that suggest that low-order connections over small clusters of individuals are the elementary building blocks of many social relationships. In such cases, making individual preference ordering judgments can often be done relatively swiftly and reliably, while making social relationship judgments over the entire product set $\mathcal{A}^n$ could entail much difficulty and hesitancy. The fact is, introducing social influence into a society will inescapably increase complexity. The issue, then, is to ensure that the complexity is no greater than it needs to be to capture the essential relationships. As observed by Palmer (1971, p. 194), "Complexity is no argument against a theoretical approach if the complexity arises not out of the theory itself but out of the material which any theory ought to handle."

Formulating conditional preference orderings takes us beyond Friedman's (1962) assertion that there is a fundamental division of labor between the psychological exercise of defining wants and the economic exercise of formulating a solution. Expressing preferences in a social environment where individuals influence each other moves the process upstream, toward the headwaters of preference origins. Endowing individuals with the social sophistication necessary to include the desires of others into their own individual desires expands the individual's sphere of interest beyond the self while at the same time preserving the essential concept of self-interest. It is no contradiction to allow an individual to expand beyond narrow self-interest regarding material benefit in order to view that benefit in a larger social context. This expansion is a response to the persistent criticism of conventional notions of individual rationality is that "The decision to group together sharply dissimilar motives under the single category of 'calculating self-interest' is said to involve an undesirable *loss of information* about rudimentary psychological and behavioral Processes" (Holmes, 1990, p. 269). To illustrate the application of conditional preferences, we consider two examples.

Example 1.1 The Three Stooges Larry, Curly, and Mo are to go to dinner at either a French (F) restaurant or an Italian (I) restaurant.[9] Larry (L) prefers French to Italian. Curly (C), however, is feeling a bit

---

[9] These charming characters will entertain us throughout this book.

contrary to Larry. He does not know Larry's preferences, but if he did he would take the opposite point of view. He would prefer French if Larry were to prefer Italian, and Italian if Larry were to prefer French. Mo (M), however, is in a very capricious mood. Although he does not know either of his friends's preferences, his convoluted thinking has him with the following preferences. If Both Larry and Curly were to prefer French, he would Prefer Italian, and if both were to prefer Italian, he would prefer French. But if Larry were to prefer French and Curly were to prefer Italian, then Mo would prefer French. However, if Larry were to prefer Italian and Curly were to prefer French, then Mo would prefer Italian.

Clearly, each member of this little society possesses individual preferences. Larry's preferences are categorical, but Curly's and Mo's preferences are more complex and nuanced. Nevertheless, they are individual preferences – they just cannot be adequately characterized by single categorical preference orderings. They are conditional preferences. The conditional conjecture profile for this network is

$$\mathfrak{P}_L = \{F \succ_L I\}$$
$$\mathfrak{P}_C = \{F \succ_{C|L} I \,|I, \; I \succ_{C|L} F \,|F\}$$
$$\mathfrak{P}_M = \{F \succ_{M|LC} I \,|II, \; I \succ_{M|LC} F \,|FF, \; F \succ_{M|LC} I \,|FI, \; I \succ_{M|LC} F \,|IF\}$$

$$(1.6)$$

This network is illustrated in Figure 1.1. The edge $L \to C$ indicates that C's ordinal preferences are conditioned on L's conjecture, and the edges from $L \to M$ and $C \to M$ indicate that M's ordinal preferences are conditioned on the conjectures by both L and C.

Example 1.2 Edwin versus Angelina This scenario is taken from Gibbard (1974), and illustrates how conditional preferences can resolve an otherwise inconsistent situation. Quoting Gibbard,

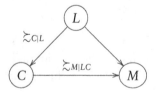

Figure 1.1: The Three Stooges Network with Ordinal Linkages.

Angelina wants to marry Edwin but will settle for the judge, who wants whatever she wants. Edwin wants to remain single, but would rather wed Angelina than see her wed the judge. There are, then, three alternatives:

$\mathbf{w}_E$: Edwin weds Angelina;
$\mathbf{w}_J$: the judge weds Angelina and Edwin remains single;
$\mathbf{w}_O$: both Edwin and Angelina remain single.

Angelina prefers them in order $\mathbf{w}_E\mathbf{w}_J\mathbf{w}_O$; Edwin in order $\mathbf{w}_O\mathbf{w}_E\mathbf{w}_J$.

Gibbard invokes a lengthy discussion concerning how to define an acyclic preference ordering for the group while adhering to the Pareto principle. He introduces the notion of "rights" to account for the fact that, although Angelina's choices can affect Edwin's choices, both of them have rights. Edwin has the right to remain single, and Angelina has the right to wed the judge.

This example motivates the development of theorems to identify social welfare functions that justify the waiving of rights to achieve Pareto efficiency. Gibbard's approach involves making decisions about waiving rights, which could involve considerable processing. His analysis shows that it is to Edwin's advantage to waive his rights, thereby conforming to the Pareto efficient social choice $\mathbf{w}_E \succsim_s \mathbf{w}_O$.

An alternative to accounting for the relationships between individuals by assessing "rights" is to express the influence directly by means of explicit conditional preference orderings. Specifically, Edwin's preference for marrying Angelina depends on her preferences for marrying the judge. Thus, a network of the form

$$\boxed{\text{Angelina}} \longrightarrow \boxed{\text{Edwin}} \qquad\qquad (1.7)$$

exists, where Angelina possesses the categorical preference ordering

$$\mathbf{w}_E \succ_A \mathbf{w}_J \succ_A \mathbf{w}_O\,, \qquad\qquad (1.8)$$

but Edwin's preferences are conditioned on conjectures for Angelina. We consider two cases: one where Edwin is an egoist, and is not willing to sacrifice his welfare to benefit Angelina, and one where Edwin is an altruist, and is willing to sacrifice his welfare to benefit Angelina.

Edwin the Egoist First, consider the conjecture $\mathbf{w}_E$ for Angelina. Then Edwin would clearly prefer to remain single to marrying Angelina, and would be indifferent between Angelina marrying the judge or remaining single, since those two options are off the table under the given conjecture. Next, consider the conjecture $\mathbf{w}_J$. Edwin would then prefer to marry Angelina to either other option, to which he would be indifferent. Finally, consider the conjecture $\mathbf{w}_O$. Then Edwin would prefer to remain single to marrying Angelina, and would be indifferent between her marrying the judge or remaining single. Thus, Edwin's conditional preference profile $\mathfrak{P}_E$ is

$$\mathbf{w}_O \succ_{E|A} \mathbf{w}_E \sim_{E|A} \mathbf{w}_J \,|\mathbf{w}_E \tag{1.9}$$

$$\mathbf{w}_E \succ_{E|A} \mathbf{w}_O \sim_{E|A} \mathbf{w}_J \,|\mathbf{w}_J \tag{1.10}$$

$$\mathbf{w}_O \succ_{E|A} \mathbf{w}_E \sim_{E|A} \mathbf{w}_J \,|\mathbf{w}_O \,. \tag{1.11}$$

Edwin the Altruist   Under this scenario, given the conjecture $\mathbf{w}_E$, Edwin prefers $\mathbf{w}_E$ to $\mathbf{w}_O$; all other conditional preferences are the same as with the egoistic case.

$$\mathbf{w}_E \succ_{E|A} \mathbf{w}_O \sim_{E|A} \mathbf{w}_J \,|\mathbf{w}_E \tag{1.12}$$

$$\mathbf{w}_E \succ_{E|A} \mathbf{w}_O \sim_{E|A} \mathbf{w}_J \,|\mathbf{w}_J \tag{1.13}$$

$$\mathbf{w}_O \succ_{E|A} \mathbf{w}_E \sim_{E|A} \mathbf{w}_J \,|\mathbf{w}_O \,. \tag{1.14}$$

It thus appears that the strategy of Edwin waiving his rights is equivalent to the strategy of Edwin the Altruist. We shall develop this concept further in Chapter 2.

This example was introduced by Gibbard (1974) to motivate the development of a theory of liberalism that is consistent with the notion of individuals possessing "rights." But this example also illustrates a scenario where direct influence is exerted on one player by another; namely, the influence that Angelina brings to bear on Edwin.

One further note regarding this example: Unlike a standard social choice problem where the society must choose one and only one outcome, this example permits Edwin and Angelina to make different choices. Thus, in addition to the possible social choice outcomes $(\mathbf{w}_E, \mathbf{w}_E)$, $(\mathbf{w}_J, \mathbf{w}_J)$, and $(\mathbf{w}_O, \mathbf{w}_O)$, the mixed outcome $(\mathbf{w}_O, \mathbf{w}_J)$ is also permitted. All other conjecture profiles result in a contradiction.   □

1.3.2 Social Models

Regarding the Three Stooges social encounter, there are a number of questions to consider. There is, of course, the obvious one: Where should they go for dinner? But one might also want to ask questions that delve deeper into the structure of this society. As the preferences

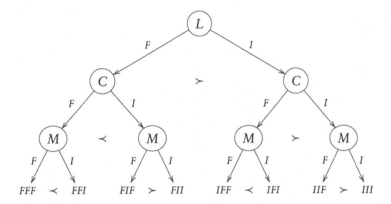

Figure 1.2: The Three Stooges Tree Diagram.

propagate through the network, do unconditional individual preference orderings emerge? Does a social preference ordering emerge? If they cannot all agree on a single destination that pleases everyone, how serious are the disagreements? Is a reasonable compromise possible? Is there any systematic way to evaluate this network in terms of its intrinsic functionality?

The tree diagram illustrated in Figure 1.2 displays the flows of influence, starting with Larry as the root vertex, then to Curly, and finally to Mo. The preference relations are indicated by the $\succ$ and $\prec$ annotations. The leaves of this tree correspond to the outcomes corresponding to all possible combinations defined by the Cartesian product $\{F, I\}^3 = \{F, I\} \times \{F, I\} \times \{F, I\}$.

The path *FIF* is the only one that simultaneously honors the preferences of all individuals; thus, a consensus cannot be reached, and they must act on a split vote. The social choice *F* is the utilitarian choice (Bentham, 2009); namely, it provides the greatest happiness for the greatest number of individuals. But one could also argue for the Rawlsian notion of social justice (Rawls, 1971) that is observed when the benefit to the least-advantaged member of society (i.e., Curly) is maximized, in which case *I* would be the preferred social choice. This example thus reveals the conundrum facing social choice theory: There is, seemingly, no unequivocally natural way to order the outcomes.

The ambiguity occurs because the decision criterion does not arise as a function of the preference orderings – it is imposed on the society by some undefined entity of convention. But who or what, is that authority and from where does it come? Did the members of the network agree to such an imposition? And if so, what was the mechanism by which that decision was made?

This conundrum is consistent with the impossibility theorem, which denies the existence of an emergent social order as a function of the individual preferences. Thus, the preference orderings must be over-laid by some exogenously imposed mapping of the set of individual preferences into a decision rule.

However, the impossibility theorem applies only to societies whose members possess categorical preferences but, since this example involves conditional preferences, the hypotheses of that theorem are not met. In a network environment where conditional preference orderings exist as a result of social influence, individuals who interact in that environment will generate social bonds and dependencies that result in varying degrees of cooperation and conflict. Such tendencies, however, are not dictated from outside the network; rather, they are intrinsic, emerging as a result of interaction. In other words, these interactions create a social structure that characterizes these innate social relationships. Such a model would enable the assessment of various attributes of the organization, such as the seriousness of disputes, the possibilities of compromise, and the propensity to coordinate behavior.

Such attributes, however, cannot be assessed from a social ordering over $\mathcal{A}$. Rather, it requires an ordering over the n-fold Cartesian product $\mathcal{A}^n = \mathcal{A} \times \cdots \times \mathcal{A}$ (n times). The ordering must be over preference profiles – sets of individual preference orderings, one for each individual. Such a model would be comprehensive, in that would account for all relevant social relationships that exist among the participants. Let $\succsim_{1:n}$ denote such an ordering.

To illustrate, consider the Three Stooges problem. Table 1.1 displays the number of individuals whose preferences are honored for each of

Table 1.1: *The Number of Stooges Whose Preferences are Honored.*

Outcome	FFF	FFI	FIF	FII	IFF	IFI	IIF	III
s	2	2	3	1	1	2	1	0

s is the number of individuals whose preferences are honored the possible outcomes. One possible concept of a group-level ordering $\succsim_{LCM}$ corresponds to the utilitarian criterion, yielding[10]

$$FIF \succ_{LCM} FFF \sim_{LCM} FFI \sim_{LCM}\sim IFI \succ_{LCM} FII$$
$$\sim_{LCM} IFF \sim_{LCM} IIF \succ_{LCM} III. \quad (1.15)$$

Although this particular ordering is exogenously imposed, it never-theless serves to illustrate the role of a social model. Setting aside for the moment the constraint that only one option may be chosen for the group, this group-level ordering provides insight about the interpersonal relationships that emerge as the individuals interact. If each individual were to go his own way, the highest alignment of interest would be the outcome *FIF*, that is, for *L* and *M* to go to *F* and *C* to go to *I*. The outcome *FFF* is in a three-way tie for the next-highest alignment, and *III* is the unique lowest alignment. Even though the individuals do not come to a consensus, the degree of alignment of interests with *FFF* is clearly greater than the degree of alignment with *III*. This ordering thus provides a complete ordering of all possible outcomes.

For simple three-agent, two-alternative scenarios such as the Three Stooges, it is straightforward, given the preference structure provided, to define a social model such as the one illustrated in (1.15). Without the specification of individual, albeit conditional, preferences, how-ever, it would be difficult to define such a model by directly considering the relationships between the eight possible outcomes. Of course, if each participant provided its own categorical preference ordering, then the solution would be trivial. It would also be uninteresting. Unless the members of the society really are asocial (and if so, why would they even want to dine together), categorical preference orderings cannot tell a complete story. Once specified, they are context free. Although removing context by abstracting the problem to a set of categorical preference orderings is one of the strengths of social choice theory, it can also be one of its weaknesses when the members of the group form a complex society.

The purpose of a social model is to provide a complete description of the social structure that emerges as influence propagates through the network. Thus, in contrast to classical social choice theory, which

---

[10] When the individuals have specific names, it will often be convenient to replace the numerical indices with literations to represent the individuals.

makes no assumptions regarding group-level preferences or choices, the social model that emerges as a result of social influence may indeed possess some, perhaps abstract, systematic notion of group-level behavior. Such systematic behavior would not be exogenously imposed; rather, it would be an innate property of the network arising from the social interactions created as social influence propagates through the network. Furthermore, since such social structure is necessarily emergent, it may be difficult to predict what form it would take before the social engagement is actualized. Thus, attempting to ascribe some ex ante contextual concept of meaningful or purposeful behavior to such a society may be problematic. Nevertheless, it may be possible to ascribe some abstract attributes to the emergent behavior. An attribute that is intrinsically void of context is the notion of *coordination*. According to the Oxford English Dictionary, "[To coordinate is] to place or arrange (things) in proper position relative to each other and to the system of which they form parts; to bring into proper combined order as parts of a whole" (Murray et al., 1991). Coordination is a neutral concept. It has to do with the degree to which the individuals (the parts) are able to combine to form an emergent organization (the whole). Individuals may coordinate cooperatively, such as with the formation of teams, they may coordinate conflictively, such as with athletic contests or military engagements, or they may coordinate in a way that does not correspond to any obvious notion of rational group-level behavior – it all depends on the way the conditional preferences combine.

To be more explicit, the purpose of a social model is to characterize the coordination characteristics of the society. It should be able to address such questions as the following: If the individuals cannot agree on a best alternative, how serious are the disputes? Is a compromise possible, or are the individuals so diametrically opposed that there is little hope for meaningful negotiations? How sensitive is the ability to coordinate to changes in individual preferences? Are there intrinsic limits to the ability of a given system to coordinate? Such questions deal with what might be termed the *ecological fitness* of the society to function in the environment that, in effect, it creates for itself as a consequence of its preference structure.

Aggregation, in the context of a social network, is much more than a process to define a social choice. It is the process of creating a social model that expresses the coordination characteristics that, in addition to revealing a fully coordinated social choice, defines the intrinsic ecological fitness of the society.

1.4 Related Research

Social psychologists and mathematicians have studied social influence network theory since the 1950s, with much of the research focusing on the organizational structure of so-called *small groups*, defined as loosely coupled collectives of mutually interacting autonomous individuals (Weick, 1995). Specifically, much of the emphasis has been placed on the structure of such organizations (cf. French (1956); DeGroot (1974); Friedkin (1986, 1990); Friedkin and Johnson (1990, 1997); Friedkin (1998); Arrow et al. (2000); Friedkin and Johnson (2011)). The basic model is that an individual's socially adjusted utility is a convex combination of its own categorical utility and a weighted sum of the categorical utilities of those agents who influence it. Karni and Schmeidler (1981) introduce the concept of state-dependent preferences where the decision maker's preferences are modulated by the state of nature. Hu and Shapley (2003a,b) apply a command structure to model player interactions by simple games. The subject of influence has also been extensively studied in the context of voting games where the individuals must vote yes or no on a given proposition. Hoede and Bakker (1982) introduce the concept of decisional power as a measure of the degree of influence of an individual or coalition of other voters to alter their vote from their original inclination (cf. Grabisch and Rusinowska (2010a,b)). Penrose (1946) and Banzhaf (1965) introduced a power index as equally divided among the voters.

To account for social relationships that exist among the members of a collective, several innovations have been applied to classical game theory. Behavioral game theory (Fehr and Schmidt, 1999; Camerer, 2003; Camerer et al., 2004; Bolton and Ockenfels, 2005; Henrich et al., 2004, 2005) is a response to the desire to introduce psychological realism and social influence into game theory by incorporating notions such as fairness and reciprocity into the utilities in addition to considerations of material benefit. The closely related field of psychological game theory (Gilboa and Schmeidler, 1988; Geanakoplos et al., 1989; Colman, 2003; Dufwenberg and Kirchsteiger, 2004; Battigalli and Dufwenberg, 2009) also employs utilities that account for beliefs as well as actions and takes into consideration belief-dependent motivations such as guilt aversion, reciprocity, regret, and shame. Regardless of the issues used to define the preferences, however, these approaches to game theory differ from the approach taken in this book in that they use unconditional linear preference orderings (i.e., categorical utilities) over the outcomes and, therefore, the solution concepts used by classical game theory continue to apply.

Other approaches to bridging the gap between individual and social interests focus on models drawn from biological and social evolutionary processes (Axelrod, 1984; Bicchieri, 1993; Sartorius, 2003; Fefferman and Ng, 2007; Bossert et al., 2012). Such approaches provide important models of the emergence of social relationships in repeated-play environments where individuals' fitness for long-term survival is taken into consideration in addition to their short-term material payoffs, and the propensity to behave in ways that extend beyond narrow self-interest is viewed as the end product of social evolution.

Although the most common approach to social choice theory is based on the assumption of individual rationality as the fundamental underlying logical concept, Bacharach (1999, 2006) and Sugden (1993, 2000, 2003) introduce a process whereby individuals can frame the decision scenario in multiple ways – one under the individual rationality framing, and one under a framing induced by concept of group identification. With the latter, individuals suspend their focus on individual payoffs and concentrate on the payoffs to the team with which they associate. When individuals identify with a group, the relationship motivates team reasoning, and the frame shifts from "What should I do?" to "What should we do?" Team reasoning thus forms the basis for generating joint intentions which then lead directly to forming a group utility. Nevertheless, the structure of the utilities remains categorical with this approach; the emphasis is on directly defining group-level preferences rather than generating a social choice from individual preferences.

An approach that differs profoundly from Arrovian-based theory is *Majority Judgment*, authored by Balinski and Laraki (2010). Their approach is to abandon the Arrovian model altogether by replacing the traditional paradigm of making comparisons between alternatives with a paradigm of making evaluations via a common language to grade and measure the merit of the alternatives, resulting in a common evaluation of all competitors. Although both this treatment and the conditional approach developed herein depart from the classical social choice model, the approach taken by Balinski and Laraki is radical – they completely reject the Arrovian model of making comparisons. The approach taken herein, however, is far from abandonment. Instead, its goal is to generalize the Arrovian model by introducing the notion of conditional comparisons. The Arrovian model then becomes a special case of the conditional model.

Behavioral social choice theory, as developed by Regenwetter et al. (2006) presents descriptive models for social behavior and offers key results regarding the evaluation of normative versus empirical evidence. They generalize the traditional binary preference relationship by considering probabilistic representations of preference and utility. Their approach builds on classical social choice and retains the basic categorical structure of preference relations. A potentially interesting and fruitful line of research would be to meld the behavioral and conditional aspects of social choice theory. Such a merging has the potential to generate substantive contributions to social choice theory.

1.5 Summary

If the model for a collective that all of its members possess categorical preference orderings and are motivated by narrow self-interest is a full characterization of the society, then this approach has little to add to conventional social choice theory. The thesis of this chapter, however, is that restricting to that view of society can be overly constrained in both the structure of the preference orderings and in the concept of self-interest. Limiting individuals to categorial preference orderings is tantamount to requiring them to express all of their values – both material and social – with a vehicle that is designed primarily to accommodate only individual benefit. Limiting individuals to a narrowly construed concept of self-interest requires them to absorb or convert any concern they have for the welfare of others into a concern for the individual welfare of themselves. Conditional individual preference orderings address both limitations. An expanded notion of individual rationality structure permits individuals to a) account for both material benefit and social benefit and b) modulate their preferences as functions of the preferences of those who socially influence them. The question remains, however, as to how to aggregate conditional preferences to create a comprehensive social model.

2 | *Aggregation*

Order is not pressure which is imposed on society from without, but an equilibrium which is set up from within.

— José Ortega y Gasset
Mirabeau: An Essay on the Nature of Statesmanship, 1975

Social choice involves two distinct problems: defining a mechanism for expressing individual preferences, and defining a mechanism for aggregating individual preferences. Chapter 1 extended the notion of individual preference to account for explicit social relationships that exist in a social network by introducing a mechanism whereby individuals can incorporate the welfare of others into their own welfare, thereby allowing them to form their preferences in the context of a social engagement. The resulting preference relationships are no longer constrained to be categorical – they can be conditional. This change in preference structure requires a corresponding change in the concept of aggregation.

Under the classical formulation of social choice, aggregation is the process by which the individual categorical preference orderings are combined to prescribe a choice for the collective. Under an expanded formulation, however, aggregation is not merely the issue of how to map a set of individual preferences into a social choice. Rather, the issue is how to create a comprehensive social model that characterizes the relationships that are formed as the conditional preferences propagate through the society, from which a social choice can be deduced that takes all such social relationships into consideration.

To appreciate the difference between classical aggregation and the expanded concept, we first review the classical approach.

2.1 Classical Aggregation

The ideal concept of aggregation, as conceived by Arrow and others, is the existence of an inherent "constitution" that would govern society according to generally agreed upon rules and conventions.[1] Establishing the existence of such a process would be a profound accomplishment, and it would be even more impressive and useful if the existence proof were constructive; that is, if existence were demonstrated by actually specifying the aggregation mechanism. The result would be a formula by which collective decisions could be made in a way that could be incontrovertibly justified as being in the best interest of the society.

Definition 2.1 Let $L(\mathcal{A})$ denote the set of linear orderings over $\mathcal{A}$. For each profile $\{\succsim_1, \ldots, \succsim_n\} \in L^n(\mathcal{A}) = L(\mathcal{A}) \times \cdots \times L(\mathcal{A})$, an *Arrovian aggregation function* is a mapping

$$g: \{\succsim_1, \ldots, \succsim_n\} \mapsto \succsim_s, \tag{2.1}$$

where $\succsim_s$ is an ordering over $\mathcal{A}$ for the collective. If $\succsim_s \in L(\mathcal{A})$, that is, if $\succsim_s$ is a linear ordering, then the function g is termed a *social welfare function*. □

Unfortunately, Arrow established that no such mechanism exists that does not violate a set of arguably desirable and reasonable conditions.[2] As a result, attention has focused on alternative concepts of aggregation. Rather than defining aggregation as a mapping from the set of preference profiles of individual linear orderings to the set of linear orderings, attention has shifted to defining aggregation as a mapping from the set of preference profiles of individual linear orderings directly to the set of alternatives.

Definition 2.2 A *social choice rule*, h, is a mapping that assigns a subset of alternatives to each preference profile. That is,

$$h: L^n(\mathcal{A}) \to \mathcal{A}. \tag{2.2}$$

---

[1] Arrow's statement of the problem is as follows: "we ask if it is formally possible to construct a procedure for passing from a set of known individual tastes to a pattern of social decision making, the procedure in question being required to satisfy certain natural conditions" (Arrow, 1951, p. 2).

[2] In addition to Arrow, other researchers, including Sen (1970), Gibbard (1973, 1974), and Satterthwaite (1975), have established impossibility theorems based on variations of Arrow's conditions.

For any preference profile $\{\succsim_1, \ldots, \succsim_n\} \in L^n(\mathcal{A})$, the set $h(\succsim_1, \ldots, \succsim_n)$ is termed a *choice set*. It represents the set of "winning" alternatives. If the choice set is a singleton set, it is termed a *social choice function*.   □

Although there are many possible solution concepts, it is convenient to narrow the search for a social choice function by defining reasonable conditions that have broad applicability. Two conditions that have received considerable traction are a) the choice rules should be symmetric among both the individuals and the alternatives and b) the choice of the collective should be consistent with the choices of sub-collectives.

Definition 2.3 A choice rule is said to be *symmetric* if it is both anonymous and neutral, where these two concepts are defined as follows:

Let π be a permutation operator over the set of individuals. For any strict profile $\{\succ_1, \ldots, \succ_n\}$, let $\{\succ_{\pi(1)}, \ldots, \succ_{\pi(n)}\}$ be the corresponding permuted profile. A social choice rule h is *anonymous* if

$$h(\succ_1, \ldots, \succ_n) = h(\succ_{\pi(1)}, \ldots, \succ_{\pi(n)}). \tag{2.3}$$

Let $\rho\colon \mathcal{A} \to \mathcal{A}$ be a permutation operator over $\mathcal{A}$. For any strict profile $\{\succ_1, \ldots, \succ_n\}$, let $\{\succ_1', \ldots, \succ_n'\}$ denote the profile such that $a \succ_i a'$ if and only if $\rho(a) \succ_i' \rho(a')$. A social choice rule h is *neutral* if for every preference profile $\{\succ_1, \ldots, \succ_n\}$ and every permutation ρ,

$$\rho[h(\succ_1', \ldots, \succ_n')] = h(\succ_1, \ldots, \succ_n). \tag{2.4}$$

Anonymity ensures that individuals are treated in an unbiased way, and neutrality assures that the alternatives are treated in an unbiased way.   □

Definition 2.4 A social choice rule h is *consistent* if the following condition holds. Let $\{X_{i_1}, \ldots, X_{i_j}\}$ and $\{X_{l_1}, \ldots, X_{l_k}\}$ be two disjoint subsets of $\{X_1, \ldots, X_n\}$, let $\{\succsim_{i_1}, \ldots, \succsim_{i_k}\}$ and $\{\succsim_{l_1}', \ldots, \succsim_{l_k}'\}$ be profiles for these two subsets, respectively, and let

$$\{\succsim_{i_1}^\dagger, \ldots, \succsim_{i_j}^\dagger, \succsim_{l_1}^\dagger, \ldots, \succsim_{l_k}^\dagger\}$$

be the profile for the union

$$\{X_{i_1}, \ldots, X_{i_j}\} \cup \{X_{l_1}, \ldots, X_{l_k}\}$$

that agrees with $\{\succsim_{i_1}, \ldots, \succsim_{i_j}\}$ on $\{X_{i_1}, \ldots, X_{i_j}\}$ and with $\{\succsim'_{l_1}, \ldots, \succsim'_{l_k}\}$ on $\{X_{l_1}, \ldots, X_{l_k}\}$. Then $h(\succsim_{i_1}, \ldots, \succsim_{i_j}) \cap h(\succsim'_{l_1}, \ldots, \succsim'_{l_k}) \neq \varnothing$ implies

$$h(\succsim_{i_1}, \ldots, \succsim_{i_j}) \cap h(\succsim'_{l_1}, \ldots, \succsim'_{l_k}) = h(\succsim^\dagger_{i_1}, \ldots, \succsim^\dagger_{i_j}, \succsim^\dagger_{l_1}, \ldots, \succsim^\dagger_{l_k}).$$
(2.5)

Thus, the winner of the combined group is the intersection of the winners of the of the two separate groups. □

Symmetry and consistency are natural attributes of many group decision situations. Young (1975) has established the relationship between these properties and numerical ordering rules called scoring functions.

Definition 2.5 A social choice rule is a *scoring rule* if a real number s_i is assigned to individual X_i's most preferred alternative. The choice set comprises the alternatives with the highest total score. □

Theorem 2.1 *A social choice rule is symmetric and consistent if and only if it is a scoring rule.*

For a proof of this result, see Young (1975). This result breaks the log jam between the implied theoretical existence of practical social choice rules and the actual construction of such rules. It constitutes a significant change from the original problem formation, however, in that it requires replacing the binary comparative relation $\succsim_i$ with a numerical score s_i. Thus, rather than finding ourselves in the uncomfortable position of there being no acceptable solution to the Arrovian aggregation process as originally envisioned, we find ourselves in the possession of an infinity of aggregation rules, each of which trivially satisfy Arrow's conditions. This situation, too, can be a bit uncomfortable, since, unlike the Arrovian ideal which would produce an endogenously generated social choice, such rules are fundamentally exogenous. They are based on information or assumptions that are not derived from the preference profile, but are imposed by some external authority. To illustrate, consider the following well-known rules.

Plurality Rules A plurality rule is a scoring rule where each individual casts one vote for its most preferred alternative and the choice set comprises those alternatives with the highest total number of votes.

Borda Rules   Perhaps the most well-known scoring rule is the Borda rank-order rule. Given a set $A = \{z_1, \ldots, z_N\}$ of alternatives, the Borda rule is to assign a value $N - 1$ to each individual's most preferred alternative, a value of $N - 2$ to each individual's second most preferred alternative and, in general, to assign a value of $N - j$ to each individual's jth most preferred alternative. Let $r_i(z_j)$ denote X_i's rank of alternative z_j, where the ranking is defined by the profile $\{\succsim_1, \ldots, \succsim_n\}$. The Borda social choice rule is

$$h(\succsim_1, \ldots, \succsim_n) = \left\{ z_j \in A : \sum_{i=1}^{n} r_i(z_j) \geq \sum_{i=1}^{n} r_i(z_k) \ \forall z_k \in A \right\}. \quad (2.6)$$

One of the important discussions regarding classical social choice theory is the concept of interpersonal comparisons of utility. Under the original Arrovian formulation, preference orderings are ordinal and relative. There is no concept of degree of intensity of preference and, consequently, there is no concept of interpersonal comparisons. One cannot say that X_1's preference for a_i over a_i' is more or less intense than X_j's preference for a_j over a_j'. But once binary comparisons are replaced by numerical scores, the concept of intensity becomes relevant, both in terms of individual intensity of preference and interpersonal comparisons. The plurality and Borda rules, however, use numerical representations as ordering devices (e.g., 1st, 2nd, 3rd, etc.), but do not necessarily correspond to intensity. Associating intensity with numerical scores, however, makes possible the introduction of choice functions that can accommodate different degrees of preference.

Utilitarian Rules   The *utilitarian* concept of aggregation is to define a group ordering over A as the sum of the individual orderings, yielding the decision rule

$$a_U = \arg \max_{a \in A} \sum_{i=1}^{n} u_i(a), \quad (2.7)$$

where $u_i(a)$ is a numerical evaluation of the benefit of a to X_i. Forming the sum of benefits makes logical sense, however, only if the benefits are expressed in the same units. Thus, the utilitarian decision rule requires that expressions are of both individual intensity and interpersonal comparability.

Social Justice Rules Another possible choice function based on intensity and interpersonal comparability is the so-called Rawlesian criterion (Rawls, 1971), where the social choice is the alternative that maximizes the minimum benefit to the individuals, or

$$a_R = \arg\max_{a \in \mathcal{A}} \min_i u_i(a) . \tag{2.8}$$

Much more could be said about social choice functions designed under the classical preference model, and much of social choice theory has focused on issues such as single-peaked preferences, manipulatability, bargaining rules, and so forth. These approaches, however, are all based on the assumption of categorical preferences, and will not be pursued further in this work.

2.2 Coordinated Aggregation

In the course of a social engagement, the individual *ex ante* conditional preferences propagate through the network, spontaneously generating *ex post* emergent social relationships. As Axelrod (1997, p. 4) observes, "Emergent properties are often surprising because it can be hard to anticipate the full consequences of even simple forms of interaction." However, general qualitative properties of emergent behavior can be characterized. For a network disposed to cooperate, the interests of the individuals will tend to align in a positive, or reinforcing, way. For a network disposed to conflict, the alignment of interests will be negative, that is, in opposition. Such an alignment in response to social influence is a manifestation of coordination. As discussed in Section 1.3.2, coordination requires two components: a) a concept of proper individual behavior and b) a concept of group order. Clearly, individual behavior is governed by the individual preferences, but any notions of orderly group behavior must emerge as a result of the *ex post* social relationships.

If all individuals possess categorical preferences, then any concept of "coordination" would arise simply by the coincidence of their material interests. However, under the pressure of social influence, it is possible for the collective to self-regulate in the sense that a functional organization emerges as they associate. In such a case, it would be of great interest to investigate what Cartwright (1965) terms "ecological control," where individuals are manipulated through their social environment to modify their behavior. This innate property of a collective is a function of, and only of, the social influence structure as determined by the social linkages. Simon (1986, p. 109) describes this emergent process: "Social institutions may be viewed as regularizations of the behavior of individuals through subjection of their behavior to stimulus-patterns socially imposed on them. It is in these patterns that an understanding of the meaning and function of organization is to be found."

For a social model to enable assessments of the propensity for coordination, the seriousness of disputes, or other manifestations of systematic behavior, it must be a function of the entire profile comprising the conjectures of all members of the society, hence the following definition.

Definition 2.6 A *coordination ordering* $\succsim_{1:n}$ is an ordering over the product set $\mathcal{A}^n$ that ranks the conjecture profiles according to the degree to which they manifest an emergent notion of systematically organized behavior. $\square$

The concept of a coordination ordering is very different from the social welfare function $\succsim_s$ defined by (2.1). Since it would be an ordering over the set of conjecture profiles, it would not compare individual alternatives on the basis of achieving either group or individual objectives. Rather, it would be a representation of the innate structure of the network with respect to connections between individual and group behavior. It would rank conjecture profiles on the basis of the shared interest that arises as a result of social influence, thereby providing a comprehensive expression of all social relationships that emerge as the *ex ante* conditional preferences propagate through the network.

If all individuals possess categorical utilities, then there is no social interaction in the sense of direct influence, and a coordination ordering would provide no information not contained in the individual preference orderings. But if the individuals possess conditional preferences, then the coordination ordering would express social behavior that goes beyond focusing on narrowly construed self-interest. It would characterize the functionality, or cohesiveness, of the group and enable the assessment of the seriousness of disputes, the aptitude for coordination, and the possibilities of compromise.

A coordination ordering would provide an emergent notion of group preference; namely, that if $(a_1, \ldots, a_n) \succsim_{1:n} (a'_1, \ldots, a'_n)$, then $(a_1, \ldots, a_n)$ generates greater coordination than $(a'_1, \ldots, a'_n)$. To illustrate such an ordering, let us focus again on the Three Stooges problem introduced in Section 1.2. Consider the tree diagram illustrated in Figure 1.2, and follow the paths to the terminating leaves, which represent the set of all possible conjecture profiles. By taking the fork at each point according to the associated preferences, we see that the outcome *FIF* is the unique path where each agent's conditional preferences are honored. By invoking the utilitarian concept of providing the greatest good for the greatest number of individuals, it is possible to construct an ordering over all of the elements of the product set, as defined by (1.15). Although this ordering is imposed by the exogenous assumption of utilitarianism and thus does not necessarily represent endogenously generated social relationships, it nevertheless illustrates how such a model can reveal the internal structure of an organization. Whereas the output of an unconstrained linear Arrovian social ordering (were it to exist) would be a group-level comparison between F and I, a social model would provide comparisons between all triples of conjectures $(a_L, a_C, a_M) \in \{F, I\} \times \{F, I\} \times \{F, I\}$. For example, according to the ordering defined by (1.15), the conjecture profile *FFF* has the second-highest level of coordination, whereas *III* has the lowest possible coordination – the only outcome for which every individual gets his less conditionally preferred outcome.

2.3 Social Coherence

A mathematical formalism may be operated in ever new, uncovenanted ways, and force on our hesitant minds the expression of a novel conception.
— Michael Polanyi
Personal Knowledge (University of Chicago Press, 1958)

As mentioned previously, the coordination ordering defined by (1.15) for the Three Stooges dinner scenario is exogenously imposed. It did not emerge as an innate property of the group, but was based on an arbitrary notion of group performance. In fact, other exogenous criteria would lead to other coordination orderings. We are interested, however, in the possibility that a coordination ordering of the form

$$\succsim_{1:ns} = f(\succsim_{i|\mathrm{pa}(i)}, \ i = 1, \ldots, n) \tag{2.9}$$

will emerge endogenously as a result of, and only of, the social interrelationships. If so, it would be result in a "constitution" for the network in much the same way that an Arrovian social choice function was envisioned to serve in that capacity for a classical social choice problem. In order to define such an endogenous coordination ordering, it will be helpful to narrow the search by insisting that any such ordering must satisfy minimal logical and rational requirements. Historically, one of the most important requirements of a social choice solution concept is that it at least satisfies a minimal notion of democracy. Indeed, the very concept of social choice as the amalgamation of individual preferences suggests that some sort of democratic principle must underlie the decision-making process, otherwise there would be no reason to consider individual preferences.

2.3.1 Democratic Social Choice

There are two extreme concepts of democracy. The notion employed by Arrow (1951) is the absence of a dictator, that is, one who unilaterally decides which alternative is chosen, regardless of the preferences of others. The other extreme notion of democracy is that of direct, or pure, democracy, where all members of the society have one vote and all votes are given equal weight. The concept of symmetry developed in Section 2.1 accords with this concept of democracy.

The assumption that underlies these concepts of democracy is that each individual possesses a categorical preference ordering. Thus, the classical analysis of democratic decision making is restricted to trivial networks. With nontrivial networks, however, the social influence that individuals have on each other renders the concept of democracy more subtle. In fact, even the concept of a direct democracy is not sufficient to ensure that a social network is operationally democratic. To illustrate, consider an election involving candidates A and B, and assume that each member of the electorate has one vote and that all votes count equally. Suppose X, a socially influential member of the community, wants candidate A to be elected. Those individuals who X influences will be swayed – not necessarily by the merits of the candidate, but by X's preference. This influence may be positive (they support candidate A since X does) or negative (they support B, who X opposes). If X's influence were positive and pervaded more than half of the electorate, then a conjecture for X that A should be elected would result in society electing A. X would be an effectual *dictator*. Alternatively, if X's influence were negative and pervaded more than half of the electorate, then a conjecture for X that A should be elected would ensure that society would elect B.

Thus, even though a society is *ostensibly* a direct democracy, where each individual gets one vote and all votes are given the same material (i.e., numerical) weight, it may turn out that, if individuals do not have equal social weight, then a single individual can effectually dictate the outcome. However, such a situation is not a true dictatorship if individuals, although faithfully complying with their conditional preferences, are empowered to define their own preferences, either categorical or conditional, free of coercion. If we assume that individuals acquiesce to the influence from others, then social influence will not violate the fundamental democratic concept of free choice.

But ensuring freedom of individual choice is not the only consideration regarding the functionality of an organization. Functionality, however, is not addressed by classical social choice. Once the decision has been made, the social choice problem is concluded and there is nothing more to be said. But for a network, a decision is rendered in a context where social relationships have been formed and the group is empowered (at least to some extent) to combine their interests in a systematic way to function as a coordinated whole. Thus, in a network environment, a more profound issue even than dictatorship is the ability of an individual to unilaterally control coordination. Suppose some member of the collective is able to assert its influence to steer or manipulate the group to behave in ways that favor its preferences, even though it may be a minority view. For example, a socially powerful individual might lose the election but still be able to modify or undermine the behavior of the group. Such an individual is capable of *subversion*.

Definition 2.7 X_i is a *subverter* if, whenever $a \succ_i a' \, \forall \, a' \in \mathcal{A} \backslash \{a\}$, then

$$(a_1, \ldots, a_{i-1}, a, a_{i+1}, \ldots, a_n) \succ_{1:n}$$
$$(a_1, \ldots, a_{i-1}, a', a_{i+1}, \ldots, a_n) \, \forall \, a' \in \mathcal{A} \backslash \{a\},$$
$$\forall \, (a_1, \ldots, a_{i-1}, a_{i+1}, \ldots, a_n) \in \mathcal{A}^{n-1}. \quad (2.10)$$

$\square$

X_i is *subversive* if, whenever $a \succ_i a' \ \forall a' \in \mathcal{A} \setminus \{a\}$, then the coordination ordering of every conjecture profile that contains a as X_i's conjecture is greater than the coordination of the conjecture profile created by replacing a with any $a' \neq a$. A subverter is different from a dictator. A dictator has the ability to decide which alternative is chosen, but a subverter effectually dictates or controls the behavior of the group.

The opposite of dictatorship is a phenomenon that Hansson (1972) and Fishburn (1973) term *suppression*. An individual is suppressed if, whenever it prefers alternative a to a', then society chooses a' over a. As Fishburn put it, one who is suppressed is "a dictator turned upside down" (Fishburn, 1973, p. 211). The concept parallel to suppression in a network environment is *subjugation*, a particularly severe form of discrimination. An individual is subjugated if, whenever it most prefers a given alternative, no matter what it is, the coordination of any conjecture profile containing that individual's most preferred alternative is less than the coordination of that same conjecture profile with any different alternative substituted for that individual's most preferred alternative. To paraphrase Fishburn, one who is subjugated is a subverter turned upside down.

Definition 2.8 X_i is *subjugated* if, for any $a \in \mathcal{A}$ such that $a \succ_i a' \ \forall a' \in \mathcal{A} \setminus \{a\}$, then

$$(a_1, \ldots, a_{i-1}, a', a_{i+1}, \ldots, a_n) \succ_{1:n}$$
$$(a_1, \ldots, a_{i-1}, a, a_{i+1}, \ldots, a_n) \ \forall a' \in \mathcal{A} \setminus \{a\},$$
$$\forall (a_1, \ldots, a_{i-1}, a_{i+1}, \ldots, a_n) \in \mathcal{A}^{n-1}. \quad (2.11)$$

$\square$

Definition 2.9 A coordination ordering is *socially coherent* if no X_i can be subjected or is capable of subversion. $\square$

Social coherence prohibits any individual either to unilaterally dominate the group's behavior or to be the victim of categorical discrimination by the group. In fact, it is straightforward to see that subjugation violates the unanimity principle: If an alternative is best for every individual, then it is best (that is, most coordinated) for the group. The unanimity principle requires that, if $a^* \succ_i a \ \forall a \in \mathcal{A} \setminus \{a^*\}$, $i = 1, \ldots, n$, then

$$(a^*, \ldots, a^*) \succ_{1:n} (a_1, \ldots, a_n) \; \forall \, (a_1, \ldots, a_n) \in \mathcal{A}^n \setminus \{(a^*, \ldots, a^*)\}.$$
$$(2.12)$$

Now suppose $a^* \succ_i a \; \forall a \in \mathcal{A} \setminus \{a^*\}$, $i = 1, \ldots n$, but X_i is subjugated. By (2.11), it must hold that, for all $a' \neq a^*$,

$$(a^*, \ldots, a^*, a', a^*, \ldots, a^*) \succ_{1:n} (a^*, \ldots, a^*, a^*, a^*, \ldots, a^*), \qquad (2.13)$$

which violates (2.12).

A society that permits either subjugation or subversion is susceptible to dysfunctional behavior. Such a society would likely be unstable; it would be susceptible to fracturing and even disintegrating. Although avoiding subjugation and subversion would not imply that the individuals are equal in any meaningful sense, it would insure that all individuals at least have a voice – a seat at the table.

There is an interesting parallel between social coherence, which denies the ability of an individual to manipulate the way a society coordinates, and the concept of strategic manipulation, as developed by Gibbard (1973) and Satterthwaite (1975), who have established conditions such that one of the following must hold: a) the voting rule is dictatorial; b) there is some candidate who can never win; or c) it is possible for a voter to gain an advantage by voting against its real preferences. The difference between strategic manipulation and social coherence is that the former deals with the ability to manipulate the outcome, while the latter deals with the coordination characteristics of the group, regardless of the outcome of the vote. Furthermore, the strategic manipulation results apply only to trivial networks and, in that environment, notions of group-level coordination due to social influence are irrelevant.

Neither subjugation nor subversion can arise when all participants possess categorical preferences and when the social choice is a function of the individual preferences. In a network, however, it is difficult to anticipate all social interactions that can take place as the individuals interact. Psychological and sociological issues bring such a richness and variability to human decision making that it is difficult to define a formal model that accounts for more than a few somewhat idealized situations. It is not assumed, therefore, that coherence is an attribute of all human societies. However, social coherence exists for many human decision-making scenarios. Furthermore, social coherence is an important design principle for an artificial society and is essential if the society is to be stable and functional.

Non-subjugation and non-subversion are rather weak constraints on the structure of the coordination preference ordering, but they are vital ones. They are perhaps the weakest conditions that must hold if each X_i can enter into negotiations with at least the theoretical possibility that its most preferred alternative can be chosen by the network. Thus, the issue of how to guarantee this minimal property of democratic social choice devolves to that of establishing social coherence.

2.3.2 An Order Isomorphism

Anyone with a background in Bayesian statistics will have noticed the obvious similarities between the concept of conditional preferences and conditional probabilities. They both involve hypothetical reasoning – a form of Bayesian conditionalization. A conditional preference ordering is a statement of the form $a_i \succ_{i|j} a_i' \mid a_j$, which means, in plain English, "If X_j conjectures a_j (the antecedent) then X_i prefers a_i to a_i' (the consequent)." Similarly, a conditional probability $P(A|B)$ is an assertion that "if B is realized (the antecedent) then the probability that A is realized is $P(A|B)$ (the consequent)." Building on this syntactical similarity, it may be fruitful to examine the features of probability theory to see if there are any analogies that relate to social coherence. To pursue any such analogies, however, requires rigorous justification since, although these two hypothetical propositions have essentially the same syntax, they involve very different semantics. Probability theory deals with the epistemological issue of belief, but utility theory deals with the behavioral issue of preference. Fortunately, however, it is straightforward to establish that the relationship is more than an analogy – it is an isomorphism.

Theorem 2.2 *An order isomorphism exists between ordering the strength of belief regarding propositions and ordering the strength of preference regarding alternatives.[3] This isomorphism applies to both categorical and conditional orderings.*

Proof Let $\{Y_1, \ldots, Y_n\}$ be a set of belief-assessing individuals defined over a finite set Ω of distinct propositions such that one and only one

---

[3] Two sets are *order isomorphic* if one of the orderings can be obtained from the other by renaming the members of the set (Itô, 1987).

element is realized, let $\{X_1, \ldots, X_n\}$ be a set of preference-assessing individuals defined over a finite set $\mathcal{A}$ of distinct alternatives such that one and only one element is actualized, and suppose that Ω and $\mathcal{A}$ are of equal cardinality.

Let $\mathrm{pa}\,(Y_i) = \{Y_{i_1}, \ldots, Y_{i_{p_i}}\}$ denote those individuals whose beliefs influence Y_i's beliefs, and let $\trianglerighteq_{i|\mathrm{pa}(i)}$ be a linear *conditional belief ordering* such that

$$\omega \trianglerighteq_{i|\mathrm{pa}(i)} \omega' \,|(\omega_{i_1}, \ldots, \omega_{i_{p_i}}) \tag{2.14}$$

means that the degree of Y_i's belief that ω is realized is at least as strong as the belief that ω' is realized, given that Y_{i_k} knows that ω_{i_k} is realized, $k = 1, \ldots, p_i$. If $\mathrm{pa}\,(Y_i) = \varnothing$, then Y_i possesses a categorical belief ordering $\trianglerighteq_i$.

Similarly, let $\mathrm{pa}\,(X_i) = \{X_{i_1}, \ldots, X_{i_{p_i}}\}$ denote those individuals whose interests influence X_i's interests, and let $\succeq_{i|\mathrm{pa}(i)}$ be a linear *conditional preference ordering* such that

$$a \succeq_{i|\mathrm{pa}(i)} a' \,|(a_{i_1}, \ldots, a_{i_{p_i}}) \tag{2.15}$$

means that the degree of X_i's preference if a is actualized is at least as high as the preference if a' is actualized, given that X_{i_k} conjectures a_{i_k}, $k = 1, \ldots, p_i$. If $\mathrm{pa}\,(X_i) = \varnothing$, then X_i possesses a categorical preference ordering $\succeq_i$.

Thus, the ordering relations in the two domains have identical syntactical structures, and any bijective mapping $h\colon \mathcal{A} \to \Omega$ such that

$$a_i \succeq_i a_i' \iff h(a_i) \trianglerighteq_i h(a_i') \tag{2.16}$$

and

$$a_i \succeq_{i|\mathrm{pa}(i)} a_i'|(a_{i_1}, \ldots a_{i_{p_i}}) \iff h(a_i) \trianglerighteq_{i|\mathrm{pa}(i)} h(a_i'|h(a_{i_1}), \ldots h(a_{i_{p_i}})) \tag{2.17}$$

is an order isomorphism. □

2.3.3 Operational Democracy

The isomorphic relationship established by Theorem 2.2 provides an incentive to explore features of probability theory that may relate to social coherence. In fact, a feature of probability theory that almost begs to be considered is the possibility of an isomorphism between the concept of subjugation and the concept of *sure loss*. A gambler suffers a sure loss if, no matter what the outcome of the gamble, the loss exceeds the reward. Such a gamble is called a Dutch book. Analogously, an individual is subjugated if, no matter what alternative the individual prefers, that alternative reduces the organizational effectiveness of the society. The key result regarding the existence of sure-loss gambles is the Dutch book theorem.

Theorem 2.3 The Dutch Book Theorem. *Suppose a gambler places a bet to win a payout of S. A fair entry fee for this gamble is bS, where b is the gambler's degree of belief of winning.*

(Necessity) If b violates the probability axioms, then it is possible to construct a bet such that the payout is always less (greater) than the entry fee – a sure loss (win).

(Sufficiency) If b conforms to the probability axioms, then it is not possible to construct a bet such that the gambler sustains a sure loss (sure gain).

A proof of this theorem is provided in Appendix A. Necessity (the original theorem) was independently established by de Finetti (1937) and Ramsey (1950), and sufficiency (the converse theorem) was independently established by Kemeny (1955) and Lehman (1955). de Finetti (1937) introduced the term *coherence* as the condition of avoiding sure loss.[4] This theorem establishes that it is possible to define a gamble that yields either a sure loss or a sure win if, and only if, the probability axioms are violated. The relevance of the Dutch book theorem regarding social coherence is established by the following theorem.

Theorem 2.4 *Subjugation is isomorphic to sure loss and subversion is isomorphic to sure gain.*

---

[4] "It is precisely in investigating the connection that must hold between evaluations of probability and decision making under conditions of uncertainty that one can arrive at criteria for measuring probabilities, for establishing conditions which they must satisfy, and for understanding the way in which one can, and indeed one must, '*reason about them*'. It turns out, in fact, that there exist simple (and in the last analysis, obvious) conditions, which we term conditions *of coherence*: any transgression of these results in decisions whose consequences are manifestly undesirable (leading to certain loss) [emphasis in original]" (de Finetti, 1937, p. 72).

Proof Suppose there exists a conjecture $a_i^* \in \mathcal{A}$ for X_i such that

$$a_i^* \succ_i a_i \, \forall \, a_i \in \mathcal{A} \backslash \{a_i^*\} \tag{2.18}$$

holds, but

$$\nexists (a_1, \ldots, a_{i-1}, a_{i+1}, \ldots, a_n) \colon (a_1, \ldots, a_{i-1}, a_i^*, a_{i+1}, \ldots, a_n) \succ_{1:n}$$
$$(a_1, \ldots, a_{i-1}, a_i, a_{i+1}, \ldots, a_n) \tag{2.19}$$

for all $a_i \neq a_i^*$. Let $\omega = h(a)$. By Theorem 2.2, (2.18) and (2.19) are isomorphic to

$$\omega_i^* \rhd_i \omega_i \, \forall \, \omega_i \in \Omega \backslash \{\omega_i^*\} \tag{2.20}$$

and

$$\nexists (\omega_1, \ldots, \omega_{i-1}, \omega_{i+1}, \ldots, \omega_n) \colon (\omega_1, \ldots, \omega_{i-1}, \omega_i^*, \omega_{i+1}, \ldots, \omega_n) \rhd_{1:n}$$
$$(\omega_1, \ldots, \omega_{i-1}, \omega_i, \omega_{i+1}, \ldots, \omega_n) \tag{2.21}$$

for all $\omega_i \neq \omega_i^*$.

If, on the basis of (2.20) one were to enter a lottery to earn \$1 if ω_i^* is realized, a fair entry fee would be \$$q > 1/2$. On the other hand, if one were to bet on the basis of (2.21) that ω_i^* will not be realized, a fair entry fee would be \$$r > 1/2$. Combing these two bets into one bet to earn \$2 requires an entry fee of \$$(q + r)$. However, since the outcomes are mutually exclusive, only one of the bets can win, thus yielding a payout of only \$1. Since $q + r > 1$, the gambler sustains a sure loss. Thus, if a sure loss is not possible, there must exist at least one joint state $(\omega_1, \ldots, \omega_{i-1}, \omega_i, \omega_{i+1}, \ldots, \omega_n)$ such that

$$(\omega_1, \ldots, \omega_{i-1}, \omega_i^*, \omega_{i+1}, \ldots, \omega_n) \rhd_{1:n} (\omega_1, \ldots, \omega_{i-1}, \omega_i, \omega_{i+1}, \ldots, \omega_n).$$
$$\tag{2.22}$$

By Theorem 2.2, there must exist at least one conjecture profile $(a_1, \ldots, a_{i-1}, a_i, a_{i+1}, \ldots, a_n)$ such that

$$(a_1, \ldots, a_{i-1}, a_i^*, a_{i+1}, \ldots, a_n) \succ_{1:n} (a_1, \ldots, a_{i-1}, a_i, a_{i+1}, \ldots, a_n),$$
$$\tag{2.23}$$

and thus subjugation is impossible.

The sure-gain condition is established as follows. Suppose

$$\omega_i^* \rhd_i \omega_i \, \forall \, \omega_i \in \Omega \backslash \{\omega_i^*\} \tag{2.24}$$

and

$$\nexists(\omega_1, \ldots, \omega_{i-1}, \omega_{i+1}, \ldots, \omega_n): (\omega_1, \ldots, \omega_{i-1}, \omega_i, \omega_{i+1}, \ldots, \omega_n) \triangleright_{1:n}$$
$$(\omega_1, \ldots, \omega_{i-1}, \omega_i^*, \omega_{i+1}, \ldots, \omega_n) \quad (2.25)$$

for all $\omega_i \neq \omega_i^*$.

If, on the basis of (2.24) one were to enter a lottery to earn \$1 if ω_i^* is not realized, a fair entry fee would be $q < 1/2$. On the other hand, if, on the basis of (2.25) one were to bet \$1 that ω_i^* is realized, a fair entry fee would $r < 1/2$. Combining the bets would earn \$1 with an entry fee of $q + r < 1$, resulting in a sure win, which, by the isomorphic relationship, would make subversion possible. Thus, to avoid subversion, there must exist at least one conjecture profile $(a_1, \ldots, a_{i-1}, a_i, a_{i+1}, \ldots, a_n)$ such that

$$(a_1, \ldots, a_{i-1}, a_i, a_{i+1}, \ldots, a_n) \succ_{1:n} (a_1, \ldots, a_{i-1}, a_i^*, a_{i+1}, \ldots, a_n).$$
$$(2.26)$$

□

Combining the results of the Theorem 2.3 and Theorem 2.4 yields the following operational definition of democratic social choice.

Definition 2.10 A network is socially coherent if, and only if, the preference orderings conform to the axioms of probability theory. □

This result is consistent with Arrow's impossibility theorem. Essentially, the impossibility theorem says that it is not possible to combine a profile of linear binary relations $\{\succsim_1, \ldots, \succsim_n\}$ to form a group-level linear binary relation $\succsim_s$ defined over all ordered pairs $(a, a') \in \mathcal{A} \times \mathcal{A}$ that satisfies a set of reasonable and desirable properties (including non-dictatorship). The classical response is to resort to numerically based social choice rules. Correspondingly, with an influence network, social coherence is impossible unless the preferences are expressed and combined in accordance with probability theory. In other words, there is no linear binary relation $\succsim_{1:n}$ over all ordered pairs $(\mathbf{a}, \mathbf{a}') \in \mathcal{A}^n \times \mathcal{A}^n$ as defined by (2.9). The response is to resort to utilities that express preference using the syntax of probability mass functions.

These results invite an interesting observation. On the one hand, expressing individual preference in terms of linear binary comparison relations, either categorically or conditionally, cannot, in general, produce a linear binary comparison relation for society. But on the other hand, expressing individual preference relations in terms of numerical functions leads to multiple numerical ways to express social preference.

This sensitivity to the way preferences are expressed raises an important question: Why should a seemingly innocuous change in the way individual preferences are expressed result in such a drastic change in the existence of a social preference? Perhaps the answer lies in what is taken as the primitive concept of preference. The syntax associated with the ordering relation $\succsim$ is a *bivariate comparison* that generates a set of ordered pairs $(a, a') \in \mathcal{A} \times \mathcal{A}$. Making comparisons is an *intrinsic* property of $\succsim$. An individual using this form of logic could offer no opinion regarding an alternative a taken in isolation, but given two alternatives, a and a', that individual could form an opinion about their relationship.

The syntax associated with a function $u: \mathcal{A} \to \mathbb{R}$ is a *univariate evaluation* defined over $\mathcal{A}$ that generates a real number for each $a \in \mathcal{A}$. An individual using this form of logic is equipped to offer an opinon regarding an alternative a viewed in isolation. To form a comparison, however, one must make two separate evaluations and then form a bivariate comparison by juxtaposing the two evaluations. Making comparisons is an *extrinsic* property of u. While it is possible for such an individual to create a unique binary relation $\succsim^\dagger$ over $\mathcal{A}$ such that $a \succsim^\dagger a'$ if $u(a) \geq u(a')$, that binary relation is not the primitive; it is not used to perform the aggregation. Thus, the change in assumptions regarding the formation of preferences is not innocuous at all. It constitutes a fundamental change in the way preferences are expressed, and it is not surprising that different primitive assumptions lead to different results. Furthermore, that this sensitivity applies to social models defined over $\mathcal{A}^n$ is also no surprise.

A demand for coherence requires that all binary preference relations must be expressed in terms of utility functions. Thus, the next step in our development must be to ensure that such a representation is consistent with probability theory. We begin by introducing the concept of *agreement*.

Definition 2.11 A linear ordering $\succsim_i$ and a utility u_i are said to *agree* if, for all $a, a' \in \mathcal{A}$,

$$a \succ_i a' \text{ if, and only if, } u_i(a) > u_i(a') \tag{2.27}$$

and

$$a \sim_i a' \text{ if, and only if, } u_i(a) = u_i(a').　\text{(2.28)}$$

Similarly, a conditional linear ordering $\succsim_{i|\text{pa}(i)}$ and a conditional utility $u_{i|\text{pa}(i)}$ *agree* if, for all $a, a' \in \mathcal{A}$,

$$a \succ_{i|\text{pa}(i)} a' \,|(a_{i_1}, \ldots, a_{i_{p_i}}) \text{ if, and only if,}$$
$$u_{i|\text{pa}(i)}(a|a_{i_1} \ldots, a_{i_{p_i}}) > u_{i|\text{pa}(i)}(a'|a_{i_1} \ldots, a_{i_{p_i}})　\text{(2.29)}$$

and

$$a \sim_{i|\text{pa}(i)} a' \,|(a_{i_1}, \ldots, a_{i_{p_i}}) \text{ if, and only if,}$$
$$u_{i|\text{pa}(i)}(a|a_{i_1} \ldots, a_{i_{p_i}}) = u_{i|\text{pa}(i)}(a'|a_{i_1} \ldots, a_{i_{p_i}})　\text{(2.30)}$$

for all conditioning conjecture profiles $(a_{i_1}, \ldots, a_{i_{p_i}}) \in \mathcal{A}^{p_i}$.　□

Fortunately, Fishburn (1986, ch. 4) has established that for any linear belief ordering over a set of propositions there exists a corresponding probability measure that agrees with it. Thus, categorical preference orderings $\succsim_i$ can be replaced with categorical utility mass functions u_i and conditional preference orderings $\succsim_{i|\text{pa}(i)}$ can be replaced with conditional utility mass functions $u_{i|\text{pa}(i)}$.

To comply with the syntax of probability theory, utilities must be mass functions; that is, they must satisfy the following normalizing conditions.

$$\begin{aligned} u_i(a) \geq 0 \,\forall a \in \mathcal{A} \\ \sum_{a \in \mathcal{A}} u_i(a) = 1 \end{aligned}　\text{(2.31)}$$

and

$$\begin{aligned} u_{i|\text{pa}(i)}(a_i|\mathbf{a}_i) \geq 0 \,\forall a \in \mathcal{A} \,\forall \mathbf{a}_i \in \mathcal{A}^{p_i} \\ \sum_{a \in \mathcal{A}} u_{i|\text{pa}(i)}(a|\mathbf{a}_i) = 1 \,\forall \mathbf{a}_i \in \mathcal{A}^{p_i} \end{aligned}　\text{(2.32)}$$

Compliance with this requirement may involve positive affine transformations of the form

$$\hat{u}(a) = \gamma u(a) + v,　\text{(2.33)}$$

where

$$\gamma = \min_{a \in \mathcal{A}} \left\{ \frac{1}{\sum_{x \in \mathcal{A}} u(x) - Nu(a)} : \sum_{x \in \mathcal{A}} u(x) - N\hat{u}(a) > 0 \right\}, \quad (2.34)$$

$$v = \frac{1 - \gamma \sum_{x \in \mathcal{A}} u(x)}{N}$$

where N is the cardinality of $\mathcal{A}$.

Requiring all utilities to be normalized forces the utilities to be cardinal; it also forces the condition of interpersonal comparability. The normalization requirement forces all utilities to have the same zero point and the same scale factor. Harsanyi (1977, p. 55) terms this condition *congruency*. We extend the notion of congruency to conditional utilities. Each X_i possesses one *utile* of benefit to apportion to the alternatives under consideration by X_i for each conditioning conjecture profile of its parents. Accordingly, we interpret the conditional utility $u_{X_1|X_2}(a_1|a_2)$ to be the proportion of X_1's utile that it ascribes to alternative a_1, given that X_2 ascribes its entire utile to alternative a_2. This constraint imposes a notion of commensurability or balance among the individuals, roughly equivalent to all voters having equal material weight. For example, consider a hierarchical organization such as the military, where influence flows from superiors to subordinates. Suppose a commander issues an order that the subordinate must carry out. Even though the commander is empowered to authorize which order should be chosen, that authority is moot if the subordinate does not execute the order. Thus, although they perform different functions, their behaviors are of operationally equivalent value. Normalized utilities are not necessarily appropriate for all social choice problems, but this constraint is appropriate for many applications.

2.4 Epistemology vis-à-vis Praxeology

Probability is not really about numbers; it is about the structure of reasoning.

— Glenn Shafer

Quoted in J. Pearl, *Probabilistic Reasoning in Intelligent Systems*
(Morgan Kaufmann, 1988)

Descartes treated belief as action that might be undertaken wisely or rashly.

— Richard Jeffrey

Probability and the Art of Judgment (Cambridge University Press, 1992)

Probability theory was placed on a solid axiomatic footing by Kolmogorov (1933), who defined probability in terms of measure theory and established it as an ahistorical and acontextual mathematical study, free of all issues that motivated previous studies. He thereby rendered probability theory free from any interpretations, including its traditional application as a way to account for epistemological uncertainty. Nevertheless, the very name "probability theory" tends to restrict the application of the mathematics, although this name stems more from its historical beginnings than from its mathematical structure. Regardless of the context, however, the use of probability theory as a mathematical model to describe a given phenomenon depends on the appropriateness of the mathematical structure of that model for the application.

The results of Section 2.3 provide strong motivation to apply probability theory and all of its mathematical machinery as an appropriate model for a social network. Applying probability theory in this way, however, should not be done carte blanche. It is not sufficient simply to apply the mathematical syntax of probability theory without rigorously justifying the appropriateness of that syntax.

The discipline of epistemology focuses on analyzing how knowledge relates to truth, belief, and justification. In such a pursuit, a systematic way to organize and evaluate evidence regarding the truth of a proposition, combine different pieces of evidence, and relate one piece of evidence to another piece of evidence is indispensable. A natural reasoning mechanism with which to address these tasks is to form hypothetical propositions of the form "if p then q" where the antecedent p is an assertion regarding the truth of one proposition and the consequent q is the resulting evaluation of belief regarding another proposition. Probability theory offers a convenient and powerful framework within which to investigate such issues.

Historically, probability theory owes its mathematical origins to the need for a systematic way to manage beliefs and expectations in an environment of uncertainty and randomness, ranging from so-called frequentist scenarios such as predicting outcomes of coin flips and dice rolls to subjective scenarios such as predicting the winners of athletic contests. Regardless of the context, however, perhaps the most important and powerful attribute of probability theory is that it provides a structure within which to express and manage hypothetical reasoning.

Therefore, it should not be surprising that the mathematical syntax of probability theory could apply in any context that involves hypothetical reasoning. In particular, it is not surprising that this theory would surface in the context of conditional preferences regarding benefit. But the need to deal with hypothetical reasoning is not, by itself, sufficient justification for simply appropriating the mathematical syntax of the theory to that context. It must be established that the reasoning structure underlying the management of preferences is compatible with the reasoning structure that probability theory uses to manage beliefs.

To examine the distinction between managing beliefs and managing preferences, let us examine two scenarios. First, given a set of propositions, the problem is to determine which of them is realized. Here, probability is used in an epistemological context to classify propositions in terms of belief and knowledge. Second, given a set of alternatives, the problem is to determine which of them should be actualized. This context, however, is not epistemological, and the concept of belief regarding the truth of a proposition is not relevant. Rather, the relevant concept is the preference for action. To emphasize this distinction, we introduce the term *praxeology*, a neologism created from the Greek roots *praxis* (action) and *logos* (reason). The Oxford English Dictionary defines *praxeology* as "the study of such actions as are necessary in order to give practical effect to a theory or technique; the science of human conduct; the science of efficient action" (Murray et al., 1991). Thus, the praxeological use of probability theory is to classify actions on the basis of preference and decisiveness.[5]

It is not sufficient, however, simply to relabel the syntactical and semantic notions that are applicable to epistemological applications

---

[5] The praxeological application of probability theory is not new. Berhold (1973) and Castagnoli and LiCalzi (1996) have interpreted normalized utility functions as probability mass functions, and Abbas and Howard (2005) and Abbas (2009) have applied probability theory to the study of multi-attribute decision problems.

of probability theory to corresponding analogous notions in the praxeological domain. These relabelings, however, can be valid only if both contexts comply with two fundamental structural constraints that often go unnoticed in the development of the theory, but are nevertheless essential. These properties are acyclicity and invariance.

An important feature of probability theory is that the simultaneous occurrence of a set of events can be expressed by the chain rule. Consider the simultaneous occurrence of B_1 and B_2. There are two ways to frame this situation. Under one framing, the probability of B_2 is viewed as influenced by the realization of B_1, and under the alternate framing, the probability of B_1 is influenced by the realization of B_2. These two framings, however, must be consistent; that is,

$$P(B_2|B_1)P(B_1) = P(B_1 \cap B_2) = P(B_2 \cap B_1) = P(B_1|B_2)P(B_2) \quad (2.35)$$

must hold.[6] Notice, however, that, although statistical dependency under these two framings is expressed in opposite directions, it is unidirectional in both cases – the influence is *acyclic*. The probability syntax does not provide for the probability of the *simultaneous* occurrence of B_1 and B_2 to be expressed as a function of both $P(B_1|B_2)$ and $P(B_2|B_1)$. As we shall see in Chapter 3, however, this constraint can be removed by eliminating simultaneity. Doing so, however, results in a dynamic, rather than static, framing of the issue.

In addition to acyclicity, there is another important constraint that must be honored: The conditional probabilities are not independent of each other. That is, $P(B_1|B_2)$ and $P(B_2|B_1)$ are functions of each other, related by the values of $P(B_1)$ and $P(B_2)$. Consequently, there is an invariance relationship between B_1 and B_2, as expressed by (2.35).

Although it is usually not explicitly stated, a necessary condition for a probabilistic model to be an appropriate characterization of a phenomenon is that invariance holds. Invariance is automatically satisfied when probability is used with frequentist scenarios such as predicting outcomes of coin flips and dice rolls.

The situation is more problematic, however, under subjective interpretations involving beliefs. Let B_1 be the event that an athletic team wins a game, and let B_2 be the event that the team's star player does not play. Suppose we wish to predict the likelihood of $B_1 \cap B_2$,

---

[6] Appendix C provides a brief tutorial of the probability concepts, terminology, and notation that is used in this work.

that is, that the team will win *and* that the star player will not play. If probability theory is to be an appropriate model with which to characterize the simultaneous realization of these events, then it must be assumed that the probability that the team wins given that the star player does not play is invariantly related to the probability that star player does not play given that the team wins. However, there is no objective mechanism that relates these conditional events in the way that the number of faces that turn up when dice are rolled are conditionally related. These latter relationships can be empirically computed, but the conditional relationships between the team winning and the star player not playing are based on subjective beliefs.

The vulnerability of subjective probability to invariance violations is often ignored in practice because the analyst would most likely use only one framing and would not be inclined to confirm consistency with alternate framings. In fact, the issue is just "swept under the rug" if it is considered at all. Nevertheless, the concept is often implicitly invoked in the construction of probability models used to characterize the way people organize information. Pearl (1988) argues that, in practice, multivariate distributions are rarely determined by specifying all of the entries in a joint-distribution table. "Probabilistic judgments on a small number of propositions are issued swiftly and reliably, while judging the likelihood of a conjunction of propositions entails much difficulty and hesitancy. This suggests that the elementary building blocks of human knowledge are not entries of a joint-distribution table. Rather, they are low-order marginal and conditional probabilities defined over small clusters of propositions" (Pearl, 1988, p. 78). Given this hypothesis, the obvious way to construct a joint distribution is to synthesize it from conditional and marginal distributions by applying the chain rule. But that is *not* how the classical development of probability theory actually works. Under the conventional development of probability theory, conditional probability mass functions are derived from joint and marginal probability mass functions, and the chain rule is a consequence, not the primary concept. Nevertheless, as Pearl observes, it is common and extremely useful to view the conditional probability mass functions as primitives with which to construct the joint mass function.

In fact, Jaynes (2003) presents a development of probability theory that, indeed, does regard conditional probabilities as the primitives and develops probability theory accordingly. In that development, the concept of invariance is a critical element. He argues that the validity of probability theory as a model of belief hinges on the assertion that the different framings of a decision problem should lead to the same result, so long as each framing uses exactly the same information. Our development follows Pearl's example and is philosophically aligned with Jaynes's approach. Our motivation is essentially the same as that used by Pearl. Research has shown that many organizational structures possess components arranged into clusters, such as branches, departments, and teams, that constrain the flow of social influence (see Burns and Stalker (1961)). Thus, we may paraphrase Pearl's remark as follows: The elementary building blocks of a social network are low-order categorical and conditional preferences defined over small clusters of individuals.

Since the goal of aggregation is to combine individual preferences, invariance is of vital importance in the praxeological domain. Thus, if the mathematics of probability theory is to be applicable to the mathematics of preference theory, then invariance must hold. Consider a two-agent society $\{X_1, X_2\}$, and suppose (in compliance with acyclicity), that X_1 possesses a categorical preference ordering $\succsim_1$ and X_2 possesses a conditional preference ordering $\succsim_{2|1}$. The coordination ordering is given by (2.9), yielding $\succsim_{12} = f(\succsim_1, \succsim_{2|1})$. Now consider the alternative framing, where X_2 possesses a categorical preference ordering $\succsim_2$ and X_1 possesses a conditional preference ordering $\succsim_{1|2}$, with coordination ordering $\succsim_{21} = f(\succsim_2, \succsim_{1|2})$. Invariance requires that $\succsim_{12} \equiv \succsim_{21}$. Complying with this constraint requires a fundamental assumption: If both individuals have access to the same information regarding their relationship, they will combine their preferences to yield the same coordination ordering, regardless of how the problem is framed.

The assumption behind invariance is that, although there are many possible ways to organize a network, if they all are based on the same information set and if the information is used in a consistent and logical way without distorting or discarding any data, then they should all generate the same social model. Admittedly, this is a goal for which honest people may strive without attaining. What is important, however, is that the *concept* be valid.

As with any model, legitimacy is dependent on the ability to predict behavior and on the light that is shed. Thus, an important aspect of defining a model for a network is to establish confidence that the modeling conditions are reasonable. This does not mean, however, that one must develop models for all possible framings. The level of investigation depends on the particular context. For example, a legitimate question is whether invariance can occur in a hierarchical society, where a superior individual, such as a company CEO or military commander, exercises influence over a subordinate. In other words, can a directed graph of the form superior $\rightarrow$ subordinate be inverted so influence flows in the opposite direction – that is, subordinate $\rightarrow$ superior? One way invariance can fail is if the CEO is an absolute dictator who rules by fiat and is completely immune to social influences. However, unless it is a trivial network, it is not likely that the individuals form their preferences in a complete social vacuum such that the preferences of others has no (even indirect or tacit) influence on their own. To the extent that the subordinate and the superior use the same information (at least conceptually), then each will take the rationality of the other into consideration when forming their preferences, regardless of the framing. The key issue in this regard is that both individuals have access to the same information and use that knowledge with compatible reasoning processes.

It is not presumed that invariance will apply to all social situations, but it is a reasonable condition that will apply to many human decision-making scenarios. Its application to the design of artificial systems, however, is less controversial. Artificial agents must operate according to the model that is used to design them. If they are designed to use all of the available information in a consistent way, then it is not unreasonable to require that their preference orderings must be invariant. In fact, it would be highly desirable as a fundamental regularity property that would reduce or eliminate inconsistent or contradictory behavior.

2.5 Coherent Aggregation

Any good mathematical commodity is worth generalizing.

— Michael Spivak
Calculus on Manifolds (W. A. Benjamin, Inc., 1965)

We have established that a comprehensive and coherent notion of coordination requires all *ex ante* preferences, both categorical and conditional, to be expressed through categorical and conditional utilities that comply with the syntax of probability theory. Thus we must replace the coordination ordering defined by (2.9) with a coordination function of the form

$$u_{1:n}(a_1, \dots, a_n) = f(u_{i|\text{pa}(i)}, \ i = 1, \dots, n). \tag{2.36}$$

We have also established that if acyclicity and invariance hold, then the network can be expressed as a directed acyclic graph whose vertices are the individuals and whose edges are the conditional utilities that serve as the connecting mechanism between the vertices. Since these edges are expressed in the syntax of probability mass functions, it is immediate that such a network is isomorphic to a Bayesian network and, therefore, the properties of Bayesian networks may be applied.

2.5.1 Bayesian Networks

Definition 2.12 A *Bayesian network* is a directed acyclic graph that satisfies the following conditions.

- The ith vertex corresponds to a discrete random variable Y_i taking values in a finite set $\mathcal{Y}_i$.
- The ith edge corresponds to the conditional probability that $Y_i = y_i \in \mathcal{Y}_i$, given that its parents $\text{pa}(Y_i) = \{Y_{i_1}, \dots, Y_{i_{q_i}}\}$ assume the values $\mathbf{y}_i = (y_{i_1}, \dots, y_{i_{q_i}}) \in \mathcal{Y}_{i_1} \times \dots \times \mathcal{Y}_{i_{q_i}}$, is specified as $p_{i|\text{pa}(i)}(y_i|\mathbf{y}_i)$. If $\text{pa}(Y_i) = \emptyset$, then $p_{i|\text{pa}(i)} = p_i$, the unconditional marginal distribution of Y_i.

□

Notice that the conditional probability mass functions are the primitive concepts in this structure. It is not assumed that a joint probability distribution for $\{Y_1, \dots, Y_n\}$ has been defined. The following theorem, which is proved in Appendix B, provides the key step in the development of a coherent coordination function.

Theorem 2.5 The Bayesian Network Theorem. *Let* $\{Y_1, \dots, Y_n\}$ *be a Bayesian Network with conditional probability mass functions for each vertex given by* $p_{i|\text{pa}(i)}(y_i|\mathbf{y}_i)$, *where* $\mathbf{y}_i = (y_{i_1}, \dots, y_{i_{q_i}})$ *are the realizations of* $\text{pa}(Y_i) = \{Y_{i_1}, \dots, Y_{i_{q_i}}\}$, *the parents of* Y_i. *Then*

$$p_{1:n}(y_1, \dots, y_n) = \prod_{i=1}^{n} p_{i|\text{pa}(i)}(y_i|\mathbf{y}_i) \tag{2.37}$$

is the unique joint mass function for $\{Y_1, \ldots, Y_n\}$ *that satisfies the conditions of the Bayesian network.*

The content of this theorem is as follows. Either when analyzing the behavior of a naturally existing set of interacting elements or when designing a set of artificial interacting elements, it is natural to start by considering the way the local behavior of specific elements is influenced by other elements that are in close proximity either spatially, temporally, or functionally. From such local models of behavior one can build a global model by piecing together the local components in appropriate ways. This theorem establishes that, if these local causal influence relationships can be expressed as a directed acyclic graph such that the influence relationships between neighboring vertices can be represented by conditional probability distributions where the conditional dependencies flow in only one way, then a unique joint probability mass function can be synthesized according to the chain rule. In other words, when *specifying* the probabilistic relationships of a DAG, one need only be concerned with how the children are influenced by their parents, and not vice versa. This approach, pioneered by Pearl (1988), provides a powerful synthesis tool for the design of artificial entities. The novelty of this approach is that it is used to synthesize a joint probability mass function from marginal and conditional mass functions as the primitive concepts, rather than, as is done with traditional probability theory, viewing the joint distribution as the primitive from which marginal and conditional distributions can be extracted. For additional discussions of Bayesian networks, see Cowell et al. (1999); Lauritzen (1996); Jensen (2001).

2.5.2 *The Aggregation Theorem*

Theorem 2.6 *Let* $\{X_1, \ldots, X_n\}$ *be an n-member acyclic network with finite alternative set* $\mathcal{A}$ *for which invariance holds, and let* $\{u_{i|\text{pa}(i)}(\cdot|\mathbf{a}_i) \, \forall \mathbf{a}_i \in \mathcal{A}^{p_i}, \, i = 1, \ldots, n\}$ *be a set of conditional utility mass functions, where* $\mathbf{a}_i = (a_{i_1}, \ldots, a_{i_{p_i}})$ *is a conditioning conjecture for* $\text{pa}(X_i) = \{X_{i_1}, \ldots, X_{i_{p_i}}\}$. *Then the coordination function* $u_{1:n}: \mathcal{A}^n \to [0, 1]$ *is socially coherent if, and only if, it is defined as*

$$u_{1:n}(a_1, \ldots, a_n) = \prod_{i=1}^{n} u_{i|\text{pa}(i)}(a_i|\mathbf{a}_i). \tag{2.38}$$

Furthermore, the coordination function is endogenous.

Proof Given the hypotheses of the theorem, the influence network is isomorphic to a Bayesian network, hence Theorem 2.5 applies.

To establish endogeny, we must assume that a desire for social coherence is an innate property of the network. Also, according to the von Neumann–Morgenstern hypothesis regarding rational behavior, if one's preferences are governed by binary preference relations, then one will behave as if one has assigned a numerical utility to each alternative and will ascribe higher preference to an alternative with a higher utility than to one with a lower utility. Thus, we may view the *ex ante* utility mass functions as innate properties of the network. Thus, just as Theorem 2.5 provides a unique statistical model for a Bayesian network, Theorem 2.6 provides a unique coordination model for a socially coherent social network.   □

We now review the process that has lead to Theorem 2.6. Our objective is to create a social model that characterizes the social environment of a collective that is endogenous and democratic. To be endogenous, it must arise from the innate properties of the collective, rather than being imposed by some external source. We argued that to achieve this objective, the aggregation must provide an assessment of innate social structure – an emergent coordination ordering – of the society as a function of all of the possible conjecture profiles defined over $\mathcal{A}^n$, and not just a ranking over $\mathcal{A}$, as is the objective of conventional aggregation. We then established that for such an aggregation to meet minimal conditions of democracy (i.e., coherence), it must comply with the axioms of probability theory. Consequently, the ordinal categorical and conditional orderings must be replaced by cardinal categorical and conditional utilities. Furthermore, if the system is acyclical and invariant, the network is isomorphic to a Bayesian network and aggregation is an application of the chain rule.

A coordination function is syntactically equivalent to a joint probability mass function for a set of discrete random variables. Just as the joint mass probability mass function captures all of the innate statistical dependencies among the random variables, the coordination function captures all of the innate social relationships among the individuals. Furthermore, all of the standard probabilistic manipulations are mathematically well defined, and it remains only to provide operational praxeological definitions for their appropriate usage.

Marginalization The utilities, either categorical or conditional, used to generate the coordination utility are *ex ante*, meaning before the social engagement. Once these utilities have propagated through the society via the chain rule to generate the coordination function, *ex post* utilities, denoted $\tilde{u}_i$, may be extracted via marginalization for each X_i yielding

$$\tilde{u}_i(a_i) = \sum_{\sim a_i} u_{1:n}(a_1, \ldots, a_n), \tag{2.39}$$

where the notation $\sum_{\sim a_i}$ means the sum is taken over all arguments of $u_{1:n}$ except a_i. It is straightforward to see that the *ex post* utilities are identical with the *ex ante* utilities of root individuals, but for non-root individuals, the *ex ante* utilities take into consideration the strength of influence that the parents have on the child. In this way, the individual accounts for the interests of others when defining its own interests, and the net result of this interrelationship is the *ex post* marginal utility.

Social Independence If all individuals possess categorical utilities, then the coordination function is simply the product of the categorical utilities, just as the joint mass function of a set of statistically independent random variables is the product of the marginal probability mass functions.

Bayes Rule In the probability context, Bayes rule provides the mechanism for transforming a prior distribution into a posterior distribution. In a praxeological context, an *ex ante* categorical utility corresponds to a prior, and posterior (i.e., *ex post*) conditional utility may be computed via Bayes rule. To illustrate, consider the two-agent network $\{X_1, X_2\}$ under framing $\{u_1, u_{2|1}\}$. First, marginalization may be used to compute the *ex post* marginal of X_2 as $\tilde{u}_2(a_2) = \sum_{a_1} u_{12}(a_1, a_2)$, and then Bayes rule may be applied to obtain the *ex post* conditional utility

$$\tilde{u}_{1|2}(a_1|a_2) = \frac{u_{2|1}(a_2|a_1)u_1(a_1)}{\tilde{u}_2(a_2)}. \tag{2.40}$$

Thus, Bayes rule provides the mechanism to convert one framing of the social model to another framing; that is,

$$u_{12}(a_1, a_2) = u_1(a_1)u_{2|1}(a_2|a_1) = \tilde{u}_{1|2}(a_1|a_2)\tilde{u}_2(a_2) = \tilde{u}_{21}(a_2, a_1). \tag{2.41}$$

2.6 Solution Concepts

The social choice literature provides many solution concepts, and it is not the intent of this book to describe them. (A useful summary of both categories may be found in Gaertner (2006, ch. 6, 7).) All of these solutions, however, are based on the classical assumption that each individual possesses only categorical utilities. This section, however, focuses attention on decision concepts that apply to socially coherent societies where the individuals possess conditional preferences.

The existence of a comprehensive social model makes it possible to develop a variety of possible solution concepts that take into account the social structure. In this section we describe one possible approach as an illustration. It should be noted that this approach is not unique, and may not universally apply. Solution concepts should be designed in accordance with the aspects of social rationality that govern the behavior of rational individuals in mutual interaction for each particular application. The coordination function may be viewed, therefore, as a framework within which solutions can be deduced that explicitly take into consideration the social complexities of the group.

The incorporation of conditional utilities opens the possibility that a meaningful notion of group preference can emerge as the conditional utilities propagate through the network. This notion of group preference, however, is not an Arrovian preference ordering, that is, a preference of the form $\succsim_s$ over $\mathcal{A}$. Rather, it is a coordination preference ordering $u_{1:n}$, defined over $\mathcal{A}^n$, the set of all conjecture profiles $(a_1, \ldots, a_n)$, where a_i is a conjecture associated with X_i.

One obvious solution concept is to define a social choice function

$$w_{1:n}(a) = u_{1:n}(a, \ldots, a), \tag{2.42}$$

from which the *coordination* solution $a_g = \arg\max_{a \in \mathcal{A}} w_{1:n}(a)$ can be derived. This result is the most coordinated outcome, but such a rule may excessively penalize some members of the society. In particular, each individual has its own individual choice function, defined by the *ex post* marginals given by (2.39).

The existence of both group and individual choice functions provides a framework for negotiation, where each individual submits a lower bound on the amount of utility it would require to agree to a solution. Let b_i denote this bound for X_i, and define the *individual negotiation* sets

$$\mathcal{N}_i = \{a \in \mathcal{A}: \tilde{u}_i(a) \geq b_i\}. \tag{2.43}$$

Under the concept of social justice advocated by (Rawls, 1971), a lower bound on the welfare for the group is the minimum benefit to any member of the group. Accordingly, the group lower bound must be determined by $\min_i b_i$. To compute this bound, we must account for the fact that the coordination distributes one unit of utility mass to N^n conjecture profiles, whereas an individual distributes one unit of utility mass to N individual conjectures. To account for this allocation difference, we must divide b_i by $N^n/N = N^{n-1}$. Thus, we let

$$b_{1:n} = \min_i b_i/N^{n-1} \tag{2.44}$$

and require the group to restrict its set of acceptable alternatives to the set

$$\mathcal{N}_{1:n} = \{a \in \mathcal{A}: w_{1:n}(a) \geq b_{1:n}\}, \tag{2.45}$$

and define the *coordination set*

$$\mathcal{C} = \mathcal{N}_{1:n} \cap \mathcal{N}_1 \cap \cdots \cap \mathcal{N}_n. \tag{2.46}$$

If $\mathcal{C} = \varnothing$, then, to obtain a solution, at least some individuals will need to reduce their values of b_i, otherwise there can be no compromise solution.

Example 2.1 Consider the Three Stooges problem introduced in Example 1.1, whose network is displayed in Figure 2.1. We may now define conditional utilities that agree with the conditional preference profile defined in (1.6). Although the requirement for coherent aggregation requires preferences to be expressed via categorical utilities, it is often useful to express these utilities parametrically,

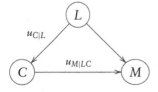

Figure 2.1: The Three-Stooges Network with Utility Linkages.

rather than with precise numerical values. Consider the following three-parameter family of utilities.

$$u_L(F) = 1 - \alpha \qquad u_L(I) = \alpha \tag{2.47}$$

for $0 \le \alpha < 1/2$;

$$\begin{aligned} u_{C|L}(F|F) &= \beta & u_{C|L}(I|F) &= 1 - \beta \\ u_{C|L}(F|I) &= 1 - \beta & u_{C|L}(I|I) &= \beta \end{aligned} \tag{2.48}$$

for $0 \le \beta < 1/2$; and

$$\begin{aligned} u_{M|LC}(F|FF) &= \gamma & u_{M|LC}(I|FF) &= 1 - \gamma \\ u_{M|LC}(F|FI) &= 1 - \gamma & u_{M|LC}(I|FI) &= \gamma \\ u_{M|LC}(F|IF) &= \gamma & u_{M|LC}(I|IF) &= 1 - \gamma \\ u_{M|LC}(F|II) &= 1 - \gamma & u_{M|LC}(I|II) &= \gamma \end{aligned} \tag{2.49}$$

for $0 \le \gamma < 1/2$.

The coordination function is computed by

$$u_{LCM}(a_L, a_C, a_M) = u_L(a_L)u_{C|L}(a_C|a_L)u_{M|LC}(a_M|a_L, a_C), \tag{2.50}$$

resulting in

$$\begin{aligned} u_{LCM}(F, F, F) &= (1 - \alpha)\beta\gamma \\ u_{LCM}(F, F, I) &= (1 - \alpha)\beta(1 - \gamma) \\ u_{LCM}(F, I, F) &= (1 - \alpha)(1 - \beta)(1 - \gamma) \\ u_{LCM}(F, I, I) &= (1 - \alpha)(1 - \beta)\gamma \\ u_{LCM}(I, F, F) &= \alpha(1 - \beta)\gamma \\ u_{LCM}(I, F, I) &= \alpha(1 - \beta)(1 - \gamma) \\ u_{LCM}(I, I, F) &= \alpha\beta(1 - \gamma) \\ u_{LCM}(I, I, I) &= \alpha\beta\gamma \end{aligned} \tag{2.51}$$

Since, by the problem statement, α, β, and γ are all constrained to the interval $[0, 1/2)$, by inspection we see immediately that the outcomes *FIF* and *III* have the largest and smallest coordination function values, respectively. This result is in agreement with the ordering defined by (1.15), which was generated by an exogenous imposition of utilitarianism, as defined by Table 1.1. The relative rankings of the intermediate outcomes, however, depend on the values of the parameters. For example, comparing the coordination function of *FFF* to the other options, $FFI \succ_{LCM} FFF$ and $FII \succ_{LCM} FFF$ for all values of the parameters, but $FFF \succ_{LCM} IFF$ for $\beta > \alpha$ and $IFF \succ_{LCM} FFF$ for $\alpha > \beta$. In other words, if the intensity of Larry's preference for French is stronger than the intensity of Curly's desire to oppose Larry, then the group will prefer IFF to FFF, regardless of Mo's preferences. By making evaluations such as these, the complex structure of the social model can be analyzed in detail.

The individual *ex post* marginals are obtained by applying (2.39), yielding

$$\begin{aligned} \tilde{u}_L(F) &= 1 - \alpha \\ \tilde{u}_L(I) &= \alpha \end{aligned}, \tag{2.52}$$

$$\begin{aligned} \tilde{u}_C(F) &= \alpha + \beta - 2\alpha\beta \\ \tilde{u}_C(I) &= 1 - \alpha + \beta - 2\alpha\beta \end{aligned}, \tag{2.53}$$

and

$$\begin{aligned} \tilde{u}_M(F) &= 1 - \gamma - \beta(1 - 2\gamma) - \alpha(1 - \beta(2 - 4\gamma) - 2\gamma) \\ \tilde{u}_M(I) &= \gamma + \beta(1 - 2\gamma) - \alpha(1 - \beta(2 - 4\gamma) - 2\gamma) \end{aligned}. \tag{2.54}$$

Straightforward analysis reveals that

$$\begin{aligned} \tilde{u}_L(F) &> \tilde{u}_L(I) \\ \tilde{u}_C(F) &< \tilde{u}_C(I) \\ \tilde{u}_M(F) &> \tilde{u}_M(I) \end{aligned} \tag{2.55}$$

for all $\alpha, \beta, \gamma \in [0, 1/2]$. As a specific numerical example, let $\alpha = \beta = \gamma = 0.4$. The coordination function values are displayed in Table 2.1,

Table 2.1: *Coordination Function for the Three Stooges Dinner Party.*

(a_L, a_C, a_M)	$u_{(LCM)}$
(F, F, F)	0.096
(F, F, I)	0.144
(F, I, F)	0.216
(F, I, I)	0.144
(I, F, F)	0.096
(I, F, I)	0.144
(I, I, F)	0.096
(I, I, I)	0.064

which confirms that the best social alternative is for Larry and Mo to go to the French Restaurant and for Curly to eat Italian, and that the worst social outcome is for them to all eat Italian. Also, since $\alpha = \beta$, it follows that $FFF \sim_{LCM} IFF$.

The corresponding individual *ex post* marginals are

$$\tilde{u}_L(F) = 0.6 \quad \tilde{u}_L(I) = 0.4$$
$$\tilde{u}_C(F) = 0.48 \quad \tilde{u}_C(I) = 0.52 \quad . \tag{2.56}$$
$$\tilde{u}_M(F) = 0.504 \quad \tilde{u}_M(I) = 0.496$$

The coordination set defined by (2.42) is $a_g = F$ with $w_{LCM}(a_g) = 0.096$. To compute the negotiation set we apply (2.44) to obtain $b_{LCM} = \min_i b_i/2^2 = 0.4/4 = 0.1$, which results in

$$\mathcal{N}_{LCM} = \{a \in \mathcal{A} : w_{LCM}(a) \geq 0.1\} = \varnothing, \tag{2.57}$$

and there is no basis for negotiation. However, if at least one individual were willing to reduce his lower bound to 0.38, then $\mathcal{N}_{LCM} = \{F\}$, a compromise would be reached and they would dine together at the French restaurant. However, the most coordinated outcome is for each to go his separate way. Thus, at least one individual must be willing to sacrifice some personal benefit for the group to stay together. □

Example 2.2 Now let us revisit Example 1.2, and perform a parametric analysis of the Edwin and Angelina problem. Suppose Angelina's categorical utility is of the form

$$u_A(\mathbf{w}_E) = \alpha \quad u_A(\mathbf{w}_J) = \beta \quad u_A(\mathbf{w}_O) = \gamma, \tag{2.58}$$

where $\alpha > \beta > \gamma \geq 0$ and $\alpha + \beta + \gamma = 1$. Next, we must specify Edwin's conditional utility $u_{E|A}$ for each of Angelina's possible conjectures. As in Section 1.3.1, we consider two cases; Edwin the Egoist, and Edwin the Altruist.

Edwin the Egoist First, suppose Angelina conjectures $\mathbf{w}_E$; that is, marrying Edwin is the outcome that should obtain. Under that hypothesis, she would not wed the judge and, consequently, any fear that Edwin would have in that regard is put to rest, thereby freeing Edwin to prefer to remain single. Thus, Edwin the Egoist would put his entire conditional mass on $\mathbf{w}_O$, yielding

$$u_{E|A}(\mathbf{w}_E|\mathbf{w}_E) = 0 \quad u_{E|A}(\mathbf{w}_J|\mathbf{w}_E) = 0 \quad u_{E|A}(\mathbf{w}_O|\mathbf{w}_E) = 1 . \quad (2.59)$$

Next, suppose Angelina were to conjecture $\mathbf{w}_J$; that is, she most prefers marrying the judge. To prevent this outcome, Edwin would reverse his preferences and place his entire conditional mass on $\mathbf{w}_E$, yielding

$$u_{E|A}(\mathbf{w}_E|\mathbf{w}_J) = 1 \quad u_{E|A}(\mathbf{w}_J|\mathbf{w}_J) = 0 \quad u_{E|A}(\mathbf{w}_O|\mathbf{w}_J) = 0 . \quad (2.60)$$

Finally, suppose Angelina were to conjecture $\mathbf{w}_O$. Under that hypothesis, Edwin could achieve his most preferred outcome by placing his entire conditional mass on $\mathbf{w}_O$, thus,

$$u_{E|A}(\mathbf{w}_E|\mathbf{w}_O) = 0 \quad u_{E|A}(\mathbf{w}_J|\mathbf{w}_O) = 0 \quad u_{E|A}(\mathbf{w}_O|\mathbf{w}_O) = 1 . \quad (2.61)$$

The resulting coordination function is obtained by applying (2.38); that is,

$$u_{EA}(a_E, a_A) = u_{E|A}(a_E|a_A)u_A(a_A) \quad (2.62)$$

for all $(a_E, a_A) \in \{\mathbf{w}_E, \mathbf{w}_J, \mathbf{w}_O\} \times \{\mathbf{w}_E, \mathbf{w}_J, \mathbf{w}_O\}$, yielding the results displayed in Table 2.2. The *ex post* marginal utilities for Edwin and Angelina are computed via (2.39), resulting in

$$\begin{aligned}
\tilde{u}_E(\mathbf{w}_E) &= \beta \\
\tilde{u}_E(\mathbf{w}_J) &= 0 \qquad , \\
\tilde{u}_E(\mathbf{w}_O) &= \alpha + \gamma
\end{aligned} \quad (2.63)$$

and

$$\begin{aligned}
\tilde{u}_A(\mathbf{w}_E) &= \alpha \\
\tilde{u}_A(\mathbf{w}_J) &= \beta \quad . \\
\tilde{u}_A(\mathbf{w}_O) &= \gamma
\end{aligned} \quad (2.64)$$

Thus, in terms of individual welfare, Edwin would maximize his benefit by remaining single, and Angelina would maximize hers by

Table 2.2: *The Coordination Function for Edwin the Egoist.*

Edwin	Angelina		
	$\mathbf{w}_E$	$\mathbf{w}_J$	$\mathbf{w}_O$
$\mathbf{w}_E$	0	β	0
$\mathbf{w}_J$	0	0	0
$\mathbf{w}_O$	α	0	γ

marrying Edwin, but this joint outcome is impossible, although it is
the outcome that would maximize coordination. Edwin's second best
outcome would be to marry Angelina, which would result in her best
outcome, but Edwin's ego will not allow him to make that sacrifice,
hence the coordination function of $(\mathbf{w}_E, \mathbf{w}_E)$ is zero. The only possible
outcome with non-zero coordination is for both Edwin and Angelina
to remain single. However, Angelina would be better off by marrying
the judge than by remaining single. The main take away from this
example is that it is a very dysfunctional group – the most coordinated
outcome would give Edwin his best outcome and Angelina her worst
outcome. Coordination is a measure of how conflictive the two are:
the higher the coordination, the more they are conflictive.

Edwin the Altruist: The only change required for Edwin the Altruist
is to replace (2.59) with

$$u_{E|A}(\mathbf{w}_E|\mathbf{w}_E) = 1 \quad u_{E|A}(\mathbf{w}_J|\mathbf{w}_E) = 0 \quad u_{E|A}(\mathbf{w}_O|\mathbf{w}_E) = 0, \qquad (2.65)$$

resulting in the coordination function displayed in Table 2.3, and the
ex post marginal utilities are

$$\begin{aligned}
\tilde{u}_E(\mathbf{w}_E) &- \alpha + \beta \\
\tilde{u}_E(\mathbf{w}_J) &= 0 \qquad , \\
\tilde{u}_E(\mathbf{w}_O) &= \gamma
\end{aligned} \qquad (2.66)$$

and Angelina's utilities remain as expressed in (2.64).

$$\tilde{u}_A(\mathbf{w}_E) = \alpha \qquad (2.67)$$
$$\tilde{u}_A(\mathbf{w}_J) = \beta \qquad (2.68)$$
$$\tilde{u}_A(\mathbf{w}_O) = \gamma . \qquad (2.69)$$

**Table 2.3: *The Coordination Function
for Edwin the Altruist.***

Edwin	Angelina		
	$\mathbf{w}_E$	$\mathbf{w}_J$	$\mathbf{w}_O$
$\mathbf{w}_E$	α	β	0
$\mathbf{w}_J$	0	0	0
$\mathbf{w}_O$	0	0	γ

Thus, the Edwin the Altruist scenario yields the highest coordination when both Edwin and Angelina obtain their most preferred outcomes, indicating a highly cooperative society. An interesting and perhaps unexpected result of Edwin's altruism is that the *ex post* benefit of him being willing to sacrifice to benefit Angelina is actually greater than it would be if he were egoistic. This result is in agreement with Gibbard (1974), who concludes that it is to Edwin's advantage to wave his rights (in other words, to be altruistic), thereby conforming with Pareto efficiency. ☐

2.7 Reframing

In Section 2.4 we established that the validity of the social model defined by Theorem 2.6 relies on invariance; that is, that all reframings of the scenario must result in the same coordination function. Consequently, we may apply Bayes rule to generate alternatives ways to frame a social choice scenario. Different framings of a network correspond to different linkages among the individuals, but when defining a network model for a human organization, there is no unique way to structure the linkages. Each framing depends on a different point of view, but if all are based on the same information set and are applied in a logical manner, they should generate the same social model. In fact, once a particular social model is created, it would be worthwhile to generate alternate framings in order to gain additional insights and to provide an additional "smell" test as a means of gaining confidence in the model.

The Three Stooges problem introduced in Section 1.3 corresponds to the framing illustrated in Figure 2.1. This is one of six possible framings of the problem. For example, let us consider the framing illustrated in Figure 2.2, where Mo possesses a categorical utility, and both Mo and Larry influence Curly. Using the values given in Table 2.1, we may compute the marginal for Mo as

$$\tilde{u}_M(a_M) = \sum_{a_L} \sum_{a_C} u_{LCM}(a_L, a_C, a_M). \tag{2.70}$$

We may also compute the conditional utility for Larry given Mo's conjectures as

$$\tilde{u}_{L|M}(a_L | a_M) = \frac{\tilde{u}_{LM}(a_L, a_M)}{\tilde{u}_M(a_M)}, \tag{2.71}$$

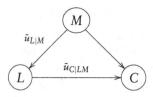

Figure 2.2: An Alternate Framing of the Three-Stooges Network with Mo Taking the Lead.

where

$$\tilde{u}_{LM}(a_L, a_M) = \sum_{a_C} u_{LCM}(a_L, a_C, a_M). \tag{2.72}$$

Finally, we may compute the conditional utility for Curly given conjectures by Larry and Mo as

$$\tilde{u}_{C|LM}(a_C|a_L, a_M) = \frac{u_{LCM}(a_L, a_C, a_M)}{\tilde{u}_{LM}(a_L, a_M)}. \tag{2.73}$$

The resulting valuations are

$$\tilde{u}_M(F) = 0.504 \qquad \tilde{u}_M(I) = 0.496, \tag{2.74}$$

$$\begin{aligned} \tilde{u}_{L|M}(F|F) &= 0.619 & \tilde{u}_{L|M}(I|F) &= 0.381 \\ \tilde{u}_{L|M}(F|I) &= 0.581 & \tilde{u}_{L|M}(I|I) &= 0.419 \end{aligned} \tag{2.75}$$

and

$$\begin{aligned} \tilde{u}_{C|LM}(F|FF) &= 0.308 & \tilde{u}_{C|LM}(I|FF) &= 0.692 \\ \tilde{u}_{C|LM}(F|FI) &= 0.5 & \tilde{u}_{C|LM}(I|FI) &= 0.5 \\ \tilde{u}_{C|LM}(F|IF) &= 0.5 & \tilde{u}_{C|LM}(I|IF) &= 0.5 \\ \tilde{u}_{C|LM}(F|II) &= 0.692 & \tilde{u}_{C|LM}(I|II) &= 0.308 \end{aligned} \tag{2.76}$$

We may interpret these results as follows. Suppose, rather than it falling on Larry to state his preferences first, it falls to Mo, who categorically prefers French to Italian cuisine. Next, Larry speaks up and states that regardless of Mo's preferences, he prefers French to Italian. Finally, Curly announces that he is opposed to both Larry and Mo if they agree, but if they do not agree, then he is indifferent.

Finally, let us examine a framing where Curly takes the lead, as illustrated in Figure 2.3. The resulting valuations for this reframing are

$$\tilde{u}_C(F) = 0.48 \qquad \tilde{u}_C(I) = 0.52, \tag{2.77}$$

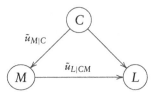

Figure 2.3: An Alternate Framing of the Three-Stooges Network with Curly Taking the Lead.

$$\tilde{u}_{M|C}(F|F) = 0.4 \qquad \tilde{u}_{M|C}(I|F) = 0.6$$
$$\tilde{u}_{M|C}(F|I) = 0.6 \qquad \tilde{u}_{M|C}(I|I) = 0.4 \text{ ,} \tag{2.78}$$

and

$$\tilde{u}_{L|CM}(F|FF) = 0.5 \qquad \tilde{u}_{L|CM}(I|FF) = 0.5$$
$$\tilde{u}_{L|CM}(F|FI) = 0.5 \qquad \tilde{u}_{L|CM}(I|FI) = 0.5$$
$$\tilde{u}_{L|CM}(F|IF) = 0.692 \qquad \tilde{u}_{L|CM}(I|IF) = 0.308 \text{ .} \tag{2.79}$$
$$\tilde{u}_{L|CM}(F|II) = 0.692 \qquad \tilde{u}_{L|CM}(I|II) = 0.308$$

With this framing with Curly in the lead, he favors Italian over French, and Mo is opposed to whatever Curly wants. Larry is indifferent if Curly prefers French to Italian, but favors French if Curly favors Italian. These three scenarios illustrate how the same information can be expressed in different, but equivalent ways.

2.8 Summary

Traditional treatments of probability theory are confined to the epistemological context, and even in that domain there are different interpretations. Savage (1954) divides these interpretations into three categories: objective (e.g, empirical), personalistic (e.g., subjective), and necessary (e.g., logical). The isomorphism established herein is with respect to the personalistic interpretation, which uses probability theory to provide a cardinal ranking of the degree of belief. The personalistic-praxeological isomorphism provides an additional interpretation that provides an exact analogy between probability and utility.

Under the personalistic interpretation, if the entire probability mass is concentrated on one proposition, then that proposition is deemed to be true and justified – it becomes knowledge. In the praxeological context, however, it is inappropriate to characterize actions in terms of belief and knowledge. Rather, the appropriate characterization is in terms of preference and decisiveness. A utility provides a mathematical characterization of the degree of preference, and if the entire utility mass is concentrated on one action, then the value of that action is incontrovertible – it is decisive. Thus, the natural praxeological analogues to the epistemological notions of belief and knowledge are, respectively, preference and decisiveness.

If all members of a society possess categorical preferences, they may be aggregated by conventional means to create a social choice. When members of the society possess conditional preferences, however, complex social relationships are created as the conditional preferences propagate through the network. In this context, aggregation creates much more than a social choice. It creates a complex social model that can be used to analyze the behavior of the network. Endogeny and democracy are essential conditions for such a model. Compliance with these conditions ensures that a) the society is self-contained in that it is not governed or influenced by assumptions or directives arising from outside the society; b) the model characterizes all social relationships that emerge as the conditional preferences propagate through the society; and c) the social model is coherent.

A key result of this chapter is a demonstration that satisfying these three conditions requires that the preferences be aggregated in a way that complies with the axioms of probability theory. Indeed, an order isomorphism exists between conditional preference orderings and conditional probabilities. It is thus established that the preferences must be expressed numerically and must be normalized to be mass functions, and must be combined according to the rules of probability theory. Accordingly, the appropriate way to aggregate the conditional utilities is via the chain rule, resulting in a coordination function that is syntactically analogous to a joint probability mass function.

The idea of applying probability theory to preference ordering is not new. Zeckhauser (1969), Fishburn (1972), and Intriligator (1973) introduced lotteries into majority rule voting procedures as a means of taking account of intensities of individuals' preferences. Coughlin (1992) discusses probabilistic election models in the context of voting. Yanovskaya (2006) has provided an axiomatization of probabilistic social choice functions. The basic idea behind these approaches is to establish a cardinal scaling by having each individual assign a probability to each alternative according to the strength of preference. It is an application of the isomorphic relationship between probability theory and utility theory. However, they differ from the approach developed herein in that they do not deal with conditional preferences. In retrospect, this limitation is somewhat surprising, since conditional reasoning is a natural human activity (at least in epistemological settings).

The notion of conditional preference orderings has been discussed by Abbas and Howard (2005) and Abbas (2009). Essentially, their approach is the polar opposite of the approach developed herein, which is to consider conditional preferences as the fundamental building blocks, or primitives, of a social organization and to use these conditional preferences to synthesize a joint preference ordering for the society. By contrast, their approach is to view multi-attribute utilities as the primitives and derive conditional utilities as the ratio of bivariate attribute utilities and single-attribute (i.e., marginal) utilities. Although the two approaches share a similar syntax, they are very different operationally. The approach developed by Abbas and Howard (2005) appropriates the standard textbook approach to constructing conditional probability distributions from joint and marginal distributions. But as was observed in Section 1.3.1, making preference judgments over the product set $\mathcal{A}^n$ is generally more difficult (and less natural) than making preference judgments (albeit conditional) over $\mathcal{A}$. In point of fact, this approach is more closely aligned with the development presented by Jaynes (2003) than with the standard textbook approach that is usually presented in introductory books on probability theory.

3 | *Deliberation*

What is the shortest word in the English language that contains the letters: abcdef? Answer: feedback. Don't forget that feedback is one of the essential elements of good communication.

— Anonymous

After their unsuccessful attempt to choose a restaurant as discussed in Example 2.1, the Three Stooges re-think their strategy. It occurs to them that whatever Larry wants, Curly does not want, and whatever Curly wants, Mo does not want. In an unfortunate attempt to resolve the impasse, Larry decides that he wants to reconsider: whatever Mo wants, he now does not want. Suppose, to start with, Larry announces his utilities, which are in favor of *F*. Curly then processes this information according to his conditional utilities, and announces he prefers *I*. Mo follows with favoring *F*, which then causes Larry to now favor *I*. Thus, after one cycle, Larry has changed his mind. Feeling a bit frustrated, but having nothing better to do, they continue the process. Eventually, they notice that their preferences are not changing at all! In fact, each one has exactly the same utility values – they are all indifferent between French and Italian dining. So they flip a coin and happily go off to dinner together (only to find that the restaurant is closed for the night).

Larry, Curly, and Mo have created an influence cycle, illustrated in Figure 3.1. This is *not* a preference cycle; it is not a manifestation of non-transitivity. An influence cycle is a form of deliberation, where the participants engage in dialogue in an attempt to negotiate a solution. By so doing, they have moved from a static situation, where all preferences are expressed simultaneously, to a dynamic situation, where preferences are expressed dynamically and are therefore subject to change.

This example illustrates an important extension to social choice theory – the ability to deliberate. If all individuals come to a social

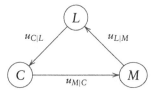

Figure 3.1: The Three Stooges Dinner Party with Cyclic Preferences.

engagement with fixed and immutable preferences, then deliberation is not possible. Indeed, there would be no reason to deliberate, because, it is assumed, each individual has already determined its own individual preferences, and has no overt concern for the welfare of others. Essentially, each individual is in a defensive position in the sense that the preferences of others can only constrain one's own welfare. But that hypothesis does not apply when social influence exists.

One of the interesting issues with regard to social choice theory is the relationship with what is termed *deliberative democracy* (Cohen, 1994; Habermas, 1994; Dryzek, 2000; Mackie, 2003; van Mill, 2006). A key feature of democracy is the opportunity for discourse – a dynamic process whereby individuals may work through a reasoning process with the hope of converging to a result that is rational, fair, and legitimate. A criticism of social choice theory is that, since individual preferences are fixed, there is no opportunity for deliberation, negotiation, and compromise. It is not the intent of this book to take a position on this debate in terms of the sociological/political motivations that govern the way groups make decisions. But one issue upon which this approach does shed some light is that it can narrow the gap between social choice theory and deliberation. In particular, the theory presented in this chapter offers a theoretical mechanism not only for dynamic preference modification to occur, but to converge to constant, or steady state, values through a dialogue process.

3.1 Dynamic Influence Models

The graph displayed in Figure 3.1 illustrates the re-formulated Three Stooges dinner party, This new formulation contains a cycle and therefore violates the acyclicity constraint discussed in Section 2.4. It is not isomorphic to a standard Bayesian network and, at first glance, the hypotheses of Theorem 2.6 do not appear to be satisfied.

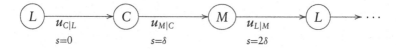

Figure 3.2: The Three Stooges dinner party viewed as a dynamic network.

A closer examination of Figure 3.1, however, reveals that it is the infinite concatenation of three Bayesian networks, $L \to C$, $C \to M$, and $M \to L$ as time s progresses, with a time lapse of δ between them, as illustrated in Figure 3.2. Three time units will pass before the cycle makes a complete circuit, which is repeated *ad infinitum* as a function of time. Consequently, the network illustrated in Figure 3.1 is isomorphic to a dynamic Bayesian network.

With an acyclic social choice problem, influence begins at the root vertices and terminates at vertices that have no children. Once propagation is complete, a solution concept is implemented, the choice is made, and the engagement is over. Obviously, the propagation of influence is not likely to be instantaneous. Some time interval is required for the transmission information between agents, but that time interval is irrelevant if the problem scenario is *stationary*, meaning that the conditional utilities do not change as influence propagates through the network. The existence of cycles, however, introduces an explicit dynamic component into the decision process. For each member of the cycle, influence propagates from one individual to another and eventually returns to the individual. Thus, even though the scenario may be stationary, the marginal preferences of each member of the cycle will be subject to continual change as time progresses. In a worst case, the marginal preferences may be unstable in the sense that they wildly oscillate, and in a best case, they will quickly converge to constant, or steady state, values. Thus, it is essential to understand the dynamic behavior of the marginal preferences.

The introduction of dynamics into a decision problem raises important questions regarding stability. A cyclic network is said to be *asymptotically stable* if the individual preferences converge to constant values as time increases. To study the convergence properties of a cyclic network, first recall that a network that satisfies the coherence condition is isomorphic to a collective of random variables. Thus, the probability syntax may be used to study cyclic networks. The key observation in this regard is that the network defined by Figure 3.1 is a Markov chain, and the convergence of such probabilistic entities is well studied. In a probabilistic context, a time series of random variables (i.e., a stochastic process) is a *Markov process* if the conditional probability distribution of future states, given the present and past states, depends only on the present state. In other words, the past and the future are independent, given the present. In the social choice context, the structure of the conditional utilities guarantees that the Markov property is satisfied. To illustrate, consider the sequence of influence relationships $X_1 \rightarrow X_2 \rightarrow X_3$. Although X_3 is directly influenced by X_2, once X_2's state is known, the history of how X_2 arrived at its current state does not affect X_3's state.

Definition 3.1   A k-member directed closed path with all edges oriented in the same direction is called a *simple k-cycle* if every vertex has exactly one incoming edge and one outgoing edge. Note that all vertices of a simple cycle must be distinct. □

Consider the simple k-cycle illustrated in Figure 3.3. Let δ denote the time interval required for information to transit between individuals, and let s denote a running time variable. At time $s = 0$, when the cycle is initiated, each X_i will be in conjecture state a_i with marginal utility $\tilde{u}_i(a_i, 0)$. Without loss of generality, assume that the

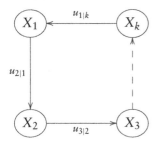

Figure 3.3: A Simple k-Cycle.

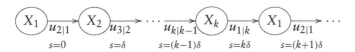

Figure 3.4: An Equivalent Dynamic Network.

cycle begins with X_1. For $s = 0, \delta, 2\delta, \cdots$, consider the equivalent dynamic network displayed in Figure 3.4.

Let us first consider the segment $\underset{s=0}{\overset{X_1 \xrightarrow{\ u_{2|1}\ } X_2}{}}$. At $s = \delta$, X_1's marginal utility is received by X_2, and the resulting coordination function for $\{X_1, X_2\}$ is, following (2.38),

$$u_{12}(a_1, a_2, \delta) = u_{2|1}(a_2|a_1)\tilde{u}_1(a_1, 0),\tag{3.1}$$

from which X_2's *ex post* marginal may be computed via (2.39), yielding

$$\tilde{u}_2(a_2, \delta) = \sum_{a_1} u_{12}(a_1, a_2, \delta).\tag{3.2}$$

Now consider the next segment $\underset{s=\delta}{\overset{X_2 \xrightarrow{\ u_{3|2}\ } X_3}{}}$. At $s = 2\delta$, the coordination function for $\{X_2, X_3\}$ is

$$u_{23}(a_2, a_3, 2\delta) = u_{3|2}(a_3|a_2)\tilde{u}_2(a_2, \delta)\tag{3.3}$$

and X_3's *ex post* marginal is

$$\tilde{u}_3(a_3, 2\delta) = \sum_{a_2} u_{23}(a_2, a_3, 2\delta).\tag{3.4}$$

Suppose this procedure continues for $s = 3\delta$, $s = 4\delta$, $\cdots$. To facilitate development of this theory, it is convenient to reformulate this process using matrix notation. Let us denote the elements of $\mathcal{A}$ as

$$\mathcal{A} = \{z_1, \ldots, z_N\}\tag{3.5}$$

and define the *utility mass vector* at time s by

$$\tilde{\mathbf{u}}_i(s) = \begin{bmatrix} \tilde{u}_i(z_1, s) \\ \vdots \\ \tilde{u}_i(z_N, s) \end{bmatrix}.\tag{3.6}$$

Next, define the *state-to-state transition matrix*

$$T_{i+1|i} = \begin{bmatrix} u_{i+1|i}(z_1|z_1) & \cdots & u_{i+1|i}(z_1|z_N) \\ \vdots & & \vdots \\ u_{i+1|i}(z_N|z_1) & \cdots & u_{i+1|i}(z_N|z_N) \end{bmatrix}.\tag{3.7}$$

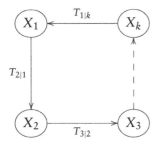

Figure 3.5: A *k*-Cycle Expressed in Terms of Transition Linkages.

With this notation, the operations defined by (3.1) and (3.2) can be combined into the single expression

$$\tilde{u}_2(\delta) = T_{1|2}\tilde{u}_1(0), \qquad (3.8)$$

and (3.3) and (3.4) can be combined to yield

$$\tilde{u}_3(2\delta) = T_{3|2}\tilde{u}_1(\delta). \qquad (3.9)$$

Figure 3.5 displays the *k*-cycle with the linkages represented by the state-to-state transition matrices. Tracing the path from X_i around the cycle back to X_i, the marginal mass vector $\tilde{u}_i$ is updated *k* times, where the indices are incremented mod *k*:

$$\tilde{u}_{i+1}(\delta) = T_{i+1|i}\tilde{u}_i(0)$$
$$\tilde{u}_{i+2}(2\delta) = T_{i+2|i+1}T_{i+1|i}\tilde{u}_i(0)$$
$$\vdots$$
$$\tilde{u}_{i+k-1}[(k-1)\delta] = T_{i+k-1|i+k-2}\cdots T_{i+2|i+1}T_{i+1|i}\tilde{u}_i(0).$$

The loop is closed with the final update of the cycle, yielding

$$\tilde{u}_{i+k}(k\delta) = T_{i+k|i+k-1}T_{i+k-1|i+k-2}\cdots T_{i+2|i+1}T_{i+1|i}\tilde{u}_i(0) \qquad (3.10)$$

or, since all indices are incremented mod *k*,

$$\tilde{u}_i(k\delta) = T_{i|i+k-1}T_{i+k-1|i+k-2}\cdots T_{i+2|i+1}T_{i+1|i}\tilde{u}_i(0). \qquad (3.11)$$

Now define the *closed-loop transition matrix*

$$T_i = T_{i|i+k-1}T_{i+k-1|i+k-2}\cdots T_{i+2|i+1}T_{i+1|i}. \qquad (3.12)$$

Also, it is convenient to express time in units equal to the interval $k\delta$, resulting in expressing (3.11) as

$$\tilde{u}_i(1) = T_i\tilde{u}_i(0) \qquad (3.13)$$

for $i = 1, \ldots, k$. The closed-loop transition matrices for the cycle are as follows.

$$T_1 = T_{1|k} T_{k|k-1} \cdots T_{3|2} T_{2|1}$$
$$T_2 = T_{2|1} T_{1|k} \cdots T_{4|3} T_{3|2}$$

$$\vdots$$

$$T_k = T_{k|k-1} T_{k-1|k-2} \cdots T_{2|1} T_{1|k} \,.$$

After t cycles,

$$\tilde{\mathbf{u}}_i(t) = T_i \tilde{\mathbf{u}}_i(t-1)$$
$$= T_i T_i \tilde{\mathbf{u}}_i(t-2)$$

$$\vdots$$

$$= T_i \cdots T_i \tilde{\mathbf{u}}_i(0)$$
$$= T_i^t \tilde{\mathbf{u}}_i(0) \,.$$

The behavior of this cycle thus devolves around the behavior of T_i^t as $t \to \infty$, which motivates a study of the convergence properties of this matrix. The following theorem, which is proved in Appendix D, establishes necessary and sufficient conditions for $\tilde{\mathbf{u}}_i(t)$ to converge as $t \to \infty$.

Definition 3.2 A transition matrix T is said to be *regular* if there exists a positive integer m such that all components of T^m are strictly greater than zero, i.e., $T^m > 0$. $\square$

Since the closed-loop transition matrices of a k-cycle are cyclic permutations of each other, either all are regular or none are regular. If the former condition holds, we say that the k-cycle is regular.

Theorem 3.1 The Markov Convergence Theorem. *Let* $\{T_1, \ldots, T_k\}$ *be a regular k-cycle. Then the limits*

$$\overline{T}_i = \lim_{t \to \infty} T_i^t, \ i = 1 \ldots, k \tag{3.14}$$

exist and there exist unique mass vectors $\overline{\mathbf{u}}_i$, $i = 1, \ldots, k$ *with*

$$T_i \overline{\mathbf{u}}_i = \overline{\mathbf{u}}_i, \ i = 1, \ldots, n, \tag{3.15}$$

where

$$\overline{\mathbf{u}}_i = \overline{T}_i \tilde{\mathbf{u}}_i(0). \tag{3.16}$$

Thus, for a regular k-cycle, each initial utility mass vector $\tilde{\mathbf{u}}(0)$ converges to $\bar{\mathbf{u}}_i$, the unique eigenvector corresponding to the unit eigenvalue of T_i. In fact,

$$\bar{T}_i = \begin{bmatrix} \bar{\mathbf{u}}_i & \cdots & \bar{\mathbf{u}}_i \end{bmatrix}. \tag{3.17}$$

This behavior may be interpreted as follows. Suppose time flows in discrete increments $t = 1, 2, \ldots$ At each time t, the utility for vertex X_i is determined by the utility vector $\tilde{\mathbf{u}}_i(t)$. As time increases, this utility vector converges to a constant value, which may be interpreted as the long-run behavior of the cycle. As transition utilities propagate through the system many times, the cumulative effect on each utility vector is to converge to a constant value. Thus, $\bar{\mathbf{u}}_i$ constitues the steady-state utility vector for X_i, $i = 1, \ldots, k$. Furthermore, the steady-state utilities are related to each other through the state-to-state transition matrices; that is,

$$\bar{\mathbf{u}}_{i+1} = T_{i+1|i}\bar{\mathbf{u}}_i, \ i = 1, \ldots, k, \text{where } k + 1 = 1 \mod k. \tag{3.18}$$

The time that it takes for influence to flow between vertices depends on the actual network under investigation. However, since, as established by Doob (1953), convergence is exponentially fast, steady state will effectively be reached after a few iterations. The limiting coordination function (2.38) thus becomes

$$\bar{u}_{1:n}(a_1, \cdots, a_n) = \prod_{i=1}^{n} \bar{u}_i(a_i). \tag{3.19}$$

Once the system has reached steady state, the k-cycle displayed in Figure 3.5 may be replaced with the graph displayed in Figure 3.6, which has no edges but with each X_i possessing an unconditional utility function defined by $\bar{u}_i$. Mathematically, these utilities are structured the same as *ex ante* categorical utilities, but they are now *ex post* utilities as the end result of social influence. In other words, the *ex ante* conditional utilities $u_{i|i-1}(a_i|a_{i-1})$ are replaced by steady-state unconditional utilities $\bar{u}_i(a_i)$.

If a network contains cycles, the earlier analysis provides necessary and sufficient conditions for the cycle to converge to a set of steady-state unconditional utility vectors for each vertex in the cycle. As a practical matter, however, the cycle cannot run to infinity, and a stopping rule must be implemented that terminates the cycle once the change in the utility vectors becomes sufficiently small.

Figure 3.6: A Converged k-Cycle.

Let $\|\cdot\|$ denote a norm on the set of utility vectors. Once the difference $\|\tilde{u}_i(t^*+1) - \tilde{u}(t^*)\| < \epsilon$ for some $\epsilon > 0$, the cycle is terminated and the $\bar{u} = \tilde{u}_i(t^*)$ is taken as the steady-state unconditional utility for X_i. Once steady state has been reached, all edges connecting the members of the cycle are dormant and the network can be evaluated in the standard way.

3.2 Closed-Loop Collaboration

Collaboration is a deliberative process that requires some linkage among the individuals whereby they may transmit information back and forth. Such a situation is tantamount to a coordination problem where the individuals iteratively seek to achieve a common goal, such as two employees who are assigned by their manager to accomplish some task. Let A and B denote two distinct approaches and suppose, for example, that X_1 initially prefers approach A, and X_2 initially prefers approach B and the group is therefore likely, at the outset, to settle for an inferior outcome. The conditional utilities, however, are defined independently of the initial preferences of either. In fact, it may turn out that both X_1 and X_2 initially prefer B, but as they take into consideration the conditional preferences of the other, they eventually (and perhaps rapidly) converge to a compromise if not a consensus.

Suppose, however, that there is no direct physical communication between the two individuals. The lack of an explicit means of transmitting information, however, does not imply the non-existence of social influence. It is possible, perhaps by methods similar to those involved in the team-reasoning and group identification concepts advocated by Bacharach (1999, 2006) and Sugden (1993, 2000, 2003), for each individual to employ *virtual deliberation*, as proposed by Misyak et al. (2014), which is a process of deciding how it would respond to the preferences of the other. This type of reasoning is consistent with Schelling's concept of focal points: "Most situations ... provide some clue for coordinating behavior, some focal point for each person's expectation of what the other expects him to expect to be expected to do" (Schelling, 1960, p. 57). The mechanism advanced by Schelling involves an imaginative process of introspection:

"In the pure-coordination game, the player's objective is to make contact with the other player through some imaginative process of introspection, of searching for shared clues"

(Schelling, 1960, p. 96).

Thus, the players could engage in thought experiments, whereby they define the model and establish convergence.

Regardless of whether influence is propagated through direct communication or by some imaginative process of virtual deliberation, the process is dynamic. In a sequential context where information is transmitted, it cannot be done instantaneously. The time increment between transmission and reception must be non-zero, and it need not be constant. All that matters is that enough communication transpires to obtain a reliable approximation to the steady-state values. In the case of implicit influence propagation, each participant performs its own convergence exercise, which is simply a matter of deliberation, and the cyclical model, along with the Markov convergence theorem, is really nothing more than a mathematical characterization of such a deliberative process.

To illustrate, we examine three examples. First, we re-visit the Three Stooges with cyclic preferences. The fundamental symmetry of this example, where the preference structure of all individuals is exactly the same, results in steady-state solutions that maintain this symmetry. The second example has a more asymmetric utility structure, and the steady-state solutions maintain that asymmetry. The third example involves a non-regular transition matrix, and confirms the claim that regularity is a necessary condition for convergence.

Example 3.1 Suppose the Stooges form a cyclic network as displayed in Figure 3.1, and let the conditional utilities be defined as

$$u_{L|M}(F|F) = \alpha \quad u_{L|M}(I|F) = 1 - \alpha$$
$$u_{L|M}(F|I) = 1 - \alpha \quad u_{L|M}(I|I) = \alpha \tag{3.20}$$

$$u_{C|L}(F|F) = \beta \quad u_{C|L}(I|F) = 1 - \beta$$
$$u_{C|L}(F|I) = 1 - \beta \quad u_{C|L}(I|I) = \beta \tag{3.21}$$

and

$$u_{M|C}(F|F) = \gamma \quad u_{M|C}(I|F) = 1 - \gamma$$
$$u_{M|C}(F|I) = 1 - \gamma \quad u_{M|C}(I|I) = \gamma . \tag{3.22}$$

The state-to-state transition matrices are then

$$T_{L|M} = \begin{bmatrix} \alpha & 1 - \alpha \\ 1 - \alpha & \alpha \end{bmatrix}, \tag{3.23}$$

$$T_{C|L} = \begin{bmatrix} \beta & 1 - \beta \\ 1 - \beta & \beta \end{bmatrix}, \tag{3.24}$$

and

$$T_{M|C} = \begin{bmatrix} \gamma & 1 - \gamma \\ 1 - \gamma & \gamma \end{bmatrix}. \tag{3.25}$$

The closed-loop transition matrices are

$$T_L = T_{L|M} T_{M|C} T_{C|L} = \begin{bmatrix} q & 1 - q \\ 1 - a & q \end{bmatrix}, \tag{3.26}$$

where $q = \alpha + \beta + \gamma - 2\alpha\beta - 2\alpha\gamma - 2\beta\gamma + 4\alpha\beta\gamma$. Similarly,

$$T_C = T_M = \begin{bmatrix} q & 1 - q \\ 1 - a & q \end{bmatrix}. \tag{3.27}$$

By inspection, we see that the eigenvectors corresponding to unit eigenvalues of these closed-loop transition matrices is

$$\bar{u}_L = \bar{u}_C = \bar{u}_M = \begin{bmatrix} 1/2 \\ 1/2 \end{bmatrix}. \tag{3.28}$$

Thus, the steady-state *ex post* utilities are that the utilities for all individuals are split equally between F and I.

Example 3.2 Suppose the network $\{X_1, X_2, X_3\}$ needs to schedule meetings at times 9:00, 10:00, and 11:00. This problem is susceptible to the famous Condorcet paradox, leading to cyclic preferences.

Table 3.1: *The Condorcet Cyclic Preference Paradox.*

| | Individual | | |
Preference	X_1	X_2	X_3
First	11:00	10:00	9:00
Second	9:00	11:00	10:00
Third	10:00	9:00	11:00

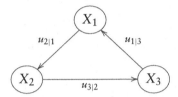

Figure 3.7: Influence Cycles for Meeting Scheduling Example.

Suppose the preferences were as specified in Table 3.1. Classical social choice theory, per se, does not provide a solution, since there is a majority regarding all three options which are mutually incompatible, thus some form of deliberation will be needed to settle the issue.

Suppose, however, that a closer examination of the preferences reveals that there are social reasons for preferring various time slots, such as how the meetings sequentially relate to each other in a social context. Suppose

X_1 prefers to meet between X_2 and X_3, otherwise, X_1 prefers 11:00
X_2 prefers to meet after X_1, meets, otherwise, X_2 prefers 10:00
X_3 prefers to meet after X_2, meets, otherwise, X_3 prefers 9:00

$$(3.29)$$

Rather than generating a preference cycle, this conditional preference structure generates an influence cycle, as illustrated in Figure 3.7. To achieve a truly coordinated decision, the social relationships must be taken into consideration. We may formulate this scenario as a network social choice problem by defining the alternative set as

$$\mathcal{A} = \{z_1, z_2, z_3\} = \{9{:}00, 10{:}00, 11{:}00\} \tag{3.30}$$

and framing the problem as a cyclic network, as illustrated in Figure 3.7, with conditional utilities of the form $u_{1|3}$, $u_{2|1}$, and $u_{3|2}$, where

$u_{i|j}(z_k|z_l)$ is the conditional utility that X_i ascribes to z_k given X_j prefers z_l.

Conditional utilities for X_1 that comply with (3.29) are

$$u_{1|3}(z_1|z_1) = 0 \qquad u_{1|3}(z_2|z_1) = \alpha_1 \qquad u_{1|3}(z_3|z_1) = 1 - \alpha_1$$
$$u_{1|3}(z_1|z_2) = 1 - \alpha_1 \qquad u_{1|3}(z_2|z_2) = 0 \qquad u_{1|3}(z_3|z_2) = \alpha_1 ,$$
$$u_{1|3}(z_1|z_3) = 1 - \alpha_1 \qquad u_{1|3}(z_2|z_3) = \alpha_1 \qquad u_{1|3}(z_3|z_3) = 0$$

$$(3.31)$$

where $\alpha_1 \in (1/2, 1]$ is the benefit to X_1 for meeting at 10:00, given the conjecture that X_3 will meet at 9:00. The corresponding state-to-state transition matrix is

$$T_{1|3} = \begin{bmatrix} u_{1|3}(z_1|z_1) & u_{1|3}(z_1|z_2) & u_{1|3}(z_1|z_3) \\ u_{1|3}(z_2|z_1) & u_{1|3}(z_2|z_2) & u_{1|3}(z_2|z_3) \\ u_{1|3}(z_3|z_1) & u_{1|3}(z_3|z_2) & u_{1|3}(z_3|z_3) \end{bmatrix} = \begin{bmatrix} 0 & 1-\alpha_1 & 1-\alpha_1 \\ \alpha_1 & 0 & \alpha_1 \\ 1-\alpha_1 & \alpha_1 & 0 \end{bmatrix}.$$

$$(3.32)$$

By similar arguments, the state-to-state transition matrices for X_2 given X_2 and for and X_2 given X_1 are

$$T_{2|1} = \begin{bmatrix} u_{2|1}(z_1|z_1) & u_{2|1}(z_1|z_2) & u_{2|1}(z_1|z_3) \\ u_{2|1}(z_2|z_1) & u_{2|1}(z_2|z_2) & u_{2|1}(z_2|z_3) \\ u_{2|1}(z_3|z_1) & u_{2|1}(z_3|z_2) & u_{2|1}(z_3|z_3) \end{bmatrix} = \begin{bmatrix} 0 & 1-\alpha_2 & 1-\alpha_2 \\ \alpha_2 & 0 & \alpha_2 \\ 1-\alpha_2 & \alpha_2 & 0 \end{bmatrix}$$

$$(3.33)$$

and

$$T_{3|2} = \begin{bmatrix} u_{3|2}(z_1|z_1) & u_{3|1}(z_1|z_2) & u_{3|2}(z_1|z_3) \\ u_{3|2}(z_2|z_1) & u_{3|2}(z_2|z_2) & u_{3|2}(z_2|z_3) \\ u_{3|2}(z_3|z_1) & u_{3|2}(z_3|z_2) & u_{3|2}(z_3|z_3) \end{bmatrix} = \begin{bmatrix} 0 & 1-\alpha_3 & \alpha_3 \\ \alpha_3 & 0 & 1-\alpha_3 \\ 1-\alpha_3 & \alpha_3 & 0 \end{bmatrix}.$$

$$(3.34)$$

The parameters α_i, $i = 1, 2, 3$, define the intensity of X_i's conditional preference. Setting $\alpha_1 = 0.8$, for example, means that X_1's preference for meeting at 10:00 is four times as high as its preference for meeting at 11:00, given the conjecture of 9:00 for X_3. For ease of analysis, let us assume that $\alpha_1 = \alpha_2 = \alpha_3 = \alpha = 0.8$. The resulting closed-loop transition matrices are:

$$T_1 = T_{1|3}T_{3|2}T_{2|1} = \begin{bmatrix} 0.136 & 0.072 & 0.168 \\ 0.768 & 0.544 & 0.672 \\ 0.096 & 0.384 & 0.160 \end{bmatrix}$$

$$(3.35)$$

$$T_2 = T_{2|1} T_{1|3} T_{3|2} = \begin{bmatrix} 0.160 & 0.168 & 0.192 \\ 0.672 & 0.160 & 0.288 \\ 0.168 & 0.672 & 0.520 \end{bmatrix} \tag{3.36}$$

$$T_3 = T_{3|2} T_{2|1} T_{1|3} = \begin{bmatrix} 0.544 & 0.192 & 0.576 \\ 0.288 & 0.136 & 0.264 \\ 0.168 & 0.672 & 0.160 \end{bmatrix}. \tag{3.37}$$

The corresponding steady utility vectors are computed as the eigenvectors corresponding to the unit eigenvalues of the closed-loop transition matrices, yielding

$$\bar{u}_1 = \begin{bmatrix} \bar{u}_1(z_1) \\ \bar{u}_1(z_2) \\ \bar{u}_1(z_3) \end{bmatrix} = \begin{bmatrix} 0.107 \\ 0.605 \\ 0.168 \end{bmatrix} \tag{3.38}$$

$$\bar{u}_2 = \begin{bmatrix} \bar{u}_2(z_1) \\ \bar{u}_2(z_2) \\ \bar{u}_2(z_3) \end{bmatrix} = \begin{bmatrix} 0.179 \\ 0.316 \\ 0.505 \end{bmatrix} \tag{3.39}$$

$$\bar{u}_3 = \begin{bmatrix} \bar{u}_3(z_1) \\ \bar{u}_3(z_2) \\ \bar{u}_3(z_3) \end{bmatrix} = \begin{bmatrix} 0.467 \\ 0.244 \\ 0.289 \end{bmatrix}, \tag{3.40}$$

and the convergent coordination function is

$$u_{123}(a_1, a_2, a_3) = \bar{u}_1(a_1)\bar{u}_2(a_2)\bar{u}_3(a_3) \tag{3.41}$$

for the conjecture profile $(a_1, a_2, a_3) \in \mathcal{A} \times \mathcal{A} \times \mathcal{A}$. The coordination values for the six non-conflicting triples are

$$\begin{aligned} u_{123}(9{:}00,\ 10{:}00,\ 11{:}00) &= 0.010 \\ u_{123}(9{:}00,\ 11{:}00,\ 10{:}00) &= 0.013 \\ u_{123}(10{:}00,\ 9{:}00,\ 11{:}00) &= 0.031 \\ u_{123}(10{:}00,\ 11{:}00,\ 9{:}00) &= 0.142 \\ u_{123}(11{:}00,\ 9{:}00,\ 10{:}00) &= 0.013 \\ u_{123}(11{:}00,\ 10{:}00,\ 9{:}00) &= 0.042\,. \end{aligned} \tag{3.42}$$

Thus, the highest coordinated non-conflicting outcome is

$$(a_1^*, a_2^*, a_3^*) = (10{:}00,\ 11{:}00,\ 9{:}00)\,, \tag{3.43}$$

where X_1 and X_2 receiving their first choices and X_3 receives its second choice.

This result is an endogenous solution rather than the result of an exogenously imposed criterion. Imposing an exogenous solution requires some entity to impose that particular choice rule, and attempting to do so could lead to a secondary level of deliberation, or even to an infinite regress with no guarantee of convergence.

On the other hand, the deliberative social choice approach relies entirely on an endogenously generated choice rule as a consequence of the social relationships that exist among the individuals, for which conditions for convergence are readily established.   □

Example 3.3 Gibbard (1974) has put forth the following scenario involving cycles to motivate the claim that there exist no social choice rules that accord rights, meaning that if alternative a is preferred to a', then a' is not in the choice set. Quoting Gibbard,

I am a perverse nonconformist: I want my bedroom walls to be a different color from Mrs. Grundy's. Grundy, on the other hand, is a conformist: She wants her bedroom walls to be the same color as mine. Exactly four social states are available: a_{ww}, a_{wy}, a_{yw}, and a_{yy}; they differ only in the color of our respective bedroom walls. The first index gives the color of my walls and the second that of Grundy's, so that in a_{wy}, for instance, mine are white and Grundy's yellow.

Clearly, this scenario involves an influence cycle of the form

$$ \tag{3.44} $$

where N is a nonconformist and C is a conformist. Let us explore this problem using conditional preferences. The transition matrix from C to N is

$$ T_{N|C} = \begin{bmatrix} 0 & 1 \\ 1 & 0 \end{bmatrix}, \tag{3.45} $$

and the transition matrix from N to C is

$$ T_{C|N} = \begin{bmatrix} 1 & 0 \\ 0 & 1 \end{bmatrix}, \tag{3.46} $$

The closed-loop transition matrix is then

$$ T_C = T_{C|N} T_{N|C} = \begin{bmatrix} 0 & 1 \\ 1 & 0 \end{bmatrix}, \tag{3.47} $$

and the utilities will simply oscillate and no steady-state solution will exist (the cycle is not regular). If C starts with white walls, then N must paint his walls yellow, but then C has to repaint her walls yellow as well, which causes N to counter by painting his white, ad infinitum.

On the other hand, suppose N is only approximate nonconformist whose behavior is governed by the

$$T_{N|C} = \begin{bmatrix} \epsilon_1 & 1-\epsilon_2 \\ 1-\epsilon_1 & \epsilon_2 \end{bmatrix} = T_N = T_C, \tag{3.48}$$

since $T_{C|N} = I$, where $0 < \epsilon_1, \epsilon_2 \ll 1$. Since this matrix does satisfy the regularity conditions of the convergence theorem, the eigenvector corresponding to the unit eigenvalue is

$$\bar{u}_N = \bar{u}_C = \begin{bmatrix} \frac{1-\epsilon_2}{2-\epsilon_1-\epsilon_2} \\ \frac{1-\epsilon_1}{2-\epsilon_1-\epsilon_2} \end{bmatrix}. \tag{3.49}$$

Thus, both will have higher utility of painting their walls white if $\epsilon_1 < \epsilon_2$. □

3.3 Non-Simple Cycles

The Markov convergence theorem also applies to networks that contain non-simple cycles. In this section we illustrate results for networks that contain sub-cycles (cycles within cycles), and embedded cycles (cycles that are influenced by individuals who are not part of the cycle.

3.3.1 Graphs with Sub-Cycles

The next level of complexity involves a more complicated cycle; namely, one with sub-cycles, as illustrated in Figure 3.8. Proceeding as before, the closed-loop transition matrix may be computed by first computing T_1. The first entry in the product, as before, is the transition from X_4 to X_1, namely,

$$T_{1|4} = \begin{bmatrix} u_{1|4}(z_1|z_1) & u_{1|4}(z_1|z_2) \\ u_{1|4}(z_2|z_1) & u_{1|4}(z_2|z_2) \end{bmatrix}. \tag{3.50}$$

The next step is to compute the transition to X_4 from its two parents, X_2 and X_3. Again assuming that the alternative set contains

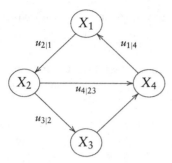

Figure 3.8: A Four-Agent Directed Cyclic Graph with a Sub-Cycle.

only two elements, that is, $\mathcal{A} = \{z_1, z_2\}$, the transition matrix from $\{X_2, X_3\}$ is the 2×4 matrix

$$T_{4|23} = \begin{bmatrix} u_{4|23}(z_1|z_1, z_1) & u_{4|23}(z_1|z_1, z_2) & u_{4|23}(z_1|z_2, z_1) & u_{4|23}(z_1|z_2, z_2) \\ u_{4|23}(z_2|z_1, z_1) & u_{4|23}(z_2|z_1, z_2) & u_{4|23}(z_2|z_2, z_1) & u_{4|23}(z_2|z_2, z_2) \end{bmatrix}.$$
$$(3.51)$$

This matrix transitions from $\{X_2, X_3\}$ to X_4 as follows:

$$\tilde{u}_4 = T_{4|23}\tilde{u}_{23} \,,$$
$$(3.52)$$

where

$$\tilde{u}_{23} = \begin{bmatrix} \tilde{u}_{23}(z_1, z_1) \\ \tilde{u}_{23}(z_1, z_2) \\ \tilde{u}_{23}(z_2, z_1) \\ \tilde{u}_{23}(z_2, z_2) \end{bmatrix}$$

$$= \begin{bmatrix} \tilde{u}_{3|2}(z_1|z_1)\tilde{u}_2(z_1) \\ \tilde{u}_{3|2}(z_2|z_1)\tilde{u}_2(z_1) \\ \tilde{u}_{3|2}(z_1|z_2)\tilde{u}_2(z_2) \\ \tilde{u}_{3|2}(z_2|z_2)\tilde{u}_2(z_2) \end{bmatrix}$$

$$= \underbrace{\begin{bmatrix} u_{3|2}(z_1|z_1) & 0 \\ u_{3|2}(z_2|z_1) & 0 \\ 0 & u_{3|2}(z_1|z_2) \\ 0 & u_{3|2}(z_2|z_2) \end{bmatrix}}_{T_{3|2}} \begin{bmatrix} \tilde{u}_2(z_1) \\ \tilde{u}_2(z_2) \end{bmatrix}.$$

Notice that this transition matrix incorporates the transition utilities linking X_2 to X_3.

The transitions from X_1 to X_2 and X_2 to X_3 are

$$T_{2|1} = \begin{bmatrix} u_{2|1}(z_1|z_1) & u_{2|1}(z_1|z_2) \\ u_{2|1}(z_2|z_1) & u_{2|1}(z_2|z_2) \end{bmatrix} \tag{3.53}$$

and

$$T_{3|2} = \begin{bmatrix} u_{3|2}(z_1|z_1) & u_{3|2}(z_1|z_2) \\ u_{3|2}(z_2|z_1) & u_{3|2}(z_2|z_2) \end{bmatrix}. \tag{3.54}$$

Thus, the closed-loop transition matrix for X_4 is

$$T_4 = T_{4|23}T_{3|2}T_{2|1}T_{1|4}, \tag{3.55}$$

from which the steady-state marginal utility vector for X_4 can be obtained as the solution to

$$\bar{u}_4 = T_4\bar{u}_4. \tag{3.56}$$

We may then compute the remaining steady-state marginal utility vectors as

$$\begin{aligned} \bar{u}_1 &= T_{1|4}\bar{u}_4 \\ \bar{u}_2 &= T_{2|1}\bar{u}_1 \\ \bar{u}_3 &= T_{3|2}\bar{u}_2 \end{aligned} \tag{3.57}$$

The equivalent steady-state graph has no edges and the coordination function is the product

$$\bar{u}_{1\ldots4}(a_1,a_2,a_3,a_4) = \prod_{i=1}^{4}\bar{u}_i(a_i). \tag{3.58}$$

3.3.2 Embedded Cycles

Definition 3.3 A directed cycle is *embedded* if there exists at least one edge connecting the cycle with a vertex that is not a member of the cycle. A vertex is called a *child of the cycle* if there exists a directed edge from at least one member of the cycle to the vertex. A vertex is called a *parent of the cycle* if there is a directed edge from the vertex to at least one member of the cycle. A cycle is termed a *root cycle* if it has no parents. □

Definition 3.4 Let $\{X_1 \to \cdots \to X_{k+1} = X_1 \pmod{k}\}$ be a simple k-root cycle embedded a graph G, and let G' denote G with all vertices of the cycle replaced by root vertices with categorical utilities composed of the corresponding limiting utility vectors, and with all other edges remaining the same. Then the *steady-state coordination function* of G is the coordination function of G'.   □

Root Cycles

Consider the graph illustrated in Figure 3.9, which has one root cycle, and let $\bar{u}_i$, $i \in \{1, 2, 3\}$ denote the steady-state utilities. Once the graph has reached steady state, it may be replaced with the equivalent graph illustrated in Figure 3.10. The corresponding coordination function is

$$\bar{u}_{1\dots6}(a_1, \dots, a_6)$$
$$= \bar{u}_1(a_1)\bar{u}_2(a_2)\bar{u}_3(a_3)u_{4|1}(a_4|a_1)u_{5|2}(a_5|a_2)u_{6|35}(a_6|a_3, a_5).$$
$$(3.59)$$

Non-Root Cycles

Assuming that all cycles are regular, the utilities of all of its members will converge to their steady-state values. For non-root cycles, these steady-state values will of course be influenced by their parents during the process of convergence but, once convergence has occurred, they

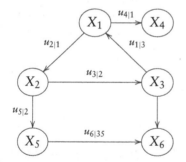

Figure 3.9: A Directed Graph with an Embedded Root Cycle.

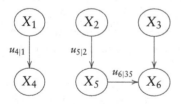

Figure 3.10: The Steady-State Equivalent Graph.

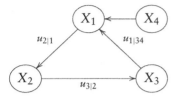

Figure 3.11: A Non-Root Cyclic Graph.

will all achieve steady-state utilities and thus will have no incoming edges. They may, however, have outgoing edges.

Figure 3.11 illustrates a 3-cycle graph with a single parent. The vertex X_1 has two parents: $\{X_3, X_4\}$, but X_4 is not part of the cycle. Thus, the marginal utility $\tilde{u}_1$ is driven by the joint utility $\tilde{u}_{34}$ according to the transition matrix $T_{1|34}$ as follows (in the interest of simplicity, $N = 2$).

$$
\begin{bmatrix} \tilde{u}_1(z_1) \\ \tilde{u}_1(z_2) \end{bmatrix} = T_{1|34} \begin{bmatrix} \tilde{u}_4(z_1) & 0 \\ \tilde{u}_4(z_2) & 0 \\ 0 & \tilde{u}_4(z_1) \\ 0 & \tilde{u}_4(z_2) \end{bmatrix} \begin{bmatrix} \tilde{u}_3(z_1) \\ \tilde{u}_3(z_2) \end{bmatrix}, \tag{3.60}
$$

with

$$
T_{1|34} = \begin{bmatrix} u_{1|34}(z_1|z_1,z_1) & u_{1|34}(z_1|z_1,z_2) & u_{1|34}(z_1|z_2,z_1) & u_{1|34}(z_1|z_2,z_2) \\ u_{1|34}(z_2|z_1,z_1) & u_{1|34}(z_2|z_1,z_2) & u_{1|34}(z_2|z_2,z_1) & u_{1|34}(z_2|z_2,z_2) \end{bmatrix}, \tag{3.61}
$$

where it is assumed that X_3 and X_4 are independent, and thus $\tilde{u}_{34}(\cdot, \cdot) = \tilde{u}_3(\cdot)\tilde{u}_4(\cdot)$. Thus, even with the exogenous input from X_4 into the cycle, the cycle itself is regular and the convergence theorem may be applied.

Since the cycle is simple, transitions from X_2 to X_3 and from X_1 to X_2 are straightforward, and the closed-loop transition matrices for the 3-cycle vertices are

$$
T_1 = T_{1|34} \begin{bmatrix} u_4(z_1) & 0 \\ 0 & u_4(z_2) \\ u_4(z_1) & 0 \\ 0 & u_4(z_2) \end{bmatrix} T_{3|2} T_{2|1}
$$

$$T_2 = T_{2|1} T_{1|34} \begin{bmatrix} u_4(z_1) & 0 \\ 0 & u_4(z_2) \\ u_4(z_1) & 0 \\ 0 & u_4(z_2) \end{bmatrix} T_{3|2}$$

$$T_3 = T_{3|2} T_{2|1} T_{1|34} \begin{bmatrix} u_4(z_1) & 0 \\ 0 & u_4(z_2) \\ u_4(z_1) & 0 \\ 0 & u_4(z_2) \end{bmatrix}, \tag{3.62}$$

yielding the steady-state equivalent graph displayed in Figure 3.12. Note that all vertices are root nodes with categorical utilities $\bar{u}_1$, $\bar{u}_2$, $\bar{u}_3$, and u_4, respectively.

Let G be a graph with an embedded cycle and let G' denote G with all vertices of the cycle replaced by root vertices with categorical utilities composed of the corresponding limiting utility vectors, and with all other edges remaining the same. Then the *steady-state coordination function* of G is the coordination function of G'.

As a final example, Figure 3.13 illustrates a graph with a non-root embedded cycle in a larger network. The equivalent steady-state graph is illustrated in Figure 3.14. The corresponding coordination function is

$$u_{1\ldots9}(a_1,\ldots,a_9) = u_1(a_1)\ddot{u}_2(a_2)\ddot{u}_3(a_3)\ddot{u}_4(a_4)\ddot{u}_5(a_5)u_{6|34}(a_6|a_3,a_4)$$
$$u_{7|1}(a_7|a_4,a_5)u_{8|3}(a_8|a_3)u_{9|7}(a_9|a_7).$$

Figure 3.12: The Equivalent Steady-State Graph with Parent.

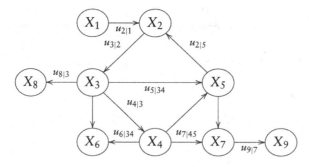

Figure 3.13: A Graph with an Embedded 4-Cycle.

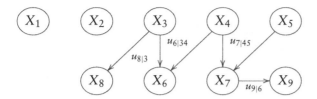

Figure 3.14: A Steady-State Embedded 4-Cycle Graph.

3.4 Summary

The constraint that social influence must be expressible as a directed acyclic graph to comply with the syntax of probability theory restricts attention to hierarchical social structures. Even with this restriction, however, the admissible set of social structures is a significant extension beyond social structures with no social influence capability; that is, societies whose graphical structure comprises a set of vertices with no edges, which is trivially acyclic.

Although cyclic probabilistic dependencies are not permitted with probability theory, there is no logical restriction against cyclic influence in a network. The issue that arises with cyclic influence is that the feedback loop creates a dynamic situation where the influence among the members of the cycle keeps changing. This chapter establishes conditions under which the influence relationships converge to steady-state values. Once convergence is achieved, the steady-state preference orderings contain the limiting values of the social influence relationships, and can be used as if they were categorical preferences.

4 | *Coordination*

The further a mathematical theory is developed, the more harmoniously and uniformly does its construction proceed, and unsuspected relations are disclosed between two separated branches of the science.

— David Hilbert

Quoted in N. Rose: *Mathematical Maxims and Minims*

(Rome Press, 1988)

It is no paradox to say that in our most theoretical moods we may be nearest to our most practical applications.

— Alfred North Whitehead

An Introduction to Mathematics (Oxford University Press, 1948)

4.1 Coordination Concepts

The concept of coordinated group behavior has received great attention in the analysis of social systems (cf. Schelling (1960), Lewis (1969), Bicchieri (1993), Cooper (1999), Malone et al. (2003), Goyal (2007), Jackson (2008), Shoham and Leyton-Brown (2009), Easley and Kleinberg (2010)). Much of the focus is on so-called coordination games, where two or more individuals must each choose one of several alternative actions. Most such studies, however, do not involve explicit notions of group-level behavior. Rather, a social engagement is deemed to be a coordination scenario if there is an opportunity for the individuals to cooperate for their mutual benefit. Games such as Hi-Lo, the Battle of the Sexes, and the Prisoner's Dilemma as discussed by Axelrod (1984) are prime examples of coordination scenarios.[1] Mutual benefit, however, is not the same as group preference. There

---

[1] It is interesting that Axelrod is careful to restrict his terminology to cooperation, rather than invoking notions of coordination.

is a difference between the behavior of individuals whose categorical preferences just happen to be aligned, even though there is no explicit social relationship between them, and the behavior of individuals who are linked together by social influence. With the former, any notions of group benefit are exogenously imposed *ex post*, but with the latter, group preference, if it exists, emerges endogenously as a consequence of the social relationships that are formed as *ex ante* social influence propagates through the network.

If all individuals possess categorical preferences, then the concept of group preference is not an innate property of the collective. It is an uncomfortable fact that game theory does not provide a definitive resolution of the so-called cooperative scenarios such as Hi-Lo and the Battle of the Sexes. Both games have multiple Nash equilibria, but game theory does not provide a definitive way to choose from among them. This limitation has motivated researchers such as Bacharach (1999, 2006) and Sugden (1993, 2000, 2003) to explore so-called *team reasoning* approaches. In addition, several other concepts of coordinated behavior, such as *tacit* coordination, as introduced by Schelling (1960), coordination by convention, as developed by Lewis (1969), and learned coordination as the end result of social evolution, as described by Bicchieri (1993), have been discussed in the literature. These concepts of coordination are all expressed in terms of categorical preference orderings and, consequently, do not comply with the dictionary's definition of coordination as the arrangement of the parts (the individuals) arranged relative to each other to form the whole (the collective) (Murray et al., 1991). Nevertheless, it is certainly possible to attribute group-level benefit to a collective of individuals who possess only categorical preferences, but such evaluations are not endogenous. They are imposed on the society by a particular solution concept, rather than as a natural consequence of the social relationships. Such notions of coordination are *exogenous* – they do not arise from the influence connections that exist among the individuals.

An alternative is to invoke the natural network structure that defines the social relationships and create a comprehensive social model that captures the dictionary concept of coordination. Once such a model is defined, it invites the concept of *endogenous* coordination. In particular, it makes possible the development of a mechanism for determining the intrinsic ability of a network to coordinate effectively.

As discussed in Section 2.2, coordination is a much more complex and sophisticated concept than cooperation. Whereas cooperation deals with the relationships between individuals with respect to the commonality of their individual interests irrespective of any concept of group interest, coordination deals with the relationship between individuals and some notion of (possibly emergent) group-level behavior or organization. Furthermore, whereas cooperation and conflict have, respectively, positive and negative connotations regarding behavior, coordination is inherently neutral. Cooperative coordination is required for effective teamwork, and conflictive coordination is required for effective competition, such as with athletic contests and military engagements.

Our goal is to develop a mathematical characterization of coordination as a function of the social structure of the network. Such a characterization would be independent of the solution concept, and would thus enable an analysis of the intrinsic ability of a group to coordinate as a function of its internal organization. Our principal mathematical tool for this development is Shannon information theory, which was developed as a means of analyzing the behavior of communication systems.

4.2 A Mathematical Characterization of Coordination

Natural science is an expansion of observing; technology, of contriving; mathematics, of understanding.

—Michael Polanyi
Personal Knowledge (University of Chicago Press, 1958)

The ability of its members to communicate with each other is a key attribute of an organization. Arrow draws an analogy between communication among members of an organization and the transmission of messages through a communications medium.

Each individual economic agent is assumed to start with the ability to receive some signals from the natural and social environments . . . The individual also starts off with a set of expectations as to the range of signals that he or anybody else might possibly receive now or in the future and probabilities of receiving the different signals. In technical terms, the individual begins with a prior probability distribution over the set of possible signals . . . A signal is then an event capable of altering the individual's probability distribution; in more technical language, the posterior distribution of signals conditional on the observation of one may, in general, differ from the prior. This transformation of probabilities is precisely what constitutes the acquisition of information (Arrow, 1974, p. 38).

This analogy likens the passing of data between economic agents to the communications activity of passing a message from a transmitter to a receiver. This latter activity is exactly the issue addressed by the engineering problem of designing a communications system, and immediately invites the application of Shannon information theory (Shannon, 1948), which provides the mathematical tools to evaluate and design such systems.

Although Arrow broached the idea of using Shannon information theory for the analysis of communication within an organization, he then evidently dismissed that pursuit: "The quantitative definition which appears in information theory is probably of only limited value for economic analysis" (Arrow, 1974, p. 38). Instead, he chose to focus only on the qualitative insight that the analogy provides. His reason for not focusing on the quantitative definition of information is that, as has been previously discussed, epistemological assertions regarding belief do not correspond to praxeological assertions regarding preference. But the fact that Arrow broached the subject at all is an indication that he intuitively saw connections. If so, then he was indeed prescient in his anticipation that Shannon information theory can be integrated into organization theory.

Shannon information theory was developed as an epistemological concept, but in the light of Theorems 2.2 and 2.6, where it is established that an isomorphic relationship can be constructed between belief and preference and that utility mass functions can be constructed that are isomorphic to a probability mass functions, it becomes fruitful to consider the existence of a praxeological analogue to Shannon information theory. Before plunging into the mathematics, however, it may be useful first to review the basic concepts in ordinary language. The fundamental issue of communication theory is to transmit a message from one location to another through some medium, called a channel, that is subject to error (typically referred to as noise). A communication system consists of a transmitter, a channel, and a receiver (e.g., a wireless telephone system). Perhaps the most simple example of such a system is a discrete binary memoryless channel, where the message to be transmitted is encoded using the binary numbering system, and thus can be expressed as a string of zeros and ones (e.g., the ASCII code). These symbols are called *binary digits*, or *bits*.

The transmitter sends the binary symbols across the channel sequentially, and the receiver then reconstructs the message. Since the sender does not know in advance what the transmitted signal will be, it can only be characterized statistically. Let Y_1 denote a random variable representing the signal to be transmitted one bit at a time chosen from the set $\{0, 1\}$. Also, let Y_2 denote the received signal, also an element of $\{0, 1\}$. If the channel is perfect (noise-free), then, $Y_2 = Y_1$ with probability one. But if the channel is imperfect, then it is possible for the transmitted signal to be distorted in a way that causes the receiver to make an error. An error occurs if either $Y_1 = 1$ and $Y_2 = 0$ or $Y_1 = 0$ and $Y_2 = 1$. Let the conditional probability mass function $p_{2|1}(y_2|y_1)$ denote the probability that $Y_2 = y_2$ will be received when $Y_1 = y_1$ is transmitted, where $y_1, y_2 \in \{0, 1\}$. Figure 4.1 illustrates the transmit-receive flow of such a communications channel, and Figure 4.2 illustrates the structure of the conditional probability model that characterizes its behavior.

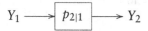

Figure 4.1: A Communications Channel.

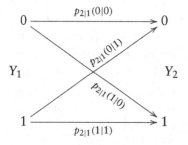

Figure 4.2: The Conditional Probability Model for a Binary Transmission Channel.

The communications problem is to design the transmitter and receiver system such that the probability of error is acceptably small and the transmission rate (the number of content bits per transmission) is acceptably large. The design problem is difficult since these two desires are in conflict. Without going into further detail, Shannon's contribution was to establish a theoretical upper bound on the transmission rate while ensuring that $p_{2|1}(1|0)$ and $p_{2|1}(0|1)$ are acceptably small. This upper bound is called the *channel capacity*. Shannon's approach was to define a quantity that he called *mutual information*, denoted $I(Y_1, Y_2)$, which is a measure of the degree to which knowing Y_2 contributes to knowing Y_1. Shannon proved that the channel capacity corresponds to the maximum possible mutual information, where the maximization is taken over all possible distributions for the input signal; that is, $C = \max_{p_1} I(Y_1, Y_2)$.[2]

Since, in our formulation, all utilities are mass functions and all manipulations, such as marginalization, the chain rule, and Bayes theorem are mathematically defined, the formalisms of information theory may be applied, but for them to be useful, they must be associated with praxeological concepts that are isomorphic to the epistemological concepts involved with Shannon information theory. Thus, it is necessary to develop operational praxeological definitions for the epistemological concepts associated with this theory. Essentially, all that is required is to establish praxeological interpretations that parallel the epistemological concepts. The primary concepts of Shannon information theory are *entropy* and *information*.

In the interest of simplicity and clarity, we first focus on a two-agent society $\{X_1, X_2\}$, where X_1 possesses a categorical utility u_1 and X_2 possesses a conditional utility $u_{2|1}$. Figure 4.3 displays the corresponding network, and Figure 4.4 displays the structure of the conditional utilities. Notice that the graphical representations of this network are identical to the communications channel illustrated in Figures 4.1 and 4.2.

---

[2] Although of great theoretical significance, Shannon's proof is not constructive; it does not define the structure or encoding mechanism with which to achieve capacity.

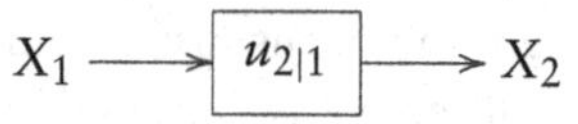

$$X_1 \longrightarrow \boxed{u_{2|1}} \longrightarrow X_2$$

Figure 4.3: A Two-Agent Network.

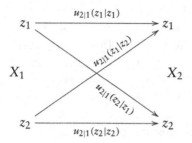

Figure 4.4: The Conditional Utility Model for a Two Agent, Two Alternative Coordination Scenario.

4.2.1 Entropy

In a probability context, *entropy* is a measure of the intrinsic randomness of a stochastic phenomenon in the sense of the ability to predict the outcome of an experiment.

Definition 4.1 Let Y be a discrete random variable taking values in the finite set $\mathcal{Y}$, governed by probability mass function p. The *surprise function* $S_p: \mathcal{Y} \to \mathbb{R}$ is defined as

$$S_p(y) = -\log_2 p(y). \tag{4.1}$$

□

As used for the study of digital communications where messages are encoded as bits, surprise is expressed with base two logarithms, and corresponds to the number of bits it would take to create a binary encoded message to express the degree of surprise experienced by the receipt of a single binary symbol. To illustrate, if $p(y) \approx 1$, then $S_p(y) \approx 0$, indicating that very little randomness is associated with the realization of an event whose probability is almost one – thus, one is hardly surprised if that event is realized. On the other hand, if $p(y) \to 0$, then $S_p(y) \to \infty$, indicating great surprise if an extremely unlikely event is actually realized, and it would take many bits to capture the degree of surprise.

In a decision-theoretic context, the notion corresponding to surprise is *opportunity cost*, defined by (Harsanyi, 1977), as the amount of utility associated with the next-best alternative. We generalize this concept by introducing the notion of *subordination* as a measure of the degree of inferiority of an alternative when compared to the ideal case where all of the mass were concentrated on one alternative. Thus, subordination is the praxeological analog to surprise.

Definition 4.2 Let X be an agent with utility mass function u. The *subordination* function $S_u: \mathcal{A} \rightarrow \mathbb{R}$ is

$$S_u(a) = -\log_2 u(a). \tag{4.2}$$

□

If $u(a) \approx 1$, then $S_u(a) \approx 0$, indicating that there is very little opportunity cost associated with an alternative that has nearly all of the utility mass associated with it. Conversely, if $u(a) \rightarrow 0$, then $S_u(a) \rightarrow \infty$, indicating that a is highly subordinated to the ideal case. The subordination function corresponds to the number of bits it would take to express the degree of inferiority of a with respect to the ideal case. Figure 4.5 displays the range of S_u over the domain $u \in [0,1]$ when the number of alternatives is $N = 2$ with $u(z_1) = u$ and $u(z_2) = 1 - u$.

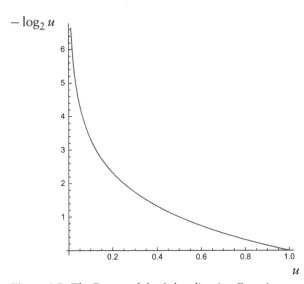

Figure 4.5: The Range of the Subordination Function.

Definition 4.3   The *entropy* associated with a probability mass function p is defined as the sum of the product of probability and surprise, that is,

$$H(p) = -\sum_{y \in \mathcal{Y}} p(y) \log_2 p(y). \tag{4.3}$$

Analogously, the entropy of a utility function is

$$H(u) = -\sum_{a \in A} u(a) \log_2 u(a). \tag{4.4}$$

□

Figure 4.6 displays entropy for a single agent with $N = 2$. Observe that entropy is maximized for $u = 1/2$, a situation where opportunity cost is maximized.

Entropy is also termed *self-information*, and is the average surprise associated with the outcome of an experiment, such as the transmission of a message through a communications medium. Given the probability distribution of the message source, one could apply statistical methods to predict the contents of the message before it is sent, but such a prediction would be subject to error. Shannon developed a quantitative measure of the average number of bits that would be required to fill in the missing content knowledge. He applies a special definition to the term *information*, and this unusual definition can cause confusion if not carefully defined and interpreted. Information, as used by Shannon, does not refer to the

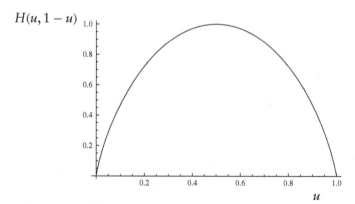

Figure 4.6: The Entropy Function for $N = 2$.

actual content knowledge of a message. Rather, it refers to the *size*, expressed as the number of bits it would take, on average, to encode the *missing* content knowledge as a result of a prediction error.[3] To illustrate, if $\mathcal{Y} = \{y_1, y_2\}$ with $p(y_1) = 1$ and $p(y_2) = 0$, then $H(p) = 0$, and the amount of missing content knowledge associated with receiving the message $y \in \mathcal{Y}$ is zero, since the content is known with probability one before the message is sent. But if $p(y_1) = p(y_2) = 0.5$, then $H(p) = 1$, then one full bit of missing content knowledge is associated with its receipt (since both possible contents are equally probable – the prediction error is maximum). But if $p(y_1) = 0.1$ and $p(y_2) = 0.9$, then $H(p) \approx 0.47$, indicating that slightly less than half a bit of content knowledge is missing, on average, in the message.

In like manner in a decision-theoretic context, self-information may be viewed as a measure of the average subordination associated with making a decision. It is a measure of the decisiveness of the individual in terms of opportunity cost, of making a choice. We stress again that information, in this context as well, is not the actual *behavior knowledge* of the individual. Rather, it is the number of bits it would take, on average, to express the *missing* behavioral knowledge that is revealed by the agent's action. To illustrate, if $\mathcal{A} = \{a_1, a_2\}$ with $u_i(a_1) = 1$ and $u_i(a_2) = 0$, then $H(u_i) = 0$, and the amount of missing behavioral knowledge that is revealed by taking $a \in \mathcal{A}$ is zero, since the behavior is obvious before the action is taken. But if $u_i(a_1) = u_i(a_2) = 0.5$, then $H(u_i) = 1$, then one full bit of missing behavioral knowledge is obtained by taking action (since both possible actions are of equal behavioral value). And if $u_i(a_1) = 0.1$ and $u_i(a_2) = 0.9$, then $H(u_i) \approx 0.47$, indicating that slightly less than half a bit of missing behavioral knowledge is revealed, on average, by the act.

---

[3] Even experts in the field often use the word *information* with both its common and technical definitions, sometimes even in the same sentence, which can be very confusing. To be as precise as possible in this treatment, however, we refer to the content of a message as *knowledge* and reserve the word *information* for its technical use. However, in other places in this book, we revert to the common usage of the word. In defense of Shannon's appropriation of the word, his usage is actually very close to its etymological roots. The Latin word *informare* means "to shape, give form to, or delineate." Thus, information *à la* Shannon admits a dimensional concept as the size or shape of the knowledge.

The notion of entropy extends to multiple random variables (and hence, to multiple agents) by defining the *joint entropy*, that is, the entropy of a joint probability distribution, yielding

$$H(p_{12}) = - \sum_{y_1,y_2} p_{12}(y_1,y_2) \log_2 p_{12}(y_1,y_2) \qquad (4.5)$$

in the probabilistic context and

$$H(u_{12}) = - \sum_{a_1,a_2} u_{12}(a_1,a_2) \log_2 u_{12}(a_1,a_2) \qquad (4.6)$$

in a praxeological context. Although entropy is a function of utility, it will often be convenient, although a slight abuse of notation, to express entropy as a function of the individuals, rather than of their associated utilities. Thus, we adopt the convention of writing $H(X_i)$ for $H(u_i)$ and $H(X_1,\ldots,X_n)$ for $H(u_{1:n})$. Thus,

$$H(X_1,\ldots,X_n) = - \sum_{a_1 \in A} \cdots \sum_{a_n \in A} u_{1:n}(a_1\ldots,a_n) \log_2 u_{1:n}(a_1,\ldots,a_n),$$

$$(4.7)$$

where $u_{1:n}$ is defined by (2.38). Joint entropy is thus a measure of the missing behavioral knowledge, expressed in bits, that is revealed by the collective when all agents take their collective action. Appendix E provides a brief tutorial on entropy and mutual information, including the proof of the following inequality:

$$H(X_1,\ldots X_n) \le H(X_1) + \cdots + H(X_n), \qquad (4.8)$$

with equality holding if, and only if, $X_1,\ldots,X_n$ are mutually socially independent. This inequality is a manifestation of the fact that, if social influence exists among a collective, the missing behavioral knowledge regarding the choice made by the group as derived from the coordination function will be less than the sum of the missing behavioral knowledge derived from the individual *ex post* marginal utilities.

4.2.2 Mutual Information

Harkening back to Figure 4.2, given the observation of Y_2, the goal of Shannon information theory is to determine the average amount of missing content knowledge contained in Y_1, given that Y_2 is observed. The joint distribution of the two random variables is

$$p_{12}(y_1, y_2) = p_1(y_2)p_{2|1}(y_2|y_1),$$ (4.9)

resulting in the joint entropy

$$H(Y_1, Y_2) = -\sum_{y_1, y_2} p_{12}(y_1, y_2) \log_2 p_{12}(y_2, y_2).$$ (4.10)

Now suppose we were to ignore the statistical dependency between Y_1 and Y_2 and assume that $p_{2|1}(y_2|y_1) = p_2(y_2)$. By making this assumption, we would essentially be discarding the content knowledge that is shared by the two random variables. This observation motivates the following definition.

Definition 4.4 The *mutual information* of Y_1 and Y_2 is the difference between the sum of the individual entropies under the assumption of statistical independence and the joint entropy:

$$I(Y_1, Y_2) = H(Y_1) + H(Y_2) - H(Y_1, Y_2).$$ (4.11)

□

Mutual information is the amount of content knowledge that is lost, on average, by assuming that Y_1 and Y_2 are statistically independent when they are not. More precisely, it is the average number of *additional* bits required to replace the content knowledge that would be lost by ignoring the statistical dependency between Y_1 and Y_2. In other words, it is a measure of the average amount of content knowledge that is shared by Y_1 and Y_2.

In the decision-theoretic context, mutual information becomes

$$I(X_1, \cdots, X_n) = \sum_{i=1}^{n} H(X_i) - H(X_1, \ldots, X_n).$$ (4.12)

Thus, mutual information is a measure, expressed in bits, of the difference in the sum of the missing behavioral knowledge of all agents viewed individually and the missing behavioral knowledge of the collective viewed as a whole. It serves as a measure of the loss in shared interest that is incurred by assuming that agents are socially independent when they are not.

It must be emphasized that the concept of shared interest is a function of the structure of the influence relationships. If all agents possess categorical preferences, then there is no shared interest *as a result of social influence.* This is true even if all individuals have identical preferences or, for that matter, if they all have opposing preferences. Such situations would be merely a coincidence of individual preferences, rather than a consequence of social relationships. Thus, if all individuals possess categorical preferences, then mutual information is zero.

4.3 Coordinatability for Networks

One cannot escape the feeling that these mathematical formulas have an independent existence and an intelligence of their own, that they are wiser than we are, wiser even than their discoverers, that we get more out of them than was originally put into them.

— Heinrich Hertz

Quoted by E. T. Bell in *Men of Mathematics*, Simon and Schuster, 1937

Recall from Section 2.5 that the aggregation process generates a coordination utility $u_{1:n}$ defined by (2.38), from which individuals may extract *ex post* marginal utility $\tilde{u}_i$, as defined by (2.39). Although these marginals now incorporate the social influences, they are now unconditional and fixed. If each individual were to render its vote on the basis of these now categorical utilities, that would be tantamount to viewing the aggregation process as simply a preliminary step used to define the individual categorical preferences, and we would be no closer to a truly coordinated solution. The collective would still need to somehow re-aggregate these preferences to form a social choice.

Although an *ex post* aggregation could certainly be done, it would result in a loss of behavioral knowledge since, just as a joint probability distribution cannot be recovered from the marginals, it is not possible to recover the coordination function from the *ex post* marginal utilities. The only way to create a coordination function from the marginals is to assume that the individuals are socially independent, yielding a constructed coordination function as the product of the marginals. The mutual information then, as given by (4.12), is the average amount of behavioral knowledge that would be lost by assuming that the individuals are socially independent when they are not. This behavioral knowledge, however, corresponds directly to the alignment of individual interests with group interests or, in other words, it quantifies the innate ability of the individuals (the parts) to combine in proper order to form an organization (the whole) – to coordinate.

Example 4.1 Let us examine the Three Stooges example discussed in Example 4.1 using the coordination function defined by (2.51). The mutual information is given by

$$I(L, C, M) = H(L) + HC) + H(M) - H(L, C, M). \qquad (4.13)$$

Figure 4.7 displays a plot of $I(L, C, M)$ for values of $\alpha = \beta = \gamma$ ranging over the interval $(0, 1/2)$. Mutual information is approximately 0.54 bit at $\alpha = \beta = \gamma = 0.1$, which means that approximately half a bit of behavioral knowledge would be destroyed by incorrectly assuming that the individuals are socially independent with marginal utilities given by (2.52), (2.53), and (2.54) evaluated at $\alpha = \beta = \gamma = 0.1$. As these parameter values approach 1/2, all three marginals approach 1/2, and all values of $u_{LCM}(a_L, a_C, a_M)$ approach 1/8. At these parameter values, the coordination function degenerates to become the product of the marginals, and the individuals become socially independent. Hence, the mutual information approaches zero.

Even with the simple scenario illustrated in Example 4.1, it is difficult to interpret the significance of mutual information in terms

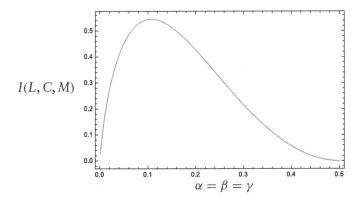

Figure 4.7: Mutual Information for the Three Stooges for $\alpha = \beta = \gamma \in (0, 1/2)$.

of the ability of the members of the collective to coordinate. It might be possible to gain more insight if we could somehow normalize the coordination measure so that the coordinatability can be expressed relative to an ideal case of maximum coordination. This desire motivates the following development.

Definition 4.5 For two individuals X_1 and X_2, the *dispersion function* $d(X_1, X_2)$ is defined by

$$d(X_1, X_2) = H(X_1, X_2) - I(X_1, X_2). \tag{4.14}$$

$\square$

It is straightforward to see that

$$d(Y_1, Y_2) = 2H(Y_1, Y_2) - H(Y_1) - H(Y_2) \tag{4.15}$$

is an alternative expression for (4.14).

Theorem 4.1 *The dispersion function $d(X_1, X_2)$ satisfies the following conditions.*

$$d(X_1, X_2) = d(X_2, X_1) \ (symmetry) \tag{4.16}$$
$$d(X_1, X_2) \geq 0 \ (non\text{-}negativity) \tag{4.17}$$
$$d(X_1, X_2) = 0 \ if \ and \ only \ if \ X_1 \vDash X_2 (strict \ positivity) \tag{4.18}$$
$$d(X_1, X_2) \leq d(X_1, X_3) + d(X_3, X_2) \ (triangle \ inequality), \tag{4.19}$$

where the notation $X_1 \vDash X_2$ means that there exists a permutation $\pi: A \to A$ such that

$$u_{2|1}(a_2|a_1) = \begin{cases} 0 & if \ a_2 \neq \pi(a_1) \\ 1 & if \ a_2 = \pi(a_1) \end{cases}.$$

Thus $d(X_1, X_2)$ is a true metric.

This theorem is proved in Appendix E. The dispersion function expresses the "distance" between the interests of X_1 and X_2. However, just as with using mutual information as a measure of "distance" (albeit mutual information is not a true metric), it is still difficult to interpret the significance of the distance. A more convenient measure of distance, therefore, is to normalize the metric by dividing by the total entropy.

Definition 4.6 The *relative dispersion* $\mathcal{D}(Y_1, Y_2)$ is defined by

$$\mathcal{D}(X_1, X_2) = \frac{d(X_1, X_2)}{H(X_1, X_2)}. \tag{4.20}$$

□

Theorem 4.2 $\mathcal{D}(X_1, X_2)$ *is also true metric with* $\mathcal{D}(X_1, X_2) \leq 1$ *for all pairs* X_1, X_2).

This theorem is also proved in Appendix E.

When $n > 2$, we may expand the definition of $d(X_1, \ldots, X_n)$ to become

$$d(X_1, \ldots, X_n) = (n-1)H(X_1, \ldots, X_n) - I(X_1, \ldots, X_n)$$
$$= nH(X_1, \ldots, X_n) - \sum_{i=1}^{n} H(X_i) \qquad . \tag{4.21}$$

The relative dispersion function for $n > 2$ becomes

$$\mathcal{D}(X_1, \ldots, X_n) = \frac{1}{n-1} \frac{d(X_1, \ldots, X_n)}{H(X_1, \ldots, X_n)}. \tag{4.22}$$

This function is symmetric and non-negative, and is zero if and only if there exists a permutation $\pi \colon \mathcal{A} \to \mathcal{A}$ such that

$$u_{i|\mathrm{pa}(i)}(a_i | \mathbf{a}_i^*) = \begin{cases} 0 & \text{if } a_i \neq a_i^* \\ 1 & \text{if } a_i = a_i^* \end{cases}, \quad i = 1, \ldots, n,$$

where $\{a_1^*, \ldots, a_n^*\} = \{\pi(a_1), \ldots, \pi(a_n)\}$. $\mathcal{D}(X_1, \ldots, X_n)$ is a measure of how much the utilities of the group are in conflict. $\mathcal{D}(X_1, \ldots, X_n)$ achieves its maximum when all of the X_i's are mutually socially independent, in which case $\mathcal{D}(X_1, \ldots, X_n) = 1$.

Definition 4.7 The *coordination index* of the network is

$$C(X_1, \ldots, X_n) = 1 - \mathcal{D}(X_1, \ldots, X_n). \tag{4.23}$$

□

The coordination index is a measure of the degree to which the members of a network are socially connected and serves as a measure of the intrinsic ability of the individuals to align their interests *as a result of direct social influence*. Alignment can be positive, in which case the individuals have compatible shared interests (e.g., teams), or it can be negative, in which case they have conflicting shared interests (e.g, athletic contests). When all of the utilities are categorical, as is the case with classical social choice theory, the individuals are mutually socially independent and the relative dispersion is maximum. Consequently, the coordination index is zero – the members have no shared social interests (although they may have shared material interests). This is true even if $u_1 = \cdots = u_n$. Common material interests do not imply shared social interests. This does not mean, of course, that mutually socially independent individuals cannot be aligned, nor does a lack of an intrinsic ability to align their interests mean that the agents will not function harmoniously. Rather, it means that if they do, it is simply by coincidence, rather than by social design.

The coordination index is the theoretical upper bound on the intrinsic ability of a network to align its interests, and is not a function of the solution concept, which may or may not exploit the coordination limits. Basically, it tells how theoretically amenable a given organizational or network structure is for coordinated behavior. But it cannot tell whether or not that structure supports the kind of coordination that one desires.

One way to think of the coordination index, then, is as a measure of the ecological fitness of a given network to function appropriately in its environment. It can also be used as a design tool to evaluate the ecological fitness of a proposed network design. A low coordination index may prompt structural changes such as the insertion of additional linkages or the modification of existing links.

Example 4.2 We again consider the Three Stooges dinner party using the same parameterized utility structure as used in Example 4.1. Figure 4.8 displays the coordination index for values of $\alpha, \beta, \gamma \in (0, \{1/2\})$. Notice that, even though mutual information displayed in Figure 4.7 is maximized near $\alpha = \beta = \gamma = 0.1$, when normalized by the total entropy, the relative entropy is $C(L, C, M) \approx 0.2$, meaning that the network is approximately 20% coordinated as is theoretically possible.

The coordination index is maximized as $\alpha = \beta = \gamma \to 0$, in which case (2.47), (2.48), and (2.49) become $u_L(F) = 1$, $u_{C|L}(I|F) = 1$, and $u_{M|LC}(F|FI) = 1$, resulting in $C(L, C, M) = 1$. The resulting coordination function (2.51) yields $u_{LCM}(F, I, F) = 1$ and the *ex post* marginals given by (2.52), (2.53), and (2.54) are $\tilde{u}_L(F) = \tilde{u}_C(I) =$

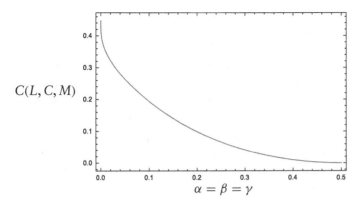

Figure 4.8: The Coordination Index for the Three Stooges for $\alpha = \beta = \gamma \in (0, 1/2)$.

$\tilde{u}_M(F) = 1$. Notice that maximal coordination does not result in agreement.

At the other extreme, as $\alpha = \beta = \gamma = 1/2$, the individuals become socially independent, resulting in $C(L, C, M) = 0$, a condition of no ability to coordinate. The coordination function is such that $u_{LCM}(a_L, a_C, a_M) = 1/8$ and the *ex post* marginal utility values are all equally apportioned between F and I.

4.4 Summary

Many concepts of coordinated decision making appear in the extant literature, but they all rely heavily on exogenous assumptions about behavior, such as knowledge regarding the rationality of the members of the society. Concepts of rational behavior, however, are not part of the mathematical structure, which comprises the members of the society, the feasible alternatives, and the individual preference orderings of the members. Concepts of coordination that derive from notions of rational behavior are *exogenous*, since they do not arise from the structure of the preference orderings.

An alternative to exogenous coordination is the concept of endogenous coordination, which is completely independent of notions of rational behavior. Instead, endogenous coordination is a function of, and only of, the mathematical structure. In particular, as conditional preferences propagate through the network, social relationships are formed, thereby creating a complex social structure. As a result of this interconnectivity of interests, the network possesses an emergent innate potential to function in a coordinated manner.

This chapter presents a mathematical approach to quantify this innate potential. The approach is to migrate the notion of mutual information, which is a key component of Shannon information theory, to the praxeological domain by establishing an isomorphism between the epistemological notion of information and the praxeological notion of interest. The result is the development of a coordination index which characterizes the degree of shared interest that arises due to the social interconnectivity among the members of the network.

5 | *Randomization*

The obvious move is to deny that the notion of knowledge has the importance generally attributed to it, and to try to make the concept of belief do the work that philosophers have generally assigned to the grander concept. I shall argue that this is the right move.

— Richard Jeffrey
Probability and the Art of Judgment (Cambridge University Press, 1992)

The development of social choice theory for networks has appropriated the syntax of probability theory in several says. We have used the concept of conditioning to form the social influence linkages between individuals, we have used the concept of coherence (avoiding sure loss) to motivate the need to express preferences in terms of conditional mass functions that are manipulated according to the probability syntax, we have applied Bayesian network theory to develop an explicit social model as a coordination ordering over profiles of conjectures, and we have applied Shannon information theory to develop operational concepts of coordination. What we have not yet done, however, is apply probability theory in its traditional usage as a means to model epistemological uncertainty.

Thus far, our discussions regarding social choice have been made under the assumption that the network model is deterministic. All members of the society are assumed to be certain of and agree on their preferences, and the choice mechanism used by the society is purely deterministic. Uncertainty, however, can enter into a social choice problem in several ways. In this chapter we discuss two manifestations of random behavior. One way for uncertainty to arise is when some of the members of the network are random variables whose realizations can influence the interests of the deterministic members of the network. Another way that uncertainty is manifest is when individuals define their preferences in terms of probability distributions rather than with fixed preference orderings.

5.1 Social Choice with Stochastic Agents

We now expand the notion of an influence network to include agents who behave as random variables that can influence and be influenced by deterministic agents. For example, agents may be influenced by phenomena beyond their control, such as environmental factors, and ignoring such factors could distort or invalidate the social model. Consider the network illustrated in Figure 5.1, where Y is a discrete random variable defined over some finite set $\mathcal{Y}$ that influences X, X is a deterministic agent defined over an alternative set $\mathcal{A}$, and Z is a discrete random variable defined over a finite set $\mathcal{Z}$.

The function $u_{X|Y}$ has the syntax of a conditional utility mass function whose conditioning entity is a stochastic phenomenon, rather than another individual, and $p_{Z|X}$ has the syntax of a conditional probability mass function whose conditioning entity is a deterministic individual, rather than another stochastic phenomenon. This structure involves the mixing of epistemological phenomena with praxeological phenomena. To develop this relationship, we observe that Theorem 2.2 establishes the isomorphic connections between probability theory and utility theory. Furthermore, social coherence requires that utilities must comply with the axioms of probability theory. Thus, the syntax of probability theory and the syntax of utility theory are compatible. It remains, however, to establish the mathematical mechanism that justifies the merging of random and deterministic influence relationships. The key issue in this regard is the concept of a transition mass function (see Appendix C for further discussion).

Definition 5.1 Let $\mathcal{Y}$ and $\mathcal{A}$ be discrete sets, let Y be a discrete random variable over $\mathcal{Y}$, and let X be an agent expressing preferences over $\mathcal{A}$. A *transition utility mass function* $u_{X|Y}$ is a mapping of $\mathcal{Y} \times \mathcal{A}$ into $[0, 1]$ such that for every $y \in \mathcal{Y}$, $u_{X|Y}(\cdot|y)$ is a utility mass function on $\mathcal{A}$.

A *transition probability mass function* $p_{Y|X}$ is a mapping of $\mathcal{A} \times \mathcal{Y}$ into $[0, 1]$ such that for every $a \in \mathcal{A}$, $p_{Y|X}(\cdot|a)$ is a probability mass function on $\mathcal{Y}$.   □

Figure 5.1: Transitions between Stochastic and Deterministic Individuals.

The following theorem, developed in Appendix C, establishes the relationship between epistemological and praxeological concepts.

Theorem 5.1 *Let $\mathcal{Y}$ and $\mathcal{A}$ be discrete sets. Let p_Y be a probability mass function over $\mathcal{Y}$, and let $u_{X|Y}$ be a transition mass function over $\mathcal{Y} \times \mathcal{A}$. Then there exists a unique mass function u_{YX} on $\mathcal{Y} \times \mathcal{A}$ such that*

$$u_{YX}(y, a) = p_Y(y) u_{X|Y}(a|y). \tag{5.1}$$

Syntactically, a transition mass function is similar to a conditional probability mass function $p_{2|1}(y_2|y_1)$, but there are two important differences. First, whereas a conditional probability mass function is defined over a single set $\mathcal{Y}$ (see Definition C.10) the events y and a lie in different sets. Second, whereas a conditional probability is defined in terms of joint and marginal mass functions (C.10), the joint mass function expressed in (5.1) is defined in terms of a transition mass function and a mass function.

Referring to Figure 5.1, the function $u_{X|Y}$ is a transition mass function between $\mathcal{Y}$ and $\mathcal{A}$, and we may define a joint mass function over $\mathcal{Y} \times \mathcal{A}$ as $u_{YX}(y, a) = p_Y(y) u_{X|Y}(a|y)$. Similarly, $p_{Z|X}$ is a transition mass function between $\mathcal{A}$ and $\mathcal{Z}$ and, accordingly, we may define a joint mass function $p_{XZ}(a, z)$. Thus, aside from the technical issue of defining the mechanism by which the linkages between epistemological and praxeological entities are created, epistemological entities can be seamlessly absorbed into the praxeological network and treated without distinction as far as constructing the coordination function is concerned.

Definition 5.2 Let $\{X_1, \ldots, X_n\}$ denote a network of n deterministic agents, and let $\{Y_1, \ldots, Y_m\}$ denote a set of discrete stochastic agents (random variables) where Y_j is defined over a finite set $\mathcal{B}_j, j = 1, \ldots, m$. The combined set of individuals $\{X_1, \ldots, X_n, Y_1, \ldots, Y_m\}$ defined over the product set $\mathcal{A}^n \times \mathcal{B}_1 \times \cdots \times \mathcal{B}_m$ comprises a *stochastic network*.

A *stochastic conjecture profile* is an array $(a_1, \ldots, a_n, b_1, \ldots, b_m) \in \mathcal{A}^n \times \mathcal{B}_1 \times \cdots \times \mathcal{B}_m$ such that $(a_1, \ldots, a_n)$ is a conjecture profile for $\{X_1, \ldots, X_n\}$ and $(b_1, \ldots, b_m)$ is a *stochastic profile* for $\{Y_1, \ldots, Y_m\}$.

A *stochastic coordination function* is a function $u_{1:n\,1:m} \colon \mathcal{A}^n \times \mathcal{B}_1 \times \cdots \times \mathcal{B}_m \to [0, 1]$ that characterizes all of the social relationships that exist among the deterministic agents, the stochastic dependency relationships that exist among the stochastic agents, the stochastic

relationships that the deterministic agents exert on the stochastic
agents, and the social relationships that the stochastic agents exert
on the deterministic agents.   □

Suppose X_i has p_i deterministic parents and q_i stochastic parents,
and Y_j has r_j deterministic parents and s_j stochastic parents, that is,

$$\text{pa}(X_i) = \{X_{i_1},\ldots,X_{i_{p_i}},Y_{k_1},\ldots,Y_{k_{q_i}}\}$$
$$\text{pa}(Y_j) = \{X_{j_1},\ldots,X_{j_{r_j}},Y_{l_1},\ldots,Y_{l_{s_j}}\}$$

(5.2)

Definition 5.3 For any stochastic conjecture profile $(a_1,\ldots,a_n,$
$b_1,\ldots,b_m)$, let

$$\mathbf{a}_i = (a_{i_1},\ldots,a_{i_{p_i}},b_{k_1},\ldots,b_{k_{q_i}})$$
$$\mathbf{b}_j = (a_{j_1},\ldots,a_{j_{r_j}},b_{l_1},\ldots,b_{l_{s_j}})$$

(5.3)

denote the conditioning conjectures of $\text{pa}(X_i)$ and $\text{pa}(Y_j)$, respectively. The *stochastic coordination function* is of the form

$$u_{1:n\,1:m}(a_1,\ldots,a_n,b_1,\ldots,b_m) = \prod_{i=1}^{n}\prod_{j=1}^{m} u_{i|\text{pa}(i)}(a_i|\mathbf{a}_i)p_{j|\text{pa}(j)}(b_j|\mathbf{b}_j).$$

(5.4)

□

Figure 5.2 provides an illustration of a stochastic network. Notice
that this network interweaves the relationships among the deterministic and stochastic agents such that deterministic agents influence both
deterministic and stochastic agents, and stochastic agents influence
both deterministic and stochastic agents.

Although the stochastic agents influence the preferences of the
deterministic agents, they are not involved in the choice; they are not
voting members. Thus, for the network to make a choice, we must
compute the deterministic marginal coordination function.

Definition 5.4 The *deterministic marginal coordination function* is
the marginal coordination function obtained by summing over the
stochastic states.

$$u_{1:n}(a_1,\ldots,a_n) = \sum_{b_1,\ldots,b_m} u_{1:n\,1:m}(a_1,\ldots,a_n,b_1,\ldots,b_m).$$ (5.5)

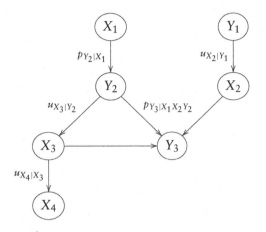

Figure 5.2: A Stochastic Network.

The deterministic marginal is the *expected coordination utility* of the stochastic network $\{X_1, \ldots, X_n, Y_1, \ldots, Y_m\}$. □

To illustrate, consider the utility-probability network displayed in Figure 5.2. The corresponding stochastic coordination function is

$$u_{X_1 : X_4 \, Y_1 : Y_3}(a_1, a_2, a_3, a_4, b_1, b_2, b_3) =$$
$$u_{X_1}(a_1) u_{X_2 | Y_1}(a_2 | b_1) u_{X_3 | Y_2}(a_3 | b_2) u_{X_4 | X_3}(a_4 | a_3)$$
$$p_{Y_1}(b_1) p_{Y_2 | X_1}(b_2 | a_1) p_{Y_3 | X_2 X_3 Y_2}(b_3 | a_2, a_3, b_2).$$

The expected coordination function is the deterministic marginal

$$u_{X_1 : X_4}(a_1, a_2, a_3, a_4) = \sum_{b_1, b_2, b_3} u_{X_1 : X_4 \, Y_1 : Y_3}(a_1, a_2, a_3, a_4, b_1, b_2, b_3).$$
$$(5.6)$$

Example 5.1 Returning to the Three Stooges dinner party, suppose Larry's preference for *F* over *I* depends on whether or not it is raining. In such a case, the state of the weather is actually part of the network since, by definition, a network must include all and only those factors that link its elements together.

Suppose it will either rain (*R*) or it will be dry (*D*). Let *W* be a weather state stochastic agent defined over the set $\mathcal{B}_W = \{R, D\}$, with probability mass function

$$p_W(R) = r \text{ and } p_W(D) = 1 - r.$$
$$(5.7)$$

If it is likely to rain on the way to the restaurant, L would prefer I (e.g., the Italian restaurant is closer than the French restaurant) but if it is more likely to be dry then L would prefer F. Larry can account for his dependency on the weather by replacing his categorical utility with utilities conditioned on the weather state, yielding the transition mass function

$$u_{L|W}(F|R) = \alpha \qquad u_{L|W}(I|R) = 1 - \alpha$$
$$u_{L|W}(F|D) = 1 - \alpha \qquad u_{L|W}(I|D) = \alpha \tag{5.8}$$

Now suppose that Curly is influenced by Larry as with the original formulation, thus his conditional utilities are unchanged, yielding

$$u_{C|L}(F|F) = \beta \qquad u_{C|L}(I|F) = 1 - \beta$$
$$u_{C|L}(F|I) = 1 - \beta \qquad u_{C|L}(I|I) = \beta \tag{5.9}$$

With regard to Mo, suppose that on some previous occasion Mo had a bad experience at the Italian restaurant, and if Larry were to conjecture I, there is a chance that it would cause Mo to throw a temper tantrum (T). If Mo did throw a tantrum, then he would categorically reject I and put all of his utility on F. But if Mo did not throw a tantrum (N), then his preferences would be as before. Let S be a stochastic agent defined over the set $\mathcal{B}_S = \{T, N\}$. Thus, Mo's conditional utilities become

$$u_{M|LCS}(F|FFT) = 1 \qquad u_{M|LCS}(I|FFT) = 0$$
$$u_{M|LCS}(F|FIT) = 1 \qquad u_{M|LCS}(I|FIT) = 0$$
$$u_{M|LCS}(F|IFT) = \gamma \qquad u_{M|LCS}(I|IFT) = 1 - \gamma$$
$$u_{M|LCS}(F|IIT) = 1 - \gamma \qquad u_{M|LCS}(I|IIT) = \gamma$$
$$u_{M|LCS}(F|FFN) = \gamma \qquad u_{M|LCS}(I|FFN) = 1 - \gamma \tag{5.10}$$
$$u_{M|LCS}(F|FIN) = 1 - \gamma \qquad u_{M|LCS}(I|FIN) = \gamma$$
$$u_{M|LCS}(F|IFN) = \gamma \qquad u_{M|LCS}(I|IFN) = 1 - \gamma$$
$$u_{M|LCS}(F|IIN) = 1 - \gamma \qquad u_{M|LCS}(I|IIN) = \gamma$$

To complete this model, we define the conditional transition mass function

$$p_{S|L}(T|F) = 0 \qquad p_{S|L}(N|F) = 1$$
$$p_{S|L}(T|I) = s \qquad p_{S|L}(N|I) = 1 - s \tag{5.11}$$

for $0 \le s \le 1$.

Consequently, a stochastic coordination function can be defined over the product set $\{F, I\}^3 \times \{R, D\} \times \{T, N\}$, yielding

$$u_{LCMWS}(a_L, a_C, a_M, w, s) =$$
$$u_{L|W}(a_L|w)u_{C|L}(a_C|a_L)u_{M|LCS}(a_C|a_L, a_C, s)p_W(w)p_{S|L}(s|a_L), \quad (5.12)$$

and the deterministic marginal coordination function is

$$u_{LCM}(a_L, a_C, a_M) = \sum_{w,s} u_{LCMWS}(a_L, a_C, a_M, w, s). \quad (5.13)$$

Figure 5.3 illustrates this augmented society comprising three deterministic agents $\{L, C, M\}$ and two stochastic agents $\{W, S\}$. □

Given the isomorphic relationship defined by Theorem 2.2, it is possible to extend a network to include random variables by simply including them as members whose utilities are epistemological rather than praxeological. Thus, it is possible for a network to be composed of arbitrary combinations of deterministic elements (rational individuals) and stochastic elements (random variables) such that entities that possess praxeological utilities maybe interspersed with entities that possess epistemological probabilities. Furthermore, it is not necessary to restrict the entities (either random or rational) to be defined over the same set (either a sample space or an alternative set). The praxeological utilities may be defined over the alternative set, and the epistemological probabilities may be defined over a sample space that is different from the alternative set.

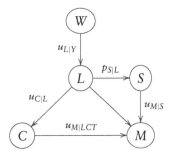

Figure 5.3: The Three Stooges Network with Stochastic Agents.

5.2 Social Choice with Randomized Preferences

Consider a social choice scenario where, instead of individuals possessing deterministic preference orderings, their preference orderings are expressed in terms of probability distributions. Take the Three Stooges dinner party for example, and suppose Larry is having trouble defining his preferences over the set $A = \{F, I\}$. He favors the ordering $F \succ_L I$, but is just not decisive enough to settle on a specific numerical utility u_L. In an attempt to help Larry, Curly suggests that he just flip a coin. If it lands heads up, then he commits to I; if it lands tails up, he commits to F. Suppose Larry has two coins in his pocket, one has probability of heads equal to r, and the other has probability of heads equal to r', where $r < r'$. If Larry were to take Curly's advice, he would replace his deterministic preference ordering $\succ$ over A with a preference ordering $\succ^*$ over the set of probability vectors $A^* = \{(1 - r, r), (1 - r', r')\}$. If Larry were willing to let the outcome of the coin toss determine which restaurant he favors, his actual *decision* would be to choose which coin to toss. Since he has a slight preference for French, this would induce a preference ordering $\succ^*$ over A^* such that $(1 - r, r) \succ^* (1 - r', r')$, and he would toss the r-coin. Regardless of which coin he were to flip, however, Larry would be letting chance decide his preferences. In game theory parlance, Larry would be invoking a *mixed strategy*.

By what rational basis can Larry justify his decision to let the outcome of a coin toss determine his preferences? To even consider such a gamble means that Larry is willing to accept the risk of an unfavorable result in order to resolve his indecisiveness. Given that he is willing, his status as a "rational" person places him under obligation to justify his behavior. This situation raises a fundamental, and surprisingly theoretically deep, rationality issue: When one is faced with a choice where the outcome is governed by a probability distribution, is there a rationally justifiable way to make a choice? This issue was resolved and made mathematically rigorous by von Neumann and Morgenstern (1944), who formalized the so-called expected utility hypothesis: When the outcome is characterized by a set of probability distribuions, or lotteries, one should choose the lottery with maximum expected value.

5.2.1 Expected Utility

Let $\mathcal{A} = \{z_1, \ldots, z_N\}$ be a finite set of alternatives, and let $\mathcal{A}^*$ denote the set of all probability vectors $\boldsymbol{\pi} = (\pi_1, \ldots, \pi_N)$, where π_j is the probability that z_i will be actualized. In particular, let $e_j = (0, \cdots, 0, 1, 0, \cdots, 0)$ denote the jth coordinate vector, where the unit appears in the jth element of e_j. Thus, e_j is the degenerate lottery that assigns all of the probability mass to z_j.

Let $\succsim^*$ denote a binary preference ordering over $\mathcal{A}^*$. That is, $\boldsymbol{\pi} \succsim^* \boldsymbol{\pi}'$ means that one prefers lottery $\boldsymbol{\pi}$ to lottery $\boldsymbol{\pi}'$ or is indifferent. We shall assume that the elements of $\mathcal{A}^*$ comply with two axioms.

Independence: If $\boldsymbol{\pi}_1, \boldsymbol{\pi}_2, \boldsymbol{\pi}_3 \in \mathcal{A}^*$ and $0 < \lambda \leq 1$, then $\boldsymbol{\pi}_1 \succsim^* \boldsymbol{\pi}_2$ if, and only if, $\lambda\boldsymbol{\pi}_1 + (1-\lambda)\boldsymbol{\pi}_3 \succsim^* \lambda\boldsymbol{\pi}_2 + (1-\lambda)\boldsymbol{\pi}_3$.

Continuity: If $\boldsymbol{\pi}_1, \boldsymbol{\pi}_2, \boldsymbol{\pi}_3 \in \mathcal{A}^*$ are such that $\boldsymbol{\pi}_1 \succ^* \boldsymbol{\pi}_2 \succ^* \boldsymbol{\pi}_3$, then there exist numbers λ and μ with $0 < \lambda, \mu < 1$ such that

$$\lambda\boldsymbol{\pi}_3 + (1-\lambda)\boldsymbol{\pi}_1 \succ^* \boldsymbol{\pi}_2 \succ^* \mu\boldsymbol{\pi}_3 + (1-\mu)\boldsymbol{\pi}_1 . \tag{5.14}$$

Definition 5.5 Let $u\colon \mathcal{A} \to \mathbb{R}$ be a utility defined over the alternative set, and define $u^*\colon \mathcal{A}^* \to \mathbb{R}$ such that

$$u^*(e_j) = u(z_j), \ j = 1, \ldots, N \tag{5.15}$$

and, for each $\boldsymbol{\pi} = (\pi_1, \ldots, \pi_N) \in \mathcal{A}^*$,

$$u^*(\boldsymbol{\pi}) = \sum_{j=1}^{N} \pi_j u^*(e_j) = \sum_{j=1}^{N} \pi_j u(z_j) . \tag{5.16}$$

The function u^* is termed a *von Neumann–Morgenstern* utility, and $u^*(\boldsymbol{\pi})$ is the *expected utility* of $\boldsymbol{\pi}$. □

Definition 5.6 A binary preference ordering $\succsim^*$ over $\mathcal{A}^*$ and a von Neumann–Morgenstern utility u^* defined over $\mathcal{A}^*$ are said to *agree* if for all $\boldsymbol{\pi}, \boldsymbol{\pi}' \in \mathcal{A}^*$, $\boldsymbol{\pi} \succ^* \boldsymbol{\pi}'$ if, and only if, $u^*(\boldsymbol{\pi}) > u^*(\boldsymbol{\pi}')$ and $\boldsymbol{\pi} \sim^* \boldsymbol{\pi}'$ if, and only if, $u^*(\boldsymbol{\pi}) = u^*(\boldsymbol{\pi}')$. □

Theorem 5.2 von Neumann–Morgenstern. *If a binary relation $\succsim^*$ on $\mathcal{A}^*$ satisfies the independence and continuity axioms, then there exists a von Neumann–Morgenstern utility u^* defined over $\mathcal{A}^*$ that agrees with $\succsim^*$. Furthermore, u^* is uniquely determined up to a positive affine transformation.*

This result was originally established by von Neumann and Morgenstern (1944) (additional in-depth treatments of this theory can be found in Blackwell and Girshick (1979), Ferguson (1967), and Kreps (1988)).

The content of the von Neumann–Morgenstern theorem is that if one has a preference ordering over a set $\mathcal{A}^*$ of lotteries, one will behave as if one has assigned a numerical utility u to the elements of $\mathcal{A}$, and $\pi \succeq^* \pi'$ if, and only if,

$$\sum_{j=1}^{N} \pi_j u(z_j) \geq \sum_{j=1}^{N} \pi_j' u(z_j). \tag{5.17}$$

5.2.2 Expected Utility on Networks

Definition 5.7   For a network $\{X_1, \ldots, X_n\}$, let $\succsim_{i|\text{pa}(i)}^*$ denote a conditional preference ordering over $\mathcal{A}^*$ for X_i that satisfies the continuity and independence axioms, and let $u_{i|\text{pa}(i)}^*$ be a von Neumann–Morgenstern utility that agrees with $\succsim_{i|\text{pa}(i)}^*$ and also complies with the syntax of probability theory. A *conjecture lottery* $\pi_i = (\pi_{i1}, \ldots, \pi_{iN}) \in \mathcal{A}^*$ for X_i is a probability vector such that $z_j \in \mathcal{A}$ is a conjecture for X_i with probability π_{ij}.

Given $\text{pa}(X_i) = \{X_{i_1}, \ldots, X_{i_{p_i}}\}$ and a conditioning conjecture lottery profile $\{\pi_{i_1}, \ldots, \pi_{i_{p_i}}\}$, the function $u_{i|\text{pa}(i)}^* : \mathcal{A}^* \to [0, 1]$ is a *conditional expected utility*. Extending Theorem 2.6 to lotteries, the *expected coordination function* becomes

$$u_{1:n}^*(\pi_1, \ldots, \pi_n) = \prod_{i=1}^{n} u_{i|\text{pa}(i)}^*(\pi_i | \pi_{i_1}, \ldots, \pi_{i_{p_i}}). \tag{5.18}$$

$\square$

It is important to contrast the coordination function defined by (2.38) with the expected coordination function defined by (5.18). Since the alternative set $\mathcal{A}$ is given to be finite, there are only a finite number of conjectures, and the coordination function can assume only a finite number of values. With the expected coordination function defined by (5.18), however, it is possible for the set $\mathcal{A}^*$ of probability distributions over $\mathcal{A}$ to be defined over a continuum of parameter values, resulting in the cardinality of $\mathcal{A}^*$ to be infinite. For example, recall from the previous discussion that Larry needs to choose from the set of probability vectors $\{(1-r,r),(1-r',r')\}$. Suppose, however, that Larry is not constrained to choose from a set comprising only two members, but can choose from the set $\{(1-r,r), 0 \leq r \leq 1\}$ that contains a continuum of members. Thus, we must consider two cases.

Finite Cardinality If $\mathcal{A}^*$ contains finitely many probability vectors, then each $\boldsymbol{\pi} \in \mathcal{A}^*$ is of the form $\boldsymbol{\pi} = (\pi_1, \ldots, \pi_n)$, where $\sum_{i=1}^{n} \pi_i = 1$. Then the procedure for calculating the ith marginal is essentially the same as defined by (2.39), namely, it is given as

$$\tilde{u}_i^*(\pi_i) = \sum_{\sim\pi_i} u_{1:n}^*(\pi_1, \ldots, \pi_n). \tag{5.19}$$

To illustrate, let $\mathcal{A} = \{z_1, z_2\}$, and let $\mathcal{A}^* = \{(1-r_1,r_1),(1-r_2,r_2)\}$. For a given utility $u(z_i)$, $i = 1, 2$, the expected utility of $(1-r_i, r_i)$ is, following (5.16),

$$u^*(1-r_i, r_i) = (1-r_i)u(z_1) + r_iu(z_2). \tag{5.20}$$

For u^* to be a mass function, we require $u(z_i) \geq 0$ and

$$\sum_{i=1}^{2} u^*(1-r_i, r_i) = 1. \tag{5.21}$$

Infinite Cardinality If $\mathcal{A}^*$ is of infinite cardinality, then there are infinitely many ways to assign a unit of probability mass to the elements of $\mathcal{A}$, and the marginal cannot be expressed as a summation. However, if the conditional utilities $u_{i|\text{pa}(i)}^*$ are expressed as densities, then the marginals can be defined as

$$\tilde{u}_i^*(\pi_i) = \int_{\sim\pi_i} u_{1:n}^*(\pi_1, \ldots, \pi_n) d{\sim}\pi_i, \tag{5.22}$$

where, as with summation, the notation $\int_{\sim\pi_i}$ means that integration is over all probability vectors except π_i.

To illustrate, let $\mathcal{A} = \{z_1, z_2\}$, and let $\mathcal{A}^* = \{(1-r,r), 0 \leq r \leq 1\}$, which defines the one-dimensional simplex $\pi_1 + \pi_2 = 1$ with $\pi_1, \pi_2 \geq 0$. For a given utility $u(z_i)$, $i = 1, 2$, the expected utility of $(1-r,r)$ is

$$u^*(1-r, r) = (1-r)u(z_1) + ru(z_2). \tag{5.23}$$

For u^* to be a density, we require $u(z_i) \geq 0$ and

$$\int_0^1 u^*(1-r,r)dr = 1. \tag{5.24}$$

Example 5.2 Let us once again return to the Three Stooges dinner problem as discussed in Section 2.6. In that scenario, Larry, Curly, and Mo possess deterministic preference orderings over the alternative set $\mathcal{A} = \{F,I\}$, as defined by (2.47), (2.48), and (2.49), respectively. We consider two cases: first with $\mathcal{A}^*$ of finite cardinality and next with $\mathcal{A}^*$ with infinite cardinality.

Finite Cardinality Suppose $\mathcal{A}^* = \{(3/4,1/4),(1/3,2/3)\}$. If the lottery $(3/4,1/4)$ is chosen, then F will be chosen with probability 3/4 and I with probability 1/4. Let

$$\begin{aligned} u_L(F) &= h \\ u_L(I) &= 0 \end{aligned} \tag{5.25}$$

where h must be chosen to ensure that u_L^* is a mass function. Applying (5.16) yields

$$\begin{aligned} u_L^*(3/4,1/4) &= 3/4u_L(F) + 1/4u_L(I) = 3/4h \\ u_L^*(1/3,2/3) &= 1/3u_L(F) + 2/3u_L(I) = 1/3h \end{aligned} \tag{5.26}$$

which requires $h = 12/13$, yielding

$$\begin{aligned} u_L^*(3/4,1/4) &= 9/13 \\ u_L^*(1/3,2/3) &= 4/13 \end{aligned} \tag{5.27}$$

To compute Curly's conditional expected utility, we let

$$\begin{aligned} u_{C|L}(F|F) &= 0 & u_{C|L}(I|F) &= h_1 \\ u_{C|L}(F|I) &= h_2 & u_{C|L}(I|I) &= 0 \end{aligned} \tag{5.28}$$

Setting $h_1 = 12/11$ and $h_2 = 12/13$ yields

$$\begin{aligned} u_{C|L}^*[(3/4,1/4) \mid (3/4,1/4)] &= 8/11 \\ u_{C|L}^*[(1/3,2/3) \mid (3/4,1/4)] &= 3/11 \\ u_{C|L}^*[(3/4,1/4) \mid (1/3,2/3)] &= 9/13 \\ u_{C|L}^*[(1/3,2/3) \mid (1/3,2/3)] &= 4/13 \end{aligned} \tag{5.29}$$

Finally, we recall that Mo's preferences were rather convoluted, depending on both Larry's and Curly's preferences. Mo should favor lotteries that prefer I to F if Larry and Curly both favor lotteries that prefer F to I. Mo should also favor lotteries that prefer I to F if Larry favors lotteries that prefer I to F and Curly favors lotteries that prefer F to I. Conversely, Mo should favor lotteries that prefer F to I if Larry favors lotteries that prefer F to I and Curly favors lotteries that prefer I to F, or if both L and C favor lotteries that prefer I to F. Thus,

$$
\begin{aligned}
u_{M|LC}(F|FF) &= 0 & u_{M|LC}(I|FF) &= h_1 \\
u_{M|LC}(F|FI) &= h_2 & u_{M|LC}(I|FI) &= 0 \\
u_{M|LC}(F|IF) &= 0 & u_{M|LC}(I|IF) &= h_3 \\
u_{M|LC}(F|II) &= h_4 & u_{M|LC}(I|II) &= 0
\end{aligned}
\tag{5.30}
$$

Applying (5.16) and solving for h_i, $i = 1, 4$, yields

$$
\begin{aligned}
u_{M|LC}^*[(3/4, 1/4) \mid (3/4, 1/4), (3/4, 1/4)] &= 3/11 \\
u_{M|LC}^*[(1/3, 2/3) \mid (3/4, 1/4), (3/4, 1/4)] &= 8/11 \\
u_{M|LC}^*[(3/4, 1/4) \mid (3/4, 1/4), (1/3, 2/3)] &= 9/13 \\
u_{M|LC}^*[(1/3, 2/3) \mid (3/4, 1/4), (1/3, 2/3)] &= 4/13 \\
u_{M|LC}^*[(3/4, 1/4) \mid (1/3, 2/3), (3/4, 1/4)] &= 3/11 \\
u_{M|LC}^*[(1/3, 2/3) \mid (1/3, 2/3), (3/4, 1/4)] &= 8/11 \\
u_{M|LC}^*[(3/4, 1/4) \mid (1/3, 2/3), (1/3, 2/3)] &= 9/13 \\
u_{M|LC}^*[(1/3, 2/3) \mid (1/3, 2/3), (1/3, 2/3)] &= 4/13
\end{aligned}
\tag{5.31}
$$

The expected utility of the network is then

$$
u_{LCM}^*(\pi_L, \pi_C, \pi_M) = u_L^*(\pi_L) u_{C|L}^*(\pi_C|\pi_L) u_{M|LCs}^*(\pi_M|\pi_L, \pi_C),
\tag{5.32}
$$

or

$$
\begin{aligned}
u_{LCM}^*[(3/4, 1/4), (3/4, 1/4), (3/4, 1/4)] &= 0.0515 \\
u_{LCM}^*[(3/4, 1/4), (3/4, 1/4), (1/3, 2/3)] &= 0.1373 \\
u_{LCM}^*[(3/4, 1/4), (1/3, 2/3), (3/4, 1/4)] &= 0.3486 \\
u_{LCM}^*[(3/4, 1/4), (1/3, 2/3), (1/3, 2/3)] &= 0.1549 \\
u_{LCM}^*[(1/3, 2/3), (3/4, 1/4), (3/4, 1/4)] &= 0.0581 \\
u_{LCM}^*[(1/3, 2/3), (3/4, 1/4), (1/3, 2/3)] &= 0.1549 \\
u_{LCM}^*[(1/3, 2/3), (1/3, 2/3), (3/4, 1/4)] &= 0.0655 \\
u_{LCM}^*[(1/3, 2/3), (1/3, 2/3), (1/3, 2/3)] &= 0.0291
\end{aligned}
\tag{5.33}
$$

and the *ex post* marginal expected utilities are

$$\tilde{u}_L^*(3/4,1/4) = 0.6923$$
$$\tilde{u}_L^*(1/3,2/3) = 0.3076 \tag{5.34}$$

$$\tilde{u}_C^*(3/4,1/4) = 0.4081$$
$$\tilde{u}_C^*(1/3,2/3) = 0.5981 \tag{5.35}$$

and

$$\tilde{u}_M^*(3/4,1/4) = 0.5237$$
$$\tilde{u}_M^*(1/3,2/3) = 0.4762 \tag{5.36}$$

From the group perspective, the expected coordination is better if all choose lottery $(3/4,1/4)$ rather than $(1/3,2/3)$, but the expected group coordination is maximized if Larry and Mo choose $(3/4,1/4)$ with Curly choosing $(1/3,2/3)$, which is consistent with the individually maximized *ex post* expected utility results. Thus, this analysis is entirely consistent with the deterministic results discussed in Section 2.6.

Infinite Cardinality We first consider Larry, whose lotteries are of the form $(1-\ell,\ell) = (P_L(F),P_L(I))$. To compute Larry's expected utility, we first must define an appropriate deterministic utility u_L. Accordingly, let

$$u_L(F) = h$$
$$u_L(I) = 0 \tag{5.37}$$

Thus,

$$u_L^*(1-\ell,\ell) = (1-\ell)u_L(F) + \ell u_L(I) = (1-\ell)h. \tag{5.38}$$

Setting h such that

$$\int_0^1 u_L(1-\ell,\ell)d\ell = h\int_0^1 (1-\ell)d\ell = 1/2h, \tag{5.39}$$

yielding $h = 2$. Thus,

$$u_L^*(1-\ell,\ell) = 2(1-\ell). \tag{5.40}$$

We next consider Curly. Let $(1-c,c) = (P_C(F),P_C(I))$ denote a lottery for Curly. Since Curly should favor lotteries that prefer I to F, given that Larry favors lotteries that prefer F to I, and vice versa, we set

$$
\begin{aligned}
u_{C|L}(F|F) &= 0 & u_{C|L}(I|F) &= 2 \\
u_{C|L}(F|I) &= 2 & u_{C|L}(I|I) &= 0
\end{aligned}
\tag{5.41}
$$

To compute Curly's conditional expected utilities, we first note that the condition that Larry favors F over L can be expressed as the relation

$$
(1 - \ell, \ell) \succ^*_L (1/2, 1/2)
\tag{5.42}
$$

or, more succinctly, as

$$
\ell \prec^*_L 1/2 .
\tag{5.43}
$$

Given this antecedent, Curly's conditional expected utility is

$$
u^*_{C|L}(1 - c, c \mid \ell \prec^*_L 1/2) = (1 - c)u_{C|L}(F|F) + cu_{C|L}(I|F) = 2c .
\tag{5.44}
$$

Also, given the antecedent $\ell \succ^*_L 1/2$,

$$
u^*_{C|L}(1 - c, c \mid \ell \succ^*_L 1/2) = (1 - c)u_{C|L}(F|I) + cu_{C|L}(I|I) = 2(1 - c) .
\tag{5.45}
$$

The deterministic conditional structure for Mo is

$$
\begin{aligned}
u_{M|LC}(F|FF) &= 0 & u_{M|LC}(I|FF) &= 2 \\
u_{M|LC}(F|FI) &= 2 & u_{M|LC}(I|FI) &= 0 \\
u_{M|LC}(F|IF) &= 0 & u_{M|LC}(I|IF) &= 2 \\
u_{M|LC}(F|II) &= 2 & u_{M|LC}(I|II) &= 0
\end{aligned}
\tag{5.46}
$$

Let $(1 - m, m) = (P_M(f), P_M(I))$ and, by analyses similar to the above, the conditional expected utilities for Mo are

$$
\begin{aligned}
u^*_{M|LC}(1 - m, m \mid \ell \prec^*_L 1/2, c \prec^*_C 1/2) &= 2m \\
u^*_{M|LC}(1 - m, m \mid \ell \succ^*_L 1/2, c \prec^*_C 1/2) &= 2m \\
u^*_{M|LC}(1 - m, m \mid \ell \prec^*_L 1/2, c \succ^*_C 1/2) &= 2(1 - m) \\
u^*_{M|LC}(1 - m, m \mid \ell \succ^*_L 1/2, c \succ^*_C 1/2) &= 2(1 - m)
\end{aligned}
\tag{5.47}
$$

The expected utility of the network is then, using an obvious notation,

$$u^*_{LCM}(\ell, c, m) = u^*_L(\ell)\, u^*_{C|L}(c|\ell)\, u^*_{M|LC}(m|\ell, c)$$

$$= \begin{cases} 8(1 - \ell)cm & \text{if } \ell < 1/2 \text{ and } c < 1/2 \\ 8(1 - \ell)(1 - c)m & \text{if } \ell > 1/2 \text{ and } c < 1/2 \\ 8(1 - \ell)c(1 - m) & \text{if } \ell < 1/2 \text{ and } c > 1/2 \\ 8(1 - \ell)(1 - c)(1 - m) & \text{if } \ell > 1/2 \text{ and } c > 1/2 \end{cases}.$$

$$(5.48)$$

Since Larry's utility is categorical, the *ex post* marginal is unchanged, thus

$$\tilde{u}^*_L(\ell) = 2(1 - \ell).$$

$$(5.49)$$

To compute $\tilde{u}^*_C$ and $\tilde{u}^*_{Ms}$, we first compute

$$\tilde{u}^*_{CM}(c, m) = \int_0^1 u^*_{LCM}(\ell, c, m)\, d\ell$$

$$= \begin{cases} \int_0^{1/2} 8(1 - \ell)cm\, d\ell + \int_{1/2}^1 8(1 - \ell)(1 - c)m\, d\ell \\ \int_0^{1/2} 8(1 - \ell)c(1 - m)\, d\ell + \int_{1/2}^1 8(1 - \ell)(1 - c)(1 - m)\, d\ell \end{cases}$$

$$= \begin{cases} (1 + 2c)m & \text{if } c < 1/2 \\ (1 + 2c)(1 - m) & \text{if } c \geq 1/2 \end{cases}.$$

$$(5.50)$$

We then compute the *ex post* marginal expected utilities for Curly and Mo as

$$\tilde{u}^*_C(c) = \int_0^1 \tilde{u}^*_{CM}c, m)dm = \frac{1 + 2c}{2}$$

$$(5.51)$$

and

$$\tilde{u}^*_M(m) = \int_0^1 \tilde{u}^*_{CM}(c, m)dc = \frac{5 - 2m}{4}.$$

$$(5.52)$$

Notice that the marginals given by (5.49), (5.51), and (5.52) are density functions, thus they integrate to unity rather than sum to unity, as is required of mass functions. Figure 5.4 illustrates the *ex post* expected utilities. Thus, Larry's and Mo's expected utilities favor F over I if $\ell, m < 1/2$, and Curly's expected utilities favor I if $c > 1/2$. These results comport well with the deterministic utilities that were

Table 5.1: *Maximum Expected Coordination Function for Three Stooges.*

Constraint	$u^*_{LCM}(\ell, c, m)$	ℓ	c	m	max
$\ell < 1/2, c < 1/2$	$(1-\ell)cm$	0	1/2	1	1/2
$\ell < 1/2, c > 1/2$	$(1-\ell)c(1-m)$	0	1	0	1
$\ell > 1/2, c < 1/2$	$(1-\ell)(1-c)m$	1/2	0	1	1/2
$\ell > 1/2, c > 1/2$	$(1-\ell)(1-c)(1-m)$	1/2	1/2	0	1/4

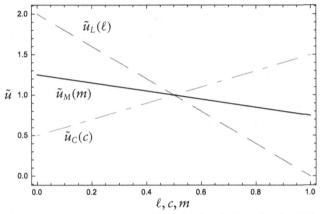

Figure 5.4: *Ex post* Expected Utilities for the Randomized Three Stooges Dinner Party. Dashed Line: $\tilde{u}_L(\ell)$, Dot-dashed Line: $\tilde{u}_C(c)$, Solid Line: $\tilde{u}_M(m)$.

assumed in the setup of the Three Stooges problem presented in Section 2.6 and with the results of the finite cardinality case previously discussed.

To maximize the coordination expected utility, we must consider each set of constraints as indicated in (5.48), yielding the results displayed in Table 5.1. The coordination expected function is maximized if Larry and Mo place all of the probabilities on F and Curly places all of his on I. This result is also consistent with the numerical results displayed in Table 2.1. □

5.3 Summary

This chapter discusses two ways in which randomness can enter a social choice problem. Section 5.1 establishes the seamless merging of epistemological notions of belief uncertainty as expressed by probability theory and praxeological notions of action uncertainty. The ability to arbitrarily interweave random phenomena and behavioral phenomena expands the concept of social choice to include stochastic as well as deterministic individuals into the community as fully integrated members of the network.

Section 5.2 extends social network theory to allow individuals to possess randomized preferences. Classical social choice theory focuses largely on scenarios where all members of the community possess fixed preferences, which leaves little flexibility on the part of the individuals when they are not fully committed to fixed priorities. At the moment of truth, when they are called upon to vote or otherwise participate in the social choice, they may prefer to cast a random vote. In the parlance of game theory, they choose to adopt a mixed strategy. The development in this section enables them to condition the probability distribution of their preferences on the probability distributions of those who influence them. The result is a generalized model for which deterministic social choice theory on networks is a special case where each individual has a degenerate probability distribution over the alternatives.

6 | *Satisficing*

Rationality, according to some, is an excess of reasonableness. We should be rational enough to confront the problems of life but there is no need to go whole hog. Indeed, doing so is something of a vice.

— Isaac Levi
The Covenant of Reason (Cambridge University Press, 1997)

6.1 Solution Concepts

Optimization is viewed by many as the *sine qua non* of decision making. It is the ultimate manifestation of narrowly construed self-interest and, as observed by Tversky and Kahenman (1986, p. 89), "No other theory of judgment and decision can ever match it in scope, power, and simplicity." Even the great mathematician Leonhard Euler rhapsodized about the principle: "Since the fabric of the world is the most perfect and was established by the wisest Creator, nothing happens in this world in which some reason of maximum or minimum would not come to light" (cited in Polya (1954)). But obsession with this principle is not without critics.

Not too long ago we were content with designing systems which merely met given specifications. ... Today, we tend, perhaps, to make a fetish of optimality. If a system is not the "best" in one sense or another, we do not feel satisfied. Indeed, we are apt to place too much confidence in a system that is, in effect, optimal by definition. At present, no completely satisfactory rule for selecting decision functions is available, and it is not very likely that one will be found in the foreseeable future. Perhaps all that we can reasonably expect is a rule which, in a somewhat equivocal manner, would delimit a set of "good" designs for a system (Zadeh, 1958, p. 3).

Perhaps the main virtue of an optimal solution is not that it is the quintessential solution – the best of the best. Rather, optimization provides a systematic mechanism for identifying a solution, such as

133

the calculus-based technique of identifying the maximum of a concave utility function by solving for the value where the first derivative is zero. What is sometimes either ignored or simply assumed is that the real choice confronting the decision maker is the choice of the criterion. Once that is established, identifying the "optimal" solution is, at least conceptually, a straightforward exercise.[1]

Optimization may be an appropriate concept at the individual level, but the issue becomes problematic when multiple decision makers are involved. Fundamentally, optimization is an *individual* concept. If a network is to optimize, it must act as if it were a sentient entity. However, although each member of a network may not obtain its globally optimal outcome by acting autonomously, each may seek a *constrained* optimal solution, typically in the form of an equilibrium state, such as a Nash equilibrium. While it may be individually appealing, constrained optimization fosters a view that others are competitors whose presence acts only to constrain their behavior, rather than partners whose presence potentially may contribute to the welfare of the network as well as the individuals. For example, the Nash equilibrium solution for the Prisoner's Dilemma game would be a very pessimistic strategy for a cooperatively disposed network.

Thus, even if a solution is "optimal," that is no guarantee that each one is happy with the outcome. One may simply be making the best of a bad situation. In other words, although optimization-based approaches are designed to distinguish between better and worse, it may not be able to distinguish between good and bad.

Because social choice theory requires a group-level decision over a single set of alternatives (in contrast to game theory, where each player has its own set of alternatives), attention focuses on group-level performance. For example, as Harsanyi (1955) shows, the optimal utilitarian solution is obtained by maximizing the expected value of the sum of the individual utilities. This approach is designed to achieve the greatest happiness for the greatest number of individuals, but it may also result in a serious disadvantage for some members of the society. By contrast, Rawls (1971) argues that the welfare of society can never be better off than the welfare of its most disadvantaged member.

---

[1] "Reason," said Bertrand Russell, "has a perfectly clear and precise meaning. It signifies the choice of the right means to an end that you wish to achieve. It has nothing whatever to do with the choice of ends." (Russell, 1954).

These two criteria represent extreme concepts of optimization. The utilitarian approach maximizes social benefit, but lets the individuals take their chances, while Rawlsianism maximizes the benefit to the weakest individual and lets society as a whole take its chances.

Although optimization is a compelling concept, it is also very rigid. It offers no provision for compromise, negotiation, or any other socially sophisticated mechanism to address and perhaps mitigate disagreements. But if society does not rely on some notion of optimization, it must rely upon some other concept of rational behavior to define and justify behavior.

One approach that has gained considerable traction is the notion of *satisficing*, as introduced by Simon (1955) as an instantiation of *bounded rationality*, the notion that, although one might wish to optimize, informational or computational limitations make it either impossible or too costly to obtain a theoretically optimal solution. Consequently, one must relax one's insistence on optimality and be content with a solution that is, in some sense that must be made specific, good enough. Simon's essential idea is to approximate an optimal solution by establishing an *aspiration level* and halting the search for better solutions once that goal is achieved (Chen and Sim, 2009). Specifying the aspiration level (the definition of "good enough"), however, is inherently heuristic: The decision maker must invoke some rule or experience-based technique or reason to justify the aspired-to level of performance. Simon is intentionally vague concerning the way aspirations are formed: "Aspirations are expectations—adjusted in the long run to realities—of the result that can reasonably be attained. They are not formed on the basis of detailed evaluation of alternative courses of action" (Simon, 1982, p. 399). One obvious criterion would be to identify a solution that meets minimum requirements in terms of material benefit, assuming such can be identified. Another criterion would be that the solution meets the social or psychological aspirations of the decision maker. More generally, the satisficing solution should meet whatever reasonableness test that is deemed appropriate by the decision maker, such as "judging heuristically that the costs of further search (for something better) will exceed the benefits of the search" (Kreps, 1990, p. 180). Many scholars have weighed in on the concept of satisficing as introduced by Simon. Byron (2004), for example, offers several views of satisficing as a practical concept for human reasoning.

Although Simonian satisficing was originally motivated by informational and computational limitations, perhaps an equally important feature of this approach is the ability to accommodate compromise in multiagent settings. What is best for me may not be best for you and vice versa, but there may nonetheless be a solution that is good enough for both of us. Thus, the essential concept of satisficing (i.e., some notion of good enough) potentially offers an alternative logical mechanism for multiagent decision making. Simon's concept of satisficing, however, has largely been restricted to individual decision making. It is surprising that satisficing has not meaningfully been considered in a multiagent setting, although a few approaches have extended the notion to multiagent/multicriterion cases (e.g., see Pazgal (1997); Bendor et al. (2009)). A possible reason for this dearth is the difficulty in defining group-level heuristics. Nevertheless, the satisficing concept of identifying solutions that can be viewed as "good enough" is a potentially attractive alternative to solutions based on optimization, and the fundamental concept naturally generalizes to multiagent scenarios.

Optimization and Simonian satisficing are extreme concepts of decision making. The former is based on the ultimate in mathematical and logical rigor for ranking and aggregating preferences, while the latter is based on heuristic notions of acceptability. Extreme cases, however, do not exhaust the possible mechanisms for rational behavior. When making performance evaluations, there are three distinct degrees of comparison: superlative, comparative, and positive. By definition, optimization-based decision theory is of the superlative degree: only the best is satisfactory. Decisions based on heuristics are of the positive degree: the choice meets a criterion that defines what it means to be "good." Arguing that a choice is "good enough," according to Simonian satisficing, is a coarsening of the superlative degree on the one hand (settling for being approximately best), and a refinement of the positive degree on the other (good enough, not just good). What might be of real interest is a non-heuristic definition of performance that is distinct from the superlative and positive degrees and qualifies as a true instantiation of the comparative degree.

Our approach is to identify a middle-ground concept that a) employs a rigorous notion of preference that is not based on optimization and b) applies a notion of "good enough" that does not rely on heuristics. The goal is to develop a formal social choice decision model that accommodates socially amenable concepts of behavior, including coordination, cooperation, compromise, altruism, and negotiation. The term *neo-satisficing* is adopted to distinguish this concept from Simonian satisficing. Neo-satisficing is founded in a mathematical formalism that rigorously defines what it means to be good enough, and therefore is as amenable to formal mathematical synthesis as are classical game theory and social choice theory solution concepts. The "satisficing" terminology is retained, however, because this usage is consistent with the issue that motivated Simon's original usage: to identify options that are, in a sense that must be made specific, good enough.

6.2 A Change in Perspective

To attain knowledge, add things every day
To attain wisdom, remove things every day.

— Lao Tzu
Tao-te Ching, ch. 48

For many multiagent decision scenarios, the interests of all individuals will not coincide, and a compromise must be achieved. When seeking a compromise, attention shifts, at least to some degree, from insisting on an outcome that maximizes success to settling for an outcome that at least avoids failure. Indeed, even from Simon's perspective on satisficing, the aspiration level can be viewed as establishing minimum requirements, which is tantamount to establishing criteria for avoiding failure.

Addressing a decision problem from the perspective of avoiding failure may seem unduly pessimistic, but that would be an unfair indictment of the concept. Setting minimum requirements is a failure-avoidance criterion. A Nash equilibrium is often nothing more than a systematic way to avoid failure (e.g., the Nash equilibrium is the next-worst outcome in the Prisoner's Dilemma – hardly an optimistic view of human behavior). On the other hand, viewing a decision problem from a failure-avoidance perspective provides flexibility that is difficult to achieve under the perspective of optimization. In particular, it allows us to distinguish between what Unger (1975, p. 55) calls absolute (limit) and relative (degree) terms. "Semantically, we may say that our absolute terms indicate, or purport to denote, an absolute *limit.* This limit is approached to the extent that the relevant relative property or properties are absent in the thing to which one might sensibly apply the absolute term, or its correlative relatives [emphasis in original]." Superlative concepts such as "best" and "worst" are clearly absolute terms. Terms such as "success" and "failure," on the other hand, can be seen as degree terms, and admit different levels of compliance. If one does not achieve the best possible outcome, then one fails, at least from the perspective of optimization, but the degree of failure if the chosen outcome were second best is not as severe as it would be if the chosen outcome were worst.

It may be tempting simply to equate the concept of failure avoidance with the heuristic concept of being good enough. Doing so, however, keeps one trapped in the perspective that the only way to evaluate an option is to compare it, either directly or by inference, to some notion of "best." Is it possible to define a criterion for avoiding failure that is fundamentally different from making comparisons to the superlative? In this chapter we establish an affirmative answer to that question. Our approach is to build on a perspective that pertains to a related problem – that of error avoidance.

6.2.1 Error Avoidance

You can test a given rule either directly, by looking at instances where it works, or indirectly, by focusing on where it does not work. ... disconfirming instances are far more powerful in establishing truth.

— Nassim Nicholas Taleb
The Black Swan (Random House, 2010)

The praxeological concept of focusing on the perspective of avoiding failure rather than seeking the best solution has an epistemological parallel. Just as "best" and "failure" are praxeological limit and degree terms, respectively, the corresponding epistemological terms are "truth" and "error." The philosopher/psychologist William James argues that the perspectives of seeking the truth and avoiding error are fundamentally different.

There are two ways of looking at our duty in the matter of opinion— ways entirely different, and yet ways about whose difference the theory of knowledge seems hitherto to have shown very little concern. We must know the truth, and we must avoid error—these are our first and great commandments as would-be knowers; but they are not two ways of stating an identical commandment, they are two separable laws ...

Believe truth! Shun error!—these, we see, are two materially different laws; and by choosing between them we may end by coloring differently our whole intellectual life. We may regard the chase for truth as paramount, and the avoidance of error as secondary; or we may, on the other hand, treat the avoidance of error as more imperative, and let truth take its chance (James, 1956, pp. 17,18).

James suggests that one whose imperative is avoiding error should go about the business of knowledge acquisition in a different way than one who views seeking truth is paramount. The epistemologist Isaac Levi (1980) subscribes to the error-avoidance perspective, and rejects the idea that convergence on truth and nothing but the truth, while perhaps the ideal, is the practical aim of inquiry. Instead, he argues that one does not have to justify one's current state of knowledge, since there is nothing other than one's current knowledge state to use as a standard. Rather, one should concentrate on expanding one's current knowledge state. Expanding one's knowledge state, however, raises the possibility of introducing error; therefore, one must proceed cautiously. Consider a set of propositions, all of which are consistent with one's current state of knowledge, but one, and only one, of them can be true. In the presence of overwhelming evidence, it may be possible to identify the true proposition with a negligibly small chance of error. But when only modest evidence is available, Levi argues that, rather than focusing solely on identifying that one true proposition, a more prudent way to proceed is by a process of elimination. Levi's approach is to view this issue as a decision-theoretic problem, termed *epistemic utility theory*. The goal of the inquiry is to ensure that the benefit of incorporating new beliefs into one's knowledge base justifies the risk of introducing error. Accordingly, he proposes two criteria with which to characterize the elements of this set: an inductive measure to quantify the strength of belief that the element is true, and an abductive measure to quantify the *informational value of rejection*, that is, how much one's knowledge would be improved if the element were eliminated from consideration.[2]

---

[2] Abductive reasoning deals with the importance or significance of a proposal independent of its truth. In scientific inquiries, abductive considerations might include the explanatory power, predictive power, and simplicity of a theory.

It may seem awkward or unnatural to evaluate propositions in terms of elimination rather than in terms of retention. This change in perspective, however, illustrates the difference between the perspective of seeking truth and the perspective of avoiding error. Rejecting, rather than accepting, hypotheses allows one to refine the set of propositions by pruning away the ones that are deemed to be discardable, thereby allowing sharper focus on those that are deemed to be worth retaining. This approach conforms with the observation by Johnson-Laird (1988, p. 218) that "The more possible states of affairs that a proposition eliminates from consideration, the more semantic information it contains."

Since the aim is to justify eliminating elements from the set of propositions, we begin by assessing the improvement in knowledge that is obtained by their removal. Let $\mathcal{P}$ denote the set of propositions under consideration, let $\mathcal{B}$ denote a Boolean algebra of subsets of $\mathcal{P}$, and let $M: \mathcal{B} \rightarrow [0,1]$ denote an *informational value of rejection probability measure*. It is helpful to view informational value as a resource to be used to assuage the demand for new information. For each $B \in \mathcal{B}$, $M(B)$ is the informational value that is conserved if B is rejected. If the non-rejected set is a singleton, then it is regarded as true, and can be conclusively added to the individual's knowledge. But if it contains multiple elements, then at least the individual has refined its knowledge by restricting focus to the non-rejected set.

Given propositions $b, b' \in \mathcal{P}$, one may establish a ranking of the informational value of rejection by ascribing more informational value of rejection to b than to b' if one is less reluctant, in terms of abductive reasoning, to eliminate b than to eliminate b'. To illustrate, suppose one is sent an encoded message that could be decoded in three equally probable ways. Let $\mathcal{P} = \{b_1, b_2, b_3\}$, where

b_1: You have won \$1.
b_2: You have won \$1,000.
b_3: You have won \$1,000,000.

The corresponding Boolean algebra is

$$\mathcal{B} = \big\{\varnothing, \{b_1\}, \{b_2\}, \{b_3\}, \{b_1, b_2\}, \{b_1, b_3\}, \{b_2, b_3\}, \mathcal{P}\big\}. \qquad (6.1)$$

Clearly, $M(\varnothing) = 0$, since rejecting none of the alternatives provides no informational value. At the other extreme, $M(\mathcal{P}) = 1$, since rejecting all alternatives creates a contradiction – a state of maximum informational value. If one were to reject $\{b_1\}$, one would focus attention on the prospect of coming into significant wealth. If one were to reject $\{b_1, b_2\}$, attention would be focused even more keenly on the prospect of significant wealth. If one were to reject $\{b_3\}$, one would resign oneself to the prospect receiving, at best, only a modest increase in wealth. Thus, in terms of abductive reasoning, a rational person would be more reluctant to reject $\{b_3\}$ than to reject $\{b_1\}$, and in this sense would consider the informational value conserved by rejecting $\{b_1\}$ to be greater than the informational value conserved by rejecting $\{b_3\}$. Also, one would be more reluctant to reject $\{b_1\}$ than to reject $\{b_1, b_2\}$; thus the informational value of rejection for $\{b_1, b_2\}$ is greater than the informational value of rejection for $\{b_1\}$. Summarizing,

$$1 = M(\mathcal{P}) > M(\{b_1, b_2\}) > M(\{b_1\}) > M(\{b_3\}) > M(\varnothing) = 0.$$

(6.2)

Thus far in our development, we have used abductive reasoning to establish a measure of the relative importance of the propositions under consideration. To complete our development, we must also employ inductive reasoning. Let $Q\colon \mathcal{B} \to [0, 1]$ be a belief probability measure. If $Q(\{b_1\}) \approx 1$, then one would have a strong belief that b_1 is the true message, and would be reluctant to reject that hypothesis on the basis of belief, even though rejecting it would conserve considerable informational value. On the other hand, although it may be that $Q(\{b_3\}) \ll 1$, one might still be reluctant to reject $\{b_3\}$, since rejecting it would conserve only a small amount of informational value. Thus, a natural way to proceed is to compare the abductive and inductive measures, and reject B if and only if $M(B) > Q(B)$; that is, reject B only if the degree of informational value conserved by rejecting B exceeds the belief probability that B contains the true state of nature. This approach generates a natural compromise between acquiring knowledge and avoiding error, and is aligned philosophically with the views of Whitehead and Popper.

It is more important that a proposition be interesting than that it be true. This statement is almost a tautology. For the energy of operation of a proposition in an occasion of experience is its interest, and is its importance. (Whitehead, 1937, part. IV, ch. XVI).

We must also stress that *truth is not the only aim of science*. We want more than truth: what we look for is *interesting truth* [emphasis in original] (Popper, 1963, p. 229).

The Levi/James approach to knowledge acquisition is to eliminate those propositions that are either uninteresting or unlikely to be true. If all but one proposition is eliminated in this way, then the lone survivor can lay claim to being the truth. In general, however, the set of propositions that are not eliminated will contain more than one element. Thus, this approach is more conservative than the classical approach of seeking to identify the one and only proposition that is then regarded as true, even though the evidence may not be convincing. It allows one to suspend judgment when the evidence does not support a conclusive choice. In effect, it allows one to be an agnostic. Of course, if one must commit immediately, one and only one element of this set must be selected. But if one is not immediately compelled to finalize a choice, the non-rejected propositions becomes the set of serious possibilities that can be used for further refinement and analysis. For example, one may be motivated to seek additional data, consult with others, or seek therapy before making a choice.

The feature of retaining more than a singleton set of serious possibilities gives the individual flexibility to negotiate with other individuals who may have different notions of belief and informational value, and its set of serious possibilities may be different. If the intersection of the two sets is not empty, they may be able to find common ground.

6.2.2 *Failure Avoidance*

Our approach is to form a praxeological analogue to the Levi/James approach to addressing epistemological questions. The notion of seeking the best and nothing but the best outcome is a natural praxeological analogue to the epistemological notion of demanding the truth and only the truth. Also, avoiding failure is a natural praxeological analogue to the epistemological concept of avoiding error. To complete the analogy, however, praxeological analogues to belief and the informational value of rejection are required. As we saw in Chapter 4, the natural analogue to belief is preference, expressed in terms of the value to the individual if the alternative is adopted. In that context, preference could entail notions of both reward and cost, but we require a more precise concept of preference that deals only with reward. Thus, we introduce the notion of *effectiveness*, to characterize an alternative in terms of preference without consideration of cost.

Table 6.1: *Optimization vis à vis Satisficing.*

Perspective	Epistemological context	Praxeological context
Optimization	Demand the truth and nothing but the truth	Demand the best and nothing but the best
Neo-satisficing	Acquire knowledge while avoiding error	Conserve resources while avoiding failure

To identify the praxeological analogue to the informational value of rejection, recall that informational value can be viewed as a resource that is conserved by rejection. In the praxeological domain, taking action requires the expenditure or consumption of some resource, such as money, energy, time, exposure to hazard, the expenditure of economic, political, social, or moral capital, or any other quantities, material, social or otherwise, that are consumed or expended by the agent in the pursuit of its objectives. Thus, the praxeological analogue to the informational value of rejecting a proposition becomes the conservational value of rejecting an alternative – its *inefficiency*, as viewed independently from its effectiveness. In other words, the more an alternative consumes resources, the higher is its inefficiency.

Accordingly, the neo-satisficing approach shifts the focus from "seeking the best and nothing but the best solution" to "conserving resources while avoiding failure" and opens the door for further analysis in an attempt to seek an acceptable compromise. Table 6.1 summarizes the analogical relationship between epistemology and praxeology in terms of the perspectives associated with optimization and neo-satisficing.

The optimization and neo-satisficing perspectives are based on different heuristic foundations. The heuristic underlying optimization is "more is preferred to less." With this perspective, one makes comparisons between alternatives – *inter-alternative comparisons*. Such comparisons are facilitated by the introduction of ordinal comparison operators such as $\succeq$. Optimization, then, is the formalization of this perspective: choose the highest-ranked alternative.

The heuristic underlying neo-satisficing, however, is quite different from the "more is preferred to less" perspective. Expressions such as "get what you pay for" and "get your money's worth" are vernacular expressions of this perspective. With this perspective one does not naturally form inter-alternative comparisons. Instead, one more naturally forms *intra-alternative comparisons* – comparisons between different attributes of an alternative.

To illustrate, suppose one needs to buy a new automobile and must choose from a finite set of alternatives. Presumably, one would evaluate each product in terms of, say, price, performance, maintenance costs, prestige, and so forth; would assign a value to each attribute; and combine them to form a score for each alternative. The scores for negative attributes such as purchase price and maintenance costs would decrease as the costs increase, and the scores for positive attributes such as performance and prestige would increase as the valuations increase. Assuming that one is not constrained by economic, social, or cultural considerations, a rational person, under this paradigm, would choose the alternative with the highest score. If more than one alternative achieves the highest rank, one could invoke a tie-breaking mechanism. There are, of course, more sophisticated ways to approach this problem, such as multi-attribute decision theory, whereby one would identify the Pareto-optimal choices.[3] But even with such more complex approaches, the ultimate objective is to identify a unique optimal choice.

Now consider this automobile purchasing problem from the neo-satisficing perspective. One would still assign scores to the various attributes, but rather than combining them all into a single numerical score, one would separate the attributes into two groups: one that views them in terms of their benefit, or *effectiveness*, and another that views them in terms of their costs, or *inefficiency*. Those alternatives for which the combined   effectiveness score is greater than the combined inefficiency score can rationally be viewed as those for which one gets one's money's worth. One can pay little and get little in return, or one can pay a lot and get a lot in return. In either case, one gets one's money's worth and, from that perspective, each alternative that so qualifies may be deemed to be "good enough" or satisficing. Success, under this paradigm, is assured by choosing a member of the satisficing subset, thereby avoiding failure.

---

[3] This approach has some links with extant work on multi-attribute decision making (Keeney and Raiffa, 1976; Dyer and Sarin, 1979; Lam et al., 2013).

Presumably, if the score attributed to the attributes under both the optimization and neo-satisficing approaches are consistent, the optimal choice would be a member of the satisficing subset. Thus, the decision maker sacrifices nothing by adopting this failure-avoidance approach. Effectively, all members of satisficing set are tied for being "good enough," although there are some obvious ways to refine the set (see (Stirling, 2003) for an extended discussion).

6.3 The Neo-Satisficing Model

A key feature of the failure-avoidance perspective is that it expands the notion of utility from a mapping defined over a finite set $\mathcal{A}$ (the outcome set) of points, to a mapping over a set of sets – a Boolean algebra of subsets of the outcome set. The goal is to identify a set of outcomes such that each element avoids failure as it has been defined. This set may then be subjected to further analysis and negotiation to arrive at a compromise. In the interest of clarity, the single-agent case is developed first and then extended to multiagent scenarios.

6.3.1 Single-Agent Satisficing

For a single agent X, let $\mathcal{F}$ denote a Boolean algebra of subsets of $\mathcal{A}$ and let $U: \mathcal{F} \to \mathbb{R}$ denote an *effectiveness utility* such that, for any $A \in \mathcal{F}$, $U(A)$ quantifies the degree to which focusing on the set A achieves the objective.[4] Also, let $V: \mathcal{F} \to \mathbb{R}$ denote an *inefficiency utility* such that, for any $A \in \mathcal{F}$, $V(A)$ quantifies the degree to which rejecting A conserves resources.

An optimization-based approach would necessarily focus on individual outcomes, but a failure-avoiding approach would relax that constraint and seek to identify collections of outcomes that have good failure-avoidance characteristics and low resource-consuming characteristics. Pursuing this latter course, however, requires the development of new mathematical structures to replace the traditional optimization-based criterion. The following list defines the attributes of these new structures that are necessary to meet these alternative criteria.

---

[4] In the epistemological domain, the probabilistic analogue to this concept is that $P(B)$ quantifies the degree to which focusing on B avoids error.

- Measures of both effectiveness and inefficiency should be nonnegative and finite. Thus, without loss of generality, these utilities may be restricted to range over the unit interval, that is, $U: \mathcal{F} \rightarrow [0,1]$ and $V: \mathcal{F} \rightarrow [0,1]$.
- Both U and V should be monotonic; that is, if $A_1 \subset A_2$, then $U(A_1) \leq U(A_2)$ and $V(A_1) \leq V(A_2)$. This condition means that the larger the set, the greater the degree of both effectiveness and inefficiency.
- $U(\varnothing) = V(\varnothing) = 0$. This condition establishes that the empty set is neither effective nor inefficient.
- $U(\mathcal{A}) = V(\mathcal{A}) = 1$. This condition ensures that the entire outcome set is completely effective and maximally inefficient.
- The incremental value, either in terms of effectiveness or inefficiency, of any two disjoint sets should be additive. That is, if $A_1 \cap A_2 = \varnothing$, then the effectiveness and inefficiency values of their union is equal to the sum of their respective individual effectiveness and inefficiency values; that is, $U(A_1 \cup A_2) = U(A_1) + U(A_2)$ and $V(A_1 \cup A_2) = V(A_1) + V(A_2)$.

These conditions imply that U and V possess the syntactical structure of probability measures over $\mathcal{F}$, although they do not possess the traditional semantic interpretations of probability. They do not quantify such attributes as belief, propensity, frequency, and so forth. Rather, they are used here to quantify resource-consuming and failure-avoidance attributes.

The goal is to choose a set $A \in \mathcal{F}$ that achieves a balance between consuming resources and achieving the objective; that is, between inefficiency and effectiveness. If A is chosen, then A^c is rejected. Consequently, the informational value of *not* rejecting A is equal to $V(A^c)$, the informational value of rejecting A^c. But $V(A^c) = 1 - V(A)$.

We may define the utility of simultaneously avoiding failure and conserving resources by retaining A as the convex combination of $U(A)$ and $V(A^c)$, namely, ·

$$\Psi(A) = \lambda U(A) + (1-\lambda)V(A^c) = \lambda U(A) + (1-\lambda)(1-V(A)), \quad (6.3)$$

where $0 \leq \lambda \leq 1$. The parameter λ represents the relative importance of avoiding failure versus conserving resources. Setting $\lambda = 1$ places a premium on effectiveness; setting $\lambda = 1/2$ places equal weight on effectiveness and inefficiency, and setting $\lambda < 1/2$ emphasizes conservation of resources over avoiding failure.

Since utilities are invariant to scale and zero level, Ψ can be transformed by a positive affine transformation of the form

$$\Phi(A) = \frac{1}{\lambda}\Psi(A) - \frac{1-\lambda}{\lambda}$$
$$= U(A) - qV(A), \tag{6.4}$$

where $q = \frac{1-\lambda}{\lambda}$. The function Φ is the *satisficing utility*. The set that maximizes this utility is termed the *satisficing set*, denoted Σ, and comprises all of the alternatives for which effectiveness dominates (as scaled by q) inefficiency; that is,

$$\Sigma = \arg\max_{A\in\mathcal{A}}\{U(A) - qV(A)\}. \tag{6.5}$$

Thus, Σ can be viewed as the set that maximizes failure avoidance (in retrospect, perhaps Euler was correct; maybe nothing does happen in this world without some notion of maximum or minimum coming to light).

The parameter q admits an interpretation as a *boldness index*. As $q \to 0$ (i.e., $\lambda \to 1$), the penalty for consuming resources decreases, and X considers more outcomes as being acceptable. The larger q becomes, however, the more actions are rejected on the basis of inefficiency, and X becomes more willing to accept failure in the interest of conserving resources. Setting $q = 1$ establishes an equal balance between avoiding failure and conserving resources. Setting $q > 1$ places higher emphasis on conserving resources than on meeting the objectives of the decision problem.

If $\mathcal{F}$ contains all singleton sets, then for any $\{a\} \in \mathcal{F}$,

$$\Phi(\{a\}) = u(a) - qv(a), \tag{6.6}$$

where u and v are mass functions corresponding to U and V, that is, $u(a) = U(\{a\})$ and $v(a) = V(\{a\})$. Thus,

$$\Phi(A) = \sum_{a\in A}\left[u(a) - qv(a)\right], \tag{6.7}$$

and the satisficing set thus becomes

$$\Sigma = \{a \in \mathcal{A}: u(a) \geq qv(a)\}. \tag{6.8}$$

The following theorem establishes sufficient conditions for the existence of a satisficing solution.

Theorem 6.3 $q \leq 1$ *implies* $\Sigma \neq \varnothing$.

Proof If $\Sigma = \varnothing$, then $u(a) < qv(a)$ for all $a \in \mathcal{A}$, in which case,

$$1 = \sum_a u(a) < q \sum_a v(a) = q, \tag{6.9}$$

resulting in a contradiction. Thus, Σ must contain at least one element.

$\square$

6.3.2 Multiple Selves

Two souls, alas, do dwell within his breast; The one is ever parting from the other.

—Johann Wolfgang von Goethe

Faust, Part I

The concept of separating attributes into different utilities is not new. Other scholars (Harsanyi (1955); Elster (1985); Margolis (1990), and Sen (1977)) have argued that it is unwise to aggregate conflicting interests into a single preference ordering. Expanding this line of reasoning, Steedman and Krause (1985) maintain that an individual, although an indivisible unit, is nevertheless capable of considering its choices from different points of view, and that separate utilities may be defined to correspond to different "facets" or "selves" of an individual.

The neo-satisficing approach is to follow Steedman and Krause (1985) and represent each agent by two selves, which effectively become the *atoms* of the decision problem.

Definition 6.1 Each X is viewed as the composite of a *selecting atom*, denoted S, and a *rejecting atom*, denoted R. $\square$

Definition 6.2 Let $u_S \colon \mathcal{A} \to [0, 1]$ denote S's *selecting utility mass function*, which evaluates alternatives in terms of effectiveness without concern for the consumption of resources, and let $u_R \colon \mathcal{A} \to [0, 1]$ denote R's *rejecting utility mass function*, which evaluates alternatives in terms of conserving resources without concern for effectiveness in meeting the objective. $\square$

Separating the attributes that affect an agent's preferences into selecting and rejecting categories provides the framework within which to formulate an operational definition of neo-satisficing; namely, an outcome is *satisficingly rational* if its selecting utility is equal to or exceeds the product of its rejecting utility and the boldness index. Colloquially, the optimality framing can be interpreted as insisting on "the best and only the best," but the neo-satisficing framing can be interpreted as being content with "getting your money's worth."

It is essential, when ascribing notions of effectiveness and efficiency to the attributes of a problem, that these concepts are not antonyms of each other. For example, it would not be appropriate to interpret efficiency as "costliness" while also interpreting effectiveness "affordable." It would be appropriate, however, to interpret efficiency as "costliness" while interpreting effectiveness as "beneficial." The operational definitions for what makes an alternative selectable must be completely distinct from the operational definition of what makes an alternative rejectable. Thus, it must be assumed that there is no direct influence between the atoms of an agent; that is, the cost of an alternative must not directly influence the benefit (although, as will be seen, indirect influence is possible).

Separating utility according to selecting and rejecting attributes permits qualitative analysis in addition to quantitative evaluations. Let N denote the cardinality of $\mathcal{A}$ and assume $q = 1$. If $u_R(a) = \frac{1}{N}$ ($u_S(a) = \frac{1}{N}$) for all $a \in \mathcal{A}$, then the rejecting (selecting) atom is in a state of complete preference neutrality regarding efficiency (effectiveness). Qualitatively, if $u_R(a) < \frac{1}{N}$ then a is deemed to be *efficient*, and if $u_S(a) > \frac{1}{N}$, then a is deemed to be *effective*. This suggests that outcomes can be partitioned into four general qualitative dispositional modes:

Gratification: $u_S(a) > \frac{1}{N}$ and $u_R(a) < \frac{1}{N}$ (effective and efficient)
Ambivalence: $u_S(a) > u_R(a) > \frac{1}{N}$ (effective and inefficient)
Dubiety: $u_R(a) < u_S(a) < \frac{1}{N}$ (ineffective and efficient)
Repulsion: $u_S(a) < u_R(a)$ (not satisficing)

These dispositional mode regions are illustrated in Figure 6.1. Gratification and repulsion are qualitative modes of *contentment*, while dubiety and ambivalence are modes of *conflict*. These qualitative categories provide additional insight that is difficult to ascertain with optimization-based approaches. Under the optimization paradigm,

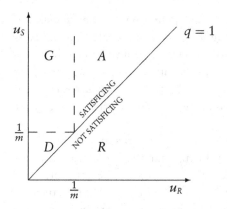

Figure 6.1: Dispositional Regions: G = Gratification, A = Ambivalence, D = Dubiety, R = Repulsion.

although the decision maker may achieve the best possible outcome (whatever comfort that knowledge affords), it may only be making the best of a bad situation. The qualitative assessments available with neo-satisficing, on the other hand, can alert the decision maker of limitations regarding its ability to cope adequately with the decision problem and may trigger a re-evaluation of the scenario. For example, the agent may be motivated to seek assistance, advice, or therapy if the dispositional mode is conflictive.

There is an obvious correspondence between this approach and cost-benefit analysis (CBA), which is often used to justify investing funds for projects under consideration by government agencies or private organizations. However, there are some important differences between CBA and the neo-satisficing approach. First, CBA requires a common unit of measurement, which requires all human economic, moral, health, and other such issues to be expressed in terms of a common transferable medium, such as money. Second, CBA is, at the end of the day, a heuristic-based form of analysis. There is no implication that a CBA decision is optimal in any sense. In fact, it may not comply with Pareto optimality, since the welfare of some participants may be improved while the welfare of others may be reduced (see Hicks (1939); Kaldor (1939)). It can also be shown that attempts to remedy this problem via side payments can actually reverse the decision (see Scitovsky (1941)).

6.3.3 *Satisficing Social Choice*

Applying the satisficing concept to social choice involves extending the formalism to the multiple agent case. For a network $\{X_1, \ldots, X_n\}$, let $\{S_1, \ldots, S_n\}$ denote the set of selecting atoms, and let $\{R_1, \ldots, R_n\}$ denote the set of rejecting atoms.

Each atom is an autonomous entity capable of forming either categorical preferences or conditional preferences as they are influenced by other atoms. For selecting atom S_i, let $\mathrm{pa}\,(S_i) = \{S_{i_1}, \ldots, S_{i_{p_i}}, R_{k_1}, \ldots, R_{k_{r_i}}\}$ denote the set of all atoms that influence it, and let $\mathrm{pa}\,(R_j) = \{S_{j_1}, \ldots, S_{j_{t_j}}, R_{l_1}, \ldots, R_{l_{v_j}}\}$ denote the set of all atoms that influence R_j. A *conditioning selecting conjecture* for S_i is a collection of conjectures, one for each member of $\mathrm{pa}\,(S_i)$, denoted $\mathbf{s}_i = (s_{i_1}, \ldots, s_{i_{p_i}}, r_{k_1}, \ldots, r_{k_{r_i}})$. Similarly, a *conditioning rejecting conjecture* for R_j is a collection of conjectures for the members of $\mathrm{pa}\,(R_j)$, denoted $\mathbf{r}_j = (s_{j_1}, \ldots, s_{j_{t_j}}, r_{l_1}, \ldots, r_{l_{v_j}})$.

Let the mass functions $u_{S_i|\,\mathrm{pa}\,(S_i)}(\cdot|\mathbf{s}_i)$ and $u_{R_j|\,\mathrm{pa}\,(R_j)}(\cdot|\mathbf{r}_j)$ respectively denote the *conditional selecting utility* and *conditional rejecting utility* for S_i and R_j, respectively.

Consider Figure 6.2, which illustrates a two-agent, four-atom network. Notice that S_1 influences R_2 which in turn influences R_1 which then in turn influences S_2. This chain of influence, however, does not constitute a cycle, although it does permit one atom to indirectly influence its cognate atom through a third atom.

These utilities are defined *ex ante*, that is, they characterize the atoms' preferences before they interact. Once they interact, influence propagates through the network according to Theorem 2.6, which is now restated in terms of the atoms.

Theorem 6.4 *Consider a network $\{X_1, \ldots, X_n\}$ with selecting and rejecting atoms $\{S_1, \ldots, S_n\}$ and $\{R_1, \ldots, R_n\}$. Given a selecting-rejecting conjecture profile $(s_1, \ldots s_n, r_1, \ldots, r_n)$, let $\mathbf{s}_i$ and $\mathbf{r}_j$ denote the conditioning conjecture subsets for $\mathrm{pa}\,(S_i)$ and $\mathrm{pa}\,(R_j)$, respectively, for $i, j, \in \{1, \ldots, n\}$. Let $u_{S_i|\,\mathrm{pa}\,(S_i)}(\cdot|\mathbf{s}_i)$ and $u_{R_j|\,\mathrm{pa}\,(R_j)}(\cdot|\mathbf{r}_j)$ be the*

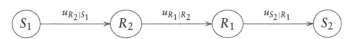

Figure 6.2: A Two-Agent, Four-Atom Network.

corresponding conditional utilities. If pa $(S_i) = \varnothing$, *then* $u_{S_i| \text{pa}(S_i)} = u_{S_i}$, *a categorical utility; similarly if* pa $(R_j) = \varnothing$. *Then the satisficing coordination function is*

$$u_{S_1:R_n}(s_1,\ldots,s_n,r_1,\ldots,r_n) = \prod_{i=1}^{n}\prod_{j=1}^{n} u_{S_i| \text{pa}(S_i)}(s_i|s_i)u_{R_j| \text{pa}(R_j)}(r_j|\mathbf{r}_j).$$

(6.10)

The satisficing coordination function provides a comprehensive representation of all social relationships that exist among the atoms. Introducing the concept of two preferentially independent selves as a refinement of an individual – one concerned exclusively with effectiveness and the other exclusively with efficiency of each feasible action – opens the possibility of developing approaches to decision making that take advantage of this refinement.

Given a satisficing coordination function $u_{S_1:R_n}$, the *selecting coordination function* may be computed by summing the satisficing coordination function over $r_1,\ldots,r_n$, yielding

$$u_{S_1:S_n}(s_1,\ldots,s_n) = \sum_{r_1,\ldots,r_n} u_{S_1:R_n}(s_1,\ldots,s_n,r_1,\ldots,r_n). \qquad (6.11)$$

Similarly, the *rejecting coordination function* is obtained by summing the satisficing coordination function over $s_1,\ldots,s_n$, yielding

$$u_{R_1:R_n}(r_1,\ldots,r_n) = \sum_{s_1,\ldots,s_n} u_{S_1:R_n}(s_1,\ldots,s_n,r_1,\ldots,r_n). \qquad (6.12)$$

The coordination functions defined earlier are functions of the conjectures of all $2n$ atoms, but only one alternative can be implemented by the group. Thus, it is necessary to collapse the coordination functions to create the *selecting social choice function* and the *rejecting social choice function* as

$$\begin{aligned} w_{S_1:S_n}(a) &= u_{S_1:S_n}(a,\ldots,a) \\ w_{R_1:R_n}(a) &= u_{R_1:R_n}(a,\ldots,a) \end{aligned}.$$

(6.13)

The *group satisficing set* then becomes

$$\Sigma_{1:n} = \{a \in \mathcal{A}: w_{S_1:S_n}(a) \geq q_{1:n}w_{R_1:R_n}(a)\}, \qquad (6.14)$$

where $q_{1:n}$ is the q-value for the network. If $\Sigma_{1:n} = \varnothing$, then no alternatives are satisficing for the network at the boldness level $q_{1:n}$.

By incrementally decreasing the value of $q_{1:n}$, however, the socially satisficing set will eventually become nonempty.

Although any element of $\Sigma_{1:n}$ satisfies the group-level criterion of being good enough, it remains possible for individuals to be disadvantaged. Consequently, it is important also to consider satisficing from the individual point of view. The *individual selecting and rejecting utilities* for each $a_i \in \mathcal{A}$ corresponding to S_i and R_i are the marginal utilities obtained by summing the joint utilities over all arguments except a_i, yielding

$$\tilde{u}_{S_i}(a_i) = \sum_{\sim a_i} u_{S_1:S_n}(a_1, \ldots a_i, \ldots, a_n) \tag{6.15}$$

and

$$\tilde{u}_{R_i}(a_i) = \sum_{\sim a_i} u_{R_1:R_n}(a_1, \ldots, a_i, \ldots, a_n) \tag{6.16}$$

for $i = 1, \ldots, n$. The *individually satisficing sets* are

$$\Sigma_i = \{a \in \mathcal{A} : \tilde{u}_{S_i}(a) \geq q_i \tilde{u}_{R_i}(a)\}. \tag{6.17}$$

Notice that each agent may have its own q-value.

The *compromise satisficing set* is the set that takes into account the interests of the group as a whole as well as each of its members, and is defined as

$$\mathcal{C} = \Sigma_{1:n} \cap \Sigma_1 \cap \cdots \cap \Sigma_n. \tag{6.18}$$

If $\mathcal{C} = \varnothing$, then a negotiation protocol maybe implemented whereby the individuals each lower their standards of acceptability by incrementally reducing their boldness values until the intersection is no longer empty. If $\mathcal{C} = \varnothing$ after each agent has reached its limit, then the network is declared to be at an impasse.

Once a non-empty compromise set has been obtained, if it is not a singleton set, the problem reduces to choosing one member of this set to implement. There are many possible tie breakers.

Utilitarian The satisficing utilitarian choice is the one that provides the greatest good for the greatest number of agents, yielding

$$a_u = \arg\max_{a \in \mathcal{C}} \sum_{i=1}^{n} [\tilde{u}_{S_i}(a) - q_i \tilde{u}_{R_i}(a)]. \tag{6.19}$$

Rawlesian   The satisficing Rawlesian choice is the one that minimizes maximum rejectability, yielding

$$a_r = \arg \min_{i \in \{1,\dots,n\}} \max_{a \in C} \tilde{u}_{R_i}(a) . \tag{6.20}$$

Group level   The *satisficing group choice* is the one that maximizes the difference between the group-level selecting and rejecting utilities, yielding

$$a_g = \arg \max_{a \in C} \{ w_{S_1 : S_n}(a) - q_{1:n} w_{R_1 : R_n}(a) \} . \tag{6.21}$$

Example 6.1   Consider a neo-satisficing model for the Three Stooges. This network comprises three selecting selves $\{S_L, S_C, S_M\}$ and three rejecting selves, denoted $\{R_L, R_C, R_M\}$. Expressing this society in terms of distinct selves, or atoms, provides a natural mechanism to characterize the individuals in more detail. When dealing with an objective such as food, a natural parsing of one's preferences would be to ascribe enjoyment of the meal with selectability (effectiveness), and to ascribe cost to rejectability (efficiency). Those may be the appropriate operational definitions for an individual, but in a social context, other factors may come into play. Recall Section 1.2, where the conditional preferences of the individuals were first presented and later expressed as conditional utilities in Section 2.6. It is clear that the conditional preferences of Curly and Mo indicate some social biases that take more than either food enjoyment or meal costs under consideration. What seems to dominate their preferences is the social situation. Curly seems more interested in opposing Larry than the financial issue, and Mo seems more interested in being generally cantankerous than anything else. Parsing these preferences into components that are desirable (selectable) and undesirable (rejectable), would paint a more vivid and precise picture of the society. Doing so, however, requires operational definitions for the notions of effectiveness regarding the achievement of the objective and the efficiency regarding conserving resources. There is no unique way to frame this problem, but an approach that complies with the operational independence of the concepts is to view the ethnicity of the food as the objective and the social compatibility as the resource resulting in the following model.

Larry   Larry's preferences are categorical, which means that his considerations of both food preference and social compatibility are not influenced by others. Since social compatibility is a nonissue for him, it is assumed that his primary interest is regarding food preference, thus

$$
\begin{aligned}
u_{S_L}(F) &= 1 - \alpha \\
u_{S_L}(I) &= \alpha
\end{aligned}
\tag{6.22}
$$

where $\alpha < 1/2$. To model Larry's complete unconcern regarding social compatibility, equal rejectability is assigned to the alternatives regarding that attribute. Thus,

$$
u_{R_L}(F) = u_{R_L}(I) = 1/2 . \tag{6.23}
$$

Curly From the problem statement, Curly appears to be more interested in opposing Larry than in the ethnicity of the food. We may account for that condition by ascribing a maximum entropy categorical utility to the alternatives, yielding

$$
u_{S_C}(F) = u_{S_C}(I) = 1/2 . \tag{6.24}
$$

Since Curly's social desire is to oppose Larry, appropriate conditional rejectability utilities for him would be

$$
\begin{aligned}
u_{R_C|S_L}(F|F) &= 1 - \beta & u_{R_C|S_L}(I|F) &= \beta \\
u_{R_C|S_L}(F|I) &= \beta & u_{R_C|S_L}(I|I) &= 1 - \beta
\end{aligned}
\tag{6.25}
$$

where $\beta < 1/2$. Thus, Curly places higher rejectability on the alternatives that oppose Larry's food enjoyment preferences.

Mo As with Curly, Mo's interests are purely social, so we ascribe a maximum entropy categorical selectability utility to him as well, yielding

$$
u_{S_M}(F) = u_{S_M}(I) = 1/2 . \tag{6.26}
$$

Mo's social preferences are represented by the following conditional rejectability structure.

$$
\begin{aligned}
u_{R_M|S_L S_C}(F|FF) &= 1 - \gamma & u_{R_M|S_L S_C}(I|FF) &= \gamma \\
u_{R_M|S_L S_C}(F|FI) &= \gamma & u_{R_M|S_L S_C}(I|FI) &= 1 - \gamma \\
u_{R_M|S_L S_C}(F|IF) &= 1 - \gamma & u_{R_M|S_L S_C}(I|IF) &= \gamma \\
u_{R_M|S_L S_C}(F|II) &= \gamma & u_{R_M|S_L S_C}(I|II) &= 1 - \gamma
\end{aligned}
\tag{6.27}
$$

where $\gamma < 1/2$.

Figure 6.3 displays the DAG associated with this network.

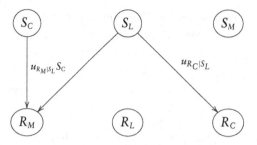

Figure 6.3: The Satisficing Model for the Three Stooges.

Setting $\alpha = \beta = \gamma = 0.4$ and $q_{LCM} = q_L = q_C = q_M = 1$, straightforward calculations yield

$$\Sigma_{LCL} = \{F\} \tag{6.28}$$

and

$$\begin{aligned} \Sigma_{LCM} &= \{F\} \\ \Sigma_L &= \{F\} \\ \Sigma_C &= \{I\} \\ \Sigma_M &= \{F, I\} \end{aligned} \tag{6.29}$$

Thus, a compromise is not possible with these q values. However, if Curly were willing to reduce q_C sufficiently, then a compromise would be possible and the group will go to the French restaurant. □

6.4 Satisficing Coordinatability

The satisficing coordinatability of the network is computed as follows. The total entropy of the $2n$ dimensional set of atoms is

$$H(S_1, \ldots, S_n, R_1, \ldots, R_n) =$$
$$- \sum_{s_1 : s_n} \sum_{r_1 : r_n} u_{S_1 : R_n}(s_1, \ldots, s_n, r_1, u_{S_1 : R_n}(s_1, \ldots, s_n, r_1, \ldots, r_n)$$
$$\log_2 u_{S_1 : R_n}(s_1, \ldots, s_n, r_1, u_{S_1 : R_n}(s_1, \ldots, s_n, r_1, \ldots, r_n). \tag{6.30}$$

The entropy of the selecting and rejecting atoms are

$$\begin{aligned} H(S_i) &= - \sum_{a_i} u_{S_i | \text{pa}(S_i)}(a_i) \log_2 u_{S_i | \text{pa}(S_i)}(a_i) \\ H(R_j) &= - \sum_{a_j} u_{R_j | \text{pa}(R_j)}(a_j) \log_2 u_{R_j | \text{pa}(R_j)}(a_j) \end{aligned} \tag{6.31}$$

The mutual information is

$$I(S_1,\ldots,S_n,R_1,\ldots,R_n) = \sum_{i=1}^{n} H(S_i) + \sum_{j=1}^{n} H(R_j) -$$
$$H(S_1,\ldots,S_n,R_1,\ldots,R_n). \quad (6.32)$$

The diversity and relative diversity are given by

$$d((S_1,\ldots,S_n,R_1,\ldots,R_n) = (2n-1)H(S_1,\ldots,S_n,R_1,\ldots,R_n)$$
$$- I(S_1,\ldots,S_n,R_1,\ldots,R_n) \quad (6.33)$$

and

$$\mathcal{D}(S_1,\ldots,S_n,R_1,\ldots,R_n) = \frac{1}{2n-1}\frac{d((S_1,\ldots,S_n,R_1,\ldots,R_n)}{H(S_1,\ldots,S_n,R_1,\ldots,R_n)}. \quad (6.34)$$

Finally, the coordination index is

$$C(S_1,\ldots,S_n,R_1,\ldots,R_n) = 1 - \mathcal{D}(S_1,\ldots,S_n,R_1,\ldots,R_n). \quad (6.35)$$

6.5 Summary

Although satisficing was originally introduced by Simon as a heuristically based response to the lack of sufficient informational or computational resources to obtain the optimal solution, the satisficing concept of seeking a solution that is "good enough" is a natural solution concept for multiagent decision problems. This chapter establishes the claim that the concept of being "good enough" need not be limited to heuristically based solution concepts by developing a mathematically rigorously notion of the "good enough" concept that naturally extends to the multiagent case.

This approach is based on a change of perspective from classical concepts of performance. Whereas an optimization-based point of view requires one to seek the best and only the best solution, an alternative point of view is, putting it in vernacular, to get one's money's worth. Thus, rather than making inter-alternative comparisons to identify the best one, our satisficing concept is to view each alternative in terms of two distinct attributes – effectiveness and efficiency – and to make intra-alternative comparisons of these attributes. All alternatives for which the effectiveness equals or exceeds the inefficiency are considered to be satisficing and may be used as the basis for negotiations.

Dutch Book Theorem

Consider a gamble where one is willing to stake one dollar for the chance to win S dollars, where $S \geq 1$. A bookmaker is one who sets the gambling odds in order to balance his gains and losses. A Dutch book is a gamble where the bookmaker takes advantage of irrational behavior on the part of the gambler that results in a loss for the gambler, no matter what the outcome. The Dutch book theorem establishes conditions under which it is impossible to devise such a gamble.

Theorem A.1 The Dutch Book Theorem. *Suppose a gambler places a bet to win a payout of S. A fair entry fee for this gamble is bS, where b is the gambler's degree of belief of winning.*
(Necessity) If b violates the probability axioms, then it is possible to construct a bet such that the payout is always less (greater) than the entry fee – a sure loss (win).
(Sufficiency) If b conforms to the probability axioms, then it is not possible to construct a bet such that the gambler sustains a sure loss (sure gain).

Proof Without loss of generality we establish this result for the special case of two bets. The proof of this theorem is essentially an exercise in separating hyperplane theory, and follows Williams (2012), who provides a general discussion of Dutch book results.

The proof of this theorem involves the following lemma, in preparation for which we establish the following notation. Consider vectors in $\mathbb{R}^2$ of the form $\mathbf{x} = (x_1, x_2)$. The l_2 norm of a vector $\mathbf{x}$ is defined as $\|\mathbf{x}\| = \langle \mathbf{x}, \mathbf{x} \rangle^{\frac{1}{2}}$, where $\langle \mathbf{x}, \mathbf{y} \rangle = x_1 y_1 + x_2 y_2$ is the inner product of $\mathbf{x}$ and $\mathbf{y}$ (also called the dot product when dealing with Euclidean spaces).

Lemma 1 *Let $C \subset \mathbb{R}^2$ be an arbitrary convex set, let $\mathbf{b} = (b_1, b_2)$, and suppose $\mathbf{b} \notin C$. Define $\mathbf{c} = \arg\min_{\mathbf{x} \in C} \|\mathbf{x} - \mathbf{b}\|$. For any $\mathbf{d} \in C$, the angle between the vectors $\mathbf{d} - \mathbf{c}$ and $\mathbf{b} - \mathbf{c}$ is obtuse.*

Proof Since $\|b - x\| \geq \|b - c\|$ for all $x \in C$, it follows that $\|b - x\|^2 \geq \|b - c\|^2$ for all $x \in C$. For any $d \in C$, let $x = c + \lambda(d - c)$ for $0 \leq \lambda \leq 1$. By convexity, $x \in C$. Thus,

$$
\begin{aligned}
0 &\geq \|b - c\|^2 - \|b - x\|^2 \\
&= \|b - c\|^2 - \|b - c - \lambda(d - c)\|^2 \\
&= \|b - c\|^2 - \langle b - c - \lambda(d - c), b - c - \lambda(d - c) \rangle \qquad \text{(A.1)} \\
&= \|b - c\|^2 - \left[\|b - c\|^2 - 2\lambda\langle b - c, d - c \rangle + \lambda^2 \|d - c\|^2 \right] \\
&= 2\lambda\langle b - c, d - c \rangle - \lambda^2 \|d - c\|^2 .
\end{aligned}
$$

Therefore,

$$
0 \geq \langle b - c, d - c \rangle - 1/2\lambda \|d - c\|^2 , \qquad \text{(A.2)}
$$

which must hold for all λ. Letting $\lambda \to 0$, it thus follows that

$$
\langle b - c, d - c \rangle \leq 0 . \qquad \text{(A.3)}
$$

Consider the diagram illustrated in Figure A.1. Since c is the element in C that is closest to b, no point outside the circle centered at b with radius $\|b - c\|$ can be closer to b than is c. Now consider the line drawn from c to y. Since it intersects the circle, no point on the line (including those within the circle) can be in C. Thus, C must lie entirely to the left of the line drawn tangent to c. Consequently, if $d \in C$, then d must be to the left of the tangent line. Hence, the angle θ formed between the vector $b - c$ and the vector $d - c$ must be obtuse.

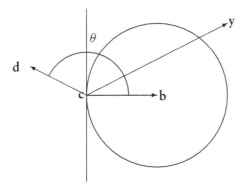

Figure A.1: Geometrical Illustration of Obtuse θ.

We have thus established that the vector $\mathbf{b} - \mathbf{c}$ separates the convex set to the left of the hyperplane defined by the vertical line from the set to the right; that is, for any vectors $\mathbf{x}$ in the left half plane and $\mathbf{y}$ in the right half plane,

$$\langle \mathbf{x}, \mathbf{b} - \mathbf{c} \rangle \leq 0 \text{ and } \langle \mathbf{y}, \mathbf{b} - \mathbf{c} \rangle \geq 0. \tag{A.4}$$

$\square$

To prove the Dutch book theorem, consider a set $\mathbf{P} = \{P_1, P_2\}$ of mutually exclusive propositions such that only one is true. A belief function is a mapping $B: \mathbf{P} \to \mathbb{R}$ such that $B(P_i)$ is the degree of belief that P_i is true. For B to be a probability, it must conform to the following axioms.

non-negativity: $B(P_i) \geq 0, i = 1, 2$
normalization: $B(P_1 \text{ or } P_2) = 1$
finite additivity: $B(P_1 \text{ or } P_2) = B(P_1) + B(P_2)$

Let $\mathbf{S} = \{S_1, S_2\}$ denote the payout vector such that a bet on P_i yields a payout of S_i if P_i is true, $i = 1, 2$.

Proof of Necessity. Let w_i denote the outcome obtained by placing a bet on P_i.

$$w_i = \begin{cases} 1 & \text{if } P_i \text{ is true} \\ 0 & \text{otherwise} \end{cases} i = 1, 2. \tag{A.5}$$

If an individual places both bets, there are four possible outcomes, denoted

$$W = \{(0,0), (1,0), (0,1), (1,1)\}, \tag{A.6}$$

and outcome vector $\mathbf{w} = (w_1, w_2) \in W$. The payout for both bets is the inner product

$$\langle \mathbf{S}, \mathbf{w} \rangle = S_1 w_1 + S_2 w_2, \tag{A.7}$$

and the entry fee for placing both bets is the inner product

$$\langle \mathbf{S}, \mathbf{b} \rangle = b_1 S_1 + b_2 S_2. \tag{A.8}$$

Let $\overline{W}$ denote the convex hull of W, as indicated in Figure A.2. Notice that a belief vector $\mathbf{b}$ satisfies the probability axioms if, and only if, $\mathbf{b} \in \overline{W}$. Now suppose the belief function B violates the probability axioms and, hence $\mathbf{b} \notin \overline{W}$, as indicated in Figure A.2.

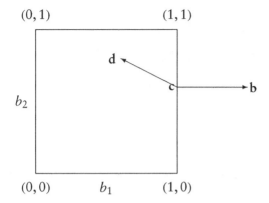

Figure A.2: Convex Hull of Belief Vectors that Satisfy the Probability Axioms.

A Dutch book will occur if the payout is less than the entry fee; that is, if

$$\langle \mathbf{S}, \mathbf{w} \rangle < \langle \mathbf{S}, \mathbf{b} \rangle \tag{A.9}$$

for all $\mathbf{w}$ or, equivalently, if

$$\langle \mathbf{S}, \mathbf{w} - \mathbf{b} \rangle < 0 \tag{A.10}$$

for all $\mathbf{w}$.

By the properties of inner products,

$$\langle \mathbf{S}, \mathbf{w} - \mathbf{b} \rangle = \|\mathbf{S}\| \|\mathbf{w} - \mathbf{b}\| \cos\theta . \tag{A.11}$$

Thus,

$$\langle \mathbf{S}, \mathbf{w} - \mathbf{b} \rangle < 0 \iff \cos(\theta) < 0 , \tag{A.12}$$

or

$$\langle \mathbf{S}, \mathbf{w} - \mathbf{b} \rangle < 0 \iff \frac{\pi}{2} < \theta < \frac{3\pi}{2} . \tag{A.13}$$

To establish the necessary conditions to avoid a Dutch book, we simply set the payout vector be $\mathbf{S} = \mathbf{b} - \mathbf{c}$ and set $\mathbf{d} = \mathbf{w}$. Substituting these values into (A.3) yields an obtuse angle θ; that is, (A.13) holds, thereby establishing that if beliefs do not conform to the probability axioms, then a sure loss cannot be avoided.

Proof of Sufficiency. To establish sufficiency, let $\mathbf{b} \in \overline{W}$, and let $\mathbf{S}$ be an arbitrary vector in $\mathbb{R}^2$. Then, as illustrated in Figure A.3, there must

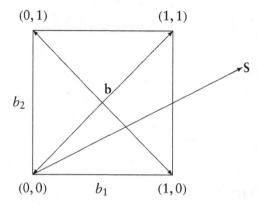

Figure A.3: Convex Hull with Beliefs that Conform to Probability Axioms.

be some elements of W such that the angle between $\mathbf{S}$ and $\mathbf{w} - \mathbf{b}$ is acute. Thus, it will always be possible to construct a bet that is not a sure loss.

Bayesian Networks

A Bayesian network is a graphical representation of a collective whose members are connected by some means of causal influence expressed in terms of conditional probability mass functions. One of the key results of Bayesian network theory is a demonstration that these linkages can be combined to synthesize a joint probability distribution as the product of the marginal and conditional probability mass functions that serve as the linkages between the vertices of the graph.

As influence flows through the network, there are three general types of connections between vertices: serial connections, diverging connections, and converging connections. These three types of connections are displayed in Figures B.1(a), (b), (c). Throughout this development, we assume that all probability mass functions are strictly positive. The key property that is exploited in this development is the notion of conditional independence.

Definition B.1 Let Y_i, Y_j, and Y_k be random variables. Y_i and Y_j are *conditionally independent*, given $Y_k = y_k$, if the joint conditional distribution factors into the product of the individual conditional distributions, that is, if

$$p_{ij|k}(y_i, y_j | y_k) = p_{i|k}(y_i | y_k) p_{j|k}(y_j | y_k).$$ (B.1)

□

Serial Connections

Consider the Bayesian network displayed in Figure B.1(a). By the construction of the network, the joint probability mass function factors as

$$p_{123}(y_1, y_2, y_3) = p_{3|2}(y_3 | y_2) p_{2|1}(y_2 | y_1) p_1(y_1),$$ (B.2)

since $\text{pa}(Y_1) = \varnothing$, $\text{pa}(Y_2) = \{Y_1\}$, and $\text{pa}(Y_3) = \{Y_2\}$. By the chain rule of probability,

(a)

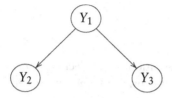

(b)

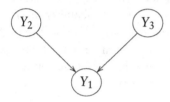

(c)

Figure B.1: Vertex Connections for Bayesian Networks: (a) Serial, (b) Diverging, (c) Converging.

$$p_{123}(y_1, y_2, y_3) = p_{13|2}(y_1, y_3|y_2)p_2(y_2)$$
$$= p_{1|23}(y_1|y_2, y_3)p_{3|2}(y_3|y_2)p_2(y_2), \qquad \text{(B.3)}$$

where the second equality is obtained via a second application of the chain rule. Since $p_{3|2}(y_3|y_2) \neq 0$, equating (B.2) and (B.3) yields

$$p_{2|1}(y_2|y_1)p_1(y_1) = p_{1|23}(y_1|y_2, y_3)p_2(y_2). \qquad \text{(B.4)}$$

Now applying Bayes theorem to the left hand side yields

$$\frac{p_{1|2}(y_1|y_2)p_2(y_2)}{p_1(y_1)}p_1(y_1) = p_{1|23}(y_1|y_2, y_3)p_2(y_2) \qquad \text{(B.5)}$$

which, upon canceling common non-zero terms, becomes

$$p_{1|2}(y_1|y_2) = p_{1|23}(y_1|y_2, y_3). \qquad \text{(B.6)}$$

Consequently,

$$
\begin{aligned}
p_{13|2}(y_1, y_3 | y_2) &= p_{1|23}(y_1 | y_2, y_3) p_{3|2}(y_3 | y_2) \\
&= p_{1|2}(y_1 | y_2) p_{3|2}(y_3 | y_2),
\end{aligned} \tag{B.7}
$$

so Y_1 and Y_3 are conditionally independent, given X_2. In the parlance of Bayesian network theory, we say that communication from the vertex associated with Y_1 to the vertex associated with Y_3 is *blocked* by the realization of Y_2. In other words, if the state of Y_2 is known, then knowledge of the state of Y_1 cannot provide information regarding the state of Y_3, and vice versa.

Diverging Connections

Consider the Bayesian network displayed in Figure B.1(b). By the construction of the network, the probability mass function factors as

$$
p_{123}(y_1, y_2, y_3) = p_{3|1}(y_3 | y_1) p_{2|1}(y_2 | y_1) p_1(y_1). \tag{B.8}
$$

By the chain rule, we also have

$$
p_{123}(y_1, y_2, y_3) = p_{3|12}(y_3 | y_1, y_2) p_{2|1}(y_2 | y_1) p_1(y_1), \tag{B.9}
$$

which means, by the strict positiveness assumption, that

$$
p_{3|12}(y_3 | y_1, y_2) = p_{3|1}(y_3 | y_1) \tag{B.10}
$$

or, in other words, Y_2 and X_3 are conditionally independent, given X_1. Again, in the parlance of Bayesian network theory, we say that the realization of Y_1 blocks communication between Y_2 and Y_3, that is, if the state of Y_1 is known, then knowledge of the state of Y_2 cannot provide information regarding the state of Y_3, and vice versa.

Converging Connections

Consider the Bayesian network displayed in Figure B.1(c). The joint probability mass function factors as

$$
p_{123}(y_1, y_2, y_3) = p_{1|23}(y_1 | y_2, y_3) p_2(y_2) p_3(y_3), \tag{B.11}
$$

Also, by the definition of conditional probability, we have that

$$
p_{3|12}(y_3 | y_1, y_2) = \frac{p_{123}(y_1, y_2, y_3)}{p_{12}(y_1, y_2)}. \tag{B.12}
$$

Substituting (B.11) into (B.12) and using the fact that $p_{23}(y_2, y_3) = p_2(y_2)p_3(y_3)$, we obtain

$$p_{3|1v_2}(y_3|y_1, y_2) = \frac{p_{1|23}(y_1|y_2, y_3)p_2(y_2)p_3(y_3)}{p_{1|2}(y_1|y_2)p_2(y_2)}$$

$$= \frac{p_{1|23}(y_1|y_2, y_3)p_3(y_3)}{p_{1|2}(y_1|y_2)}. \qquad (B.13)$$

For Y_2 and Y_3 to be conditionally independent given Y_1, the left side of the above expression must equal $p_{3|1}(y_3|y_1)$ for all possible distributions. Perhaps the most constructive way to invalidate this general claim is to provide a counter example. Let

$$Y_1 = \begin{cases} 1 & \text{lawn wet} \\ 0 & \text{lawn dry} \end{cases} \quad Y_2 = \begin{cases} 1 & \text{rain} \\ 0 & \text{not rain} \end{cases} \quad Y_3 = \begin{cases} 1 & \text{sprinklers on} \\ 0 & \text{sprinklers off} \end{cases}.$$

Since either rain or sprinklers will wet the lawn with probability one, we have $p_{1|23}(1|1, 1) = p_{1|23}(1|1, 0) = p_{1|23}(1|0, 1)$ and $p_{1|23}(1|0, 0) = 1$. This defines the joint distribution $p_{123}(y_1|y_2, y_3)$. Furthermore,

$$p_{1|2}(1|1) = p_{1|23}(1|1, 1)p_3(1) + p_{1|23}(1|1, 0)p_3(0)$$
$$= p_3(1) + p_3(0) = 1 \qquad (B.14)$$

By a similar argument, we also conclude that $P_{1|3}(1|1) = 1$. It is also reasonable to assume that the lawn is not always wet, that is, that $P_1(1) < 1$.

Substituting the above values into (B.13) yields

$$p_{3|12}(1|1, 1) = \frac{p_{1|23}(1|1, 1)p_3(1)}{p_{1|2}(1|1)} = p_2(1).$$

However, we have that

$$p_{3|1}(1|1) = \frac{p_{1|3}(1|1)p_3(1)}{p_1(1)} = \frac{p_3(1)}{p_1(1)}.$$

Since $p_1(1) < 1$, we conclude that $p_{3|12}(1|1, 1) \neq p_{3|1}(1|1)$; that is, Y_3 and Y_2 are *not* conditionally independent, given Y_1. In other words, if Y_1 is instantiated, the communication between Y_2 and Y_3 is *not* blocked. However, if Y_1 is *not* instantiated, then there is no communication between Y_2 and Y_3 – the vertex Y_2 is blocked from the vertex Y_3. We thus observe that, while it is true that knowledge of Y_2 alone does not provide information about Y_3, knowledge of Y_1, coupled with knowledge of Y_2, does provide information about Y_3. This is the so-called *explaining away* property of probability theory: the events "rain" and "sprinklers on" are independent when considered alone, but if the event "lawn wet" is instantiated, then the additional possibility of "rain" does indeed modify the probability that "sprinklers on."

d-Separation

The above analyses of communication for the three types of connections in a DAG define the notion of *d*-separation.

Definition B.2 Let Y_j and Y_i be vertices of a DAG. These vertices are said to be *d-separated* if, for all paths between Y_j and Y_i, there is an intermediate vertex Y_k, distinct from Y_j and Y_i, such that a) the connection at Y_k is either serial or diverging and Y_k is instantiated, or b) the connection is converging and neither Y_k nor any of its descendants are instantiated. We say that the path $Y_j \mapsto Y_i$ is *blocked* by Y_k. A path that is not blocked is said to be *active*. □

The notion of *d*-separation provides the connecting principle between the graphical representation of this flow of influence and a probabilistic model of conditional dependence. The following theorem establishes the mechanism by which the joint probability mass function is synthesized.

Theorem B.2 The Bayesian Network Theorem *Let* $\{Y_1, \ldots, Y_n\}$ *be a Bayesian Network with conditional probability mass functions for each vertex given by* $p_{i|\mathrm{pa}(i)}(y_i|y_i)$. *Then the joint probability mass function is*

$$p_{1:n}(y_1, \ldots, y_n) = \prod_{i=1}^{n} p_{i|\mathrm{pa}(i)}(y_i|y_i). \tag{B.15}$$

Proof Without loss of generality, we may assume that the vertices of the network are enumerated such that all children of any given vertex have a higher-numbered index, otherwise the indexing is arbitrary. By the chain rule of probability, the joint probability mass function may be factored into the form

$$p_{1:n} = p_{n|n-1\cdots1}p_{n-1|n-2\cdots1}p_{n-2|n-3\cdots1} \cdots p_{3|21}p_{2|1}p_1, \tag{B.16}$$

where, in the interest of clarity, we have suppressed the argument list. Now consider an arbitrary term in the factorization, say $p_{i|i-1\cdots1}$. Suppose there are q_i parents of Y_i, denoted $\text{pa}\,(Y_i) = \{Y_{i_1}, \ldots, Y_{i_{q_i}}\}$. By the enumeration scheme, we have that $i_k < i$ for $k = 1, \ldots, i$, so each of the vertices in the parent set lie in the conditioning argument list of $p_{i|i-1\cdots1}$. By the indexing convention, all neighbors of Y_i in this argument list are also members of the parent set, so if all elements of the argument set are neighbors, then $p_{i|i-1\cdots1} = p_{i|\text{pa}(i)}$. Suppose Y_ℓ is in the argument list but $Y_\ell \notin \text{pa}\,(Y_i)$. Then Y_ℓ is connected to Y_i with either a serial connection, a diverging connection, or a converging connection via a path that passes through a parent vertex, say Y_{i_k}. For both serial and diverging connections, however, since Y_{i_k} is instantiated, it blocks Y_i from Y_ℓ. For a converging connection, since neither Y_i or any of its children is instantiated (that is, does not lie in the conditioning argument list), Y_{i_k} also blocks communication between Y_i and Y_ℓ. Thus, Y_i and Y_ℓ are conditionally independent given Y_{i_k} and Y_ℓ may be dropped from the conditioning argument list. In this way, all non-parent elements in the conditioning argument list maybe removed, yielding

$$p_{i|i-1\cdots1} = p_{i|i_1\cdots i_k} = p_{i|\text{pa}(i)} \,. \tag{B.17}$$

If $\text{pa}\,(Y_i) = \varnothing$, then Y_i and Y_j are conditionally independent for all $j < i$, and $p_{i|i-1\cdots1}$ may be replaced by the unconditional marginal mass function p_i. Thus, (B.16) reduces to $\prod_{i=1}^{n} p_{v_i|\,\text{pa}\,(v_i)}$. $\qquad\square$

Probability Concepts

By its very name, probability theory is viewed primarily as the study of random phenomena, and much of the terminology is focused on that application. More generally speaking, however, probability theory is a branch of mathematics that exists independently of any particular application or context. In addition to its traditional application, this book uses probability theory in unconventional ways, primarily as a mathematical model for conditional utility. In this appendix we review many of the basic probabilistic concepts and notation as presented in the traditional epistemological setting in order to facilitate the migration of the concepts into the alternative contexts discussed in the book.

Probability Space

General measure theory is a vast topic that permeates virtually all of mathematics. In this appendix, however, we restrict attention to a very small but also very important subset of that theory – probability theory. In particular, we shall focus only on measure theory involving finite sets. Given a finite sample space $\Omega = \{\omega_1, \ldots, \omega_N\}$, the set of possible outcomes of an experiment, such that one, and only one, outcome will be realized, a *probability measure P* is a function defined over subsets of Ω that provides a numerical assessment of the chance that the outcome that is realized belongs to that subset. Measure theory provides a rigorous mathematical framework within which to make such assessments.

Definition C.1 A *Boolean algebra*, denoted $\mathcal{F}$, is a collection of subsets of Ω that possesses the following properties.

1. $\Omega \in \mathcal{F}$.
2. If $B \in \Omega$ then $B^c \in \Omega$, where $B^c = \Omega \setminus B$ is the complement of B.
3. If $B_1 \in \Omega$ and $B_2 \in \Omega$, then $B_1 \cup B_2 \in \Omega$.

A Boolean algebra is thus said to be *closed under complementation and finite unions*. Thus, it also holds that $\varnothing \in \mathcal{F}$ and $B_1 \cap B_2 \in \mathcal{F}$. The pair $(\Omega, \mathcal{F})$ is termed a *measurable space*.   □

The smallest possible Boolean algebra is $\{\Omega, \varnothing\}$, the *trivial* Boolean algebra. The next smallest Boolean algebra is $\{B, B^c, \Omega, \varnothing\}$ for any $B \subset \Omega$. For our applications, however, we will focus exclusively on the largest possible Boolean algebra; namely, the one that contains all singleton sets of Ω. We denote singleton sets by the notation $\{\omega\}$. Thus, whereas we write $\omega \in \Omega$, we write $\{\omega\} \subset \Omega$ and $\{\omega\} \in \mathcal{F}$.

Definition C.2 A *probability measure* is a mapping $P \colon \mathcal{F} \to [0,1]$ such that

1. $0 \leq P(B) \leq 1$ for every $B \in \mathcal{F}$.
2. $P(\Omega) = 1$.
3. For sets $B_1, \dots, B_n$ such that $B_i \cap B_j = \varnothing$, then

$$P\left(\cup_{i=1}^{n} B_i \right) = \sum_{i=1}^{n} P(B_i).$$ (C.1)

The triple $(\Omega, \mathcal{F}, P))$ is termed a *probability space*.   □

Since set intersection is commutative, it follows that $P(B_1 \cap B_2) = P(B_2 \cap B_2)$.

Definition C.3 The events B_1 and B_2 are said to be *statistically independent* if

$$P(B_1 \cap B_2) = p(B_1)P(B_2).$$ (C.2)

□

Definition C.4 A *conditional probability measure* is a probability measure defined by

$$P(B_i | B_j) = \frac{P(B_i \cap B_j)}{P(B_j)}, i, j, \in \{1, 2\}\, i \neq j,$$ (C.3)

provided that $P(B_j) > 0$. Thus, if B_i and B_j are independent, then $P(B_i | B_j) = P(B_j)$ □

Definition C.5 The simultaneous occurrence of the set of events $B_1, \dots, B_n$ is given by the *chain rule of probability*, defined as

$$P(B_1 \cap \cdots \cap B_n) = P(B_n | B_{n-1} \cap \cdots \cap B_1) P(B_{n-1} | B_{n-2} \cap \cdots \cap B_1)$$
$$\cdots P(B_3 | B_2 \cap B_1) P(B_2 | B_1) P(B_1) . \quad \text{(C.4)}$$

Furthermore, by the commutative property, for any permutation π over this set of events, it must hold that

$$P(B_1 \cap \cdots \cap B_n) = P(B_{\pi(1)} \cap \cdots \cap B_{\pi(n)}) , \quad \text{(C.5)}$$

where $P(B_{\pi(1)} \cap \cdots \cap B_{\pi(n)})$ is computed by the chain rule according to the permuted ordering of events. $\qquad \square$

Random Variables

Definition C.6 A *random variable* $Y: \Omega \to \mathcal{Y}$ is a numerical valuation of elements of Ω such that the inverse image of any $A \subset \mathcal{Y}$ is an element of $\mathcal{F}$, that is,

$$Y^{-1}(A) = \{\omega \in \Omega: Y(\omega) \in A\} \in \mathcal{F} . \quad \text{(C.6)}$$

$\qquad \square$

Definition C.7 A *probability mass function* for a random variable Y is defined by

$$p(y) = P(Y^{-1}(\{y\})) = P(\{\omega: Y(\omega) = y\}) . \quad \text{(C.7)}$$

$\qquad \square$

Definition C.8 Given two random variables Y_1 and Y_2, the *joint probability mass function* is defined by

$$p_{12}(y_1, y_2) = P\big(Y_1^{-1}(\{y_1\}) \cap Y_2^{-1}(\{y_2\})\big)$$
$$= P\big(\{(\omega_1, \omega_2) \in \Omega \times \Omega: Y_1(\omega_1) = y_1 \text{ and } Y_2(\omega_2) = y_2\}\big) . \quad \text{(C.8)}$$

$\qquad \square$

By the commutative property, $p_{12}(y_1, y_2) = p_{21}(y_2, y_1)$.

Definition C.9 Given a joint probability mass function p_{ij}, $i, j \in \{1, 2\}$, $i \neq j$, the *marginal probability mass function* for Y_i is defined as

$$p_i(y_i) = \sum_{y_j} p_{ij}(y_i, y_j).$$ (C.9)

□

Definition C.10 A *conditional probability mass function* for Y_i given $Y_j = y_j$ is defined by

$$p_{i|j}(y_i|y_j) = \frac{p_{ij}(y_i, y_j)}{p_j(y_j)},$$ (C.10)

provided $p_j(y_j) > 0$.

□

An obvious consequence of this definition is that the joint probability mass function can be reconstructed as product of the marginal of one and the conditional of the other, that is,

$$p_{ij}(y_i, y_j) = p_i(y_i)p_{j|i}(y_j|y_i) = p_j(y_j)p_{i|j}(y_i|y_j),$$ (C.11)

which is equivalent to *Bayes rule*

$$p_{j|i}(y_j|y_i) = \frac{p_{i|j}(y_i|y_j)p_j(y_j)}{p_i(y_i)}.$$ (C.12)

Definition C.11 The random variables Y_i and Y_j are said to be *independent* if

$$p_{i|j}(y_i|y_j) = p_i(y_j) \,\forall\, y_j.$$ (C.13)

□

If Y_i and Y_j are independent, then the joint probability mass function can be reconstructed from the marginals, yielding

$$p_{ij}(y_i, y_j) = p_i(y_i)p_j(y_j).$$ (C.14)

Transition Probabilities

Definition C.12 Let $(\Omega_1, \mathcal{F}_1)$ and $(\Omega_2, \mathcal{F}_2)$ be two measurable spaces. A *transition probability* P_1^2 is a mapping of $\Omega_1 \times \mathcal{F}_2$ into $[0, 1]$ such that for every $\omega_1 \in \Omega_1$, $P_1^2(\omega_1, \cdot)$ is a probability measure on $\mathcal{F}_2$. □

We interpret the expression $P_1^2(\omega_1, B_2)$ as the probability that the event $B_2 \subset \Omega_2$ is realized, given that $\omega_1 \in B_1$ is realized.

Definition C.13 Let $(\Omega_1, \mathcal{F}_1)$ and $(\Omega_2, \mathcal{F}_2)$ be two measurable spaces. The measurable space $(\Omega_1 \times \Omega_2, \mathcal{F}_1 \otimes \mathcal{F}_2)$ is termed a *joint measurable space*, where $\mathcal{F}_1 \otimes \mathcal{F}_2$ is the smallest Boolean algebra that contains all *measurable rectangles* $B_1 \times B_2$ where $B_i \in \mathcal{F}_i$, $i = 1, 2$. □

Theorem C.3 *Let $(\Omega_1, \mathcal{F}_1)$ and $(\Omega_2, \mathcal{F}_2)$, be two measurable spaces, let P_1 be a probability on $(\Omega_1, \mathcal{F}_1)$, and let P_1^2 be a transition probability on $\Omega_1 \times \mathcal{F}_2$. Then there exists a unique probability P_{12} on $(\Omega_1 \times \Omega_2, \mathcal{F}_1 \otimes \mathcal{F}_2)$ such that*

$$P_{12}(B_1 \times B_2) = \int_{\Omega_2} P_1(d\omega_1) P_1^2(\omega_1, B_2) \quad \forall B_1 \in \mathcal{F}_1, \; B_2 \in \mathcal{F}_2.$$

(C.15)

For a proof of this result, see Neveu (1965).

Definition C.14 Let Ω_1 and Ω_2 be discrete sample spaces, and let Y_1 and Y_2 be discrete random variables over Ω_1 and Ω_2, respectively. A *transition probability mass function* p_1^2 is a mapping of $\Omega_1 \times \Omega_2$ into $[0, 1]$ such that for every $\omega_1 \in \Omega_1$ p_1^2 is a probability mass function on Ω_2. □

The expression $p_1^2(\omega_1, \omega_2)$ is the probability that the event $\omega_2 \in \Omega_2$ is realized, given that $\omega_1 \in \Omega_1$ is realized.

Corollary 1 *Let Ω_1 and Ω_2 be discrete sample spaces, and let Y_1 and Y_2 be discrete random variables defined on Ω_1 and Ω_2. Let p_1 be a probability mass function on Ω_1, and let p_1^2 be a transition probability mass function on $\Omega_1 \times \Omega_2$. Then there exists a unique probability mass function p_{12} on $\Omega_1 \times \Omega_2$ such that*

$$p_{12}(\omega_1, \omega_2) = p_1(\omega_1) p_1^2(\omega_1, \omega_2).$$

(C.16)

It should be emphasized that a transition probability mass function is not a conditional mass function in the sense expressed by Definition C.10, since it is not defined as the ratio of joint and marginal probability mass functions. Instead, it is used to *create* the joint probability mass function (C.16). Once this distinction is appreciated, it is more convenient to revert to the familiar notation associated with conditional mass functions. Therefore, we write

$$p_{2|1}(\omega_2|\omega_1) = p_1^2(\omega_1, \omega_2).$$

(C.17)

Markov Convergence Theorem

The key step in the proof of the Markov convergence theorem is a fundamental matrix-theoretic result regarding positive matrices. For additional discussions of these results see (Gantmacher, 1959; Doob, 1953; Luenberger, 1979).

Positive Matrices

Definition D.1 Let $T = [t_{jk}]$ be a square matrix with t_{jk} denoting the entry in the jth row and kth column. T is nonnegative, denoted $T \nless 0$, if $t_{jk} \nless 0 \, \forall j, k$. T is positive, denoted $T \geq 0$, if $t_{jk} \nless 0 \, \forall j, k$ and $t_{jk} > 0$ for at least one element. T is strictly positive, denoted $T > 0$, if $t_{jk} > 0 \, \forall j, k$. ☐

In this section we establish that a positive matrix has a positive dominant eigenvalue. The key result regarding positive matrices is the following theorem established by Perron (1907) and Frobenius (1912).

Theorem D.4 (Frobeneius–Perron) *If a square matrix $T > 0$ then a) there exists a positive eigenvalue λ_0 and a positive eigenvector x_0; b) if $\lambda \neq \lambda_0$ is an eigenvalue of T, then $|\lambda| < \lambda_0$; c) λ_0 has geometric and algebraic multiplicity one.*

To prove this theorem we follow Luenberger (1979).

Proof To prove part a), let λ_0 be defined by

$$\lambda_0 = \max\{\lambda \colon Tx \geq \lambda x, \ x \geq 0\}. \tag{D.1}$$

Clearly, $0 < \lambda_0 < \infty$. Let $x_0 \geq 0$ be a vector corresponding to λ_0, that is, $Tx_0 \geq \lambda_0 x_0$. Since $T > 0$ it follows that $Tx > 0$ for any $x \geq 0$. Therefore $T[Tx_0 - \lambda_0 x_0] > 0$ unless $Tx_0 = \lambda_0 x_0$. Suppose $Tx_0 > \lambda_0 x_0$. Then for $y_0 = Tx_0 > 0$, it would follow that $Ty_0 - \lambda_0 y_0$ or, equivalently, $Ty_0 > \lambda_0 y_0$. But if this were true then λ_0 could be increased slightly without violating the inequality (D.1), which contradicts the definition of λ_0. Therefore, it follows that

$$T\mathbf{x}_0 = \lambda_0 \mathbf{x}_o \text{ and } \mathbf{x} > 0. \tag{D.2}$$

To prove b), let $\lambda \neq \lambda_0$ be an eigenvalue of T and let $\mathbf{y}$ be a corresponding eigenvector: $T\mathbf{y} = \lambda\mathbf{y}$. Let $\tilde{\mathbf{y}}$ denote the vector whose components are the absolute values of the components of $\mathbf{y}$ and consider the vector $T\tilde{\mathbf{y}}$. The first component of this vector is $t_{11}|y_1| + \cdots + t_{1n}|y_n|$. Since the t_{ij} are all positive, it must hold that

$$t_{11}|y_1| + \cdots + t_{1n}|y_n| \geq |t_{11}y_1 + \cdots + t_{1n}y_n|, \tag{D.3}$$

with a similar result holding for all other components. Thus,

$$T\tilde{\mathbf{y}} \geq |T\mathbf{y}| \geq |\lambda\tilde{\mathbf{y}}| = |\lambda|\tilde{\mathbf{y}}. \tag{D.4}$$

From the definition of λ_0 it immediately follows that $|\lambda| \leq \lambda_0$.

To prove that strict inequality holds, consider the matrix $T_\delta = T - \delta I$ where $\delta > 0$ is chosen small enough so that T_δ is still strictly positive. Then $\lambda_0 - \delta$ and $\lambda - \delta$ are eigenvalues of T_δ and, because T_δ is strictly positive, it follows that $|\lambda - \delta| \leq |\lambda_0|$. However, if $|\lambda| = \lambda_0$, $\lambda \neq \lambda_0$, it follows by direct computation of the absolute value that $|\lambda - \delta| > |\lambda_0 - \delta|$, which is a contradiction.

To prove that the geometric multiplicity is 1 it must be shown that (to within a scalar multiple) $\mathbf{x}_0$ is the only eigenvector associated with λ_0. Suppose there were another. Then, since T is real, there will be a real eigenvector $\mathbf{y}_0$ that is linearly independent of $\mathbf{x}_0$. Since $\mathbf{x}_0 > 0$, it is possible to find a linear combination $\mathbf{w} = \alpha\mathbf{x}_0 + \mathbf{y}_0$ such that $\mathbf{w} \geq 0$ but not $\mathbf{w} = 0$. However, since $T\mathbf{w} = \lambda_0\mathbf{w}$ is strictly positive, we have a contradiction. Therefore, the geometric multiplicity of λ_0 is 1.

Finally, suppose the algebraic multiplicity of λ_0 is greater than 1. Then, since the geometric multiplicity is 1, there mut be a Jordan chain of length at least two associated with λ_0. Thus, there is a vector $\mathbf{z}$ such that $(T - \lambda_0 I)\mathbf{z} = \mathbf{y}$ and $(T - \lambda_0 I)\mathbf{y} = 0$. In view if what was shown above, $\mathbf{y}$ must be a multiple of $\mathbf{x}_0$ and thus, without loss of generality, it can be assumed that $(T - \lambda_0 I)\mathbf{z} = \mathbf{x}_0$. Now let $\mathbf{f}_0$ be the strictly positive eigenvector of T^T corresponding to λ_0. Then $\mathbf{f}_0^T$ is a left eigenvector of T and it follows that

$$0 = \mathbf{f}_0^T(T - \lambda_0 I)\mathbf{z} = \mathbf{f}_0^T\mathbf{x}_0. \tag{D.5}$$

But $\mathbf{f}_0^T \mathbf{x}_0$ is positive because both $\mathbf{f}_0$ and $\mathbf{x}_0$ are strictly positive. Thus, we have a contradiction and it follows that the algebraic multiplicity of λ_0 is 1.   □

The results of the Frobenius–Perron theorem can be extended to the following result, which is stated without proof.

Theorem D.5 *Let* $T \geq 0$ *be such that* $T^m > 0$ *for some positive integrer m. Then the conclusions of Theorem D.4 apply to T.*

Markov Chains

Definition D.2 A finite *Markov chain* is a discrete-time stochastic process which at any time can be in one of N states. Let $u_i(s)$ denote the probability that the process is in state i at time s, and let $\mathbf{u}(s) = (u_1(s), \ldots, u_N(s))$ denote the *probability mass vector* that defines the distribution of the state at time s.

A *transition probability mass vector* is a conditional probability mass vector $(t_{j|1}, \ldots, t_{j|N})$ such that $t_{j|i}$ is the probability that the process will be in state j at time $s + 1$, given that it is in state i at time s.

A square matrix T such that each column is a transition probability mass vector is termed a *transition matrix*. A transition matrix T is said to be *regular* if $T^m > 0$ for some finite m.   □

With this construction, the probability of transitioning between states during the step from time s to time $s + 1$ is given by

$$\mathbf{u}(s+1) T \mathbf{u}(s). \tag{D.6}$$

Thus, for $N = 3$, we write

$$\mathbf{u}(s+1) = \begin{bmatrix} u_1(s+1) \\ u_2(s+1) \\ u_3(s+1) \end{bmatrix} = \begin{bmatrix} t_{1|1} & t_{1|2} & t_{1|3} \\ t_{2|1} & t_{2|2} & t_{2|3} \\ t_{3|1} & t_{3|2} & t_{3|3} \end{bmatrix} \begin{bmatrix} u_1(s) \\ u_2(s) \\ u_3(s) \end{bmatrix} = T\mathbf{u}(s). \tag{D.7}$$

Theorem D.6 The Markov Convergence Theorem *If T is a regular transition matrix, there exists a unique probability mass vector* $\bar{\mathbf{u}}$ *such that a)* $T\bar{\mathbf{u}} = \bar{\mathbf{u}}$; *b) for any initial state i corresponding to an initial probability mass vector equal to the ith coordinate vector*

$\mathbf{e}_i = \begin{bmatrix} 0 & \cdots & 0 & 1 & 0 \cdots & 0 \end{bmatrix}^T$, *where the unit appears in the ith position, the steady-state probability mass vector is*

$$\bar{\mathbf{u}} = \lim_{s \to \infty} T^s \mathbf{e}_i \qquad (D.8)$$

and c)

$$\lim_{s \to \infty} T^s = \overline{T}. \qquad (D.9)$$

Proof Part a) follows from the Frobenius–Perron Theorem and the fact that the dominant eigenvalue is $\lambda_0 = 1$. To prove b), we note that since $\lambda_0 = 1$ is a simple root, it follows that $T^s \mathbf{e}_i$ must converge to a scalar multiple of $\bar{\mathbf{u}}$. However, since each $T^s \mathbf{e}_i$ is a probability mass vector, the multiple must be unity. Part c) is simply a restatement of b), since each row of T^s converges to $\bar{\mathbf{u}}$. □

Corollary 2 *If T is a regular transition matrix and* $\mathbf{u}(0)$ *is any initial probability mass vector, then*

$$\bar{\mathbf{u}} = \overline{T}\mathbf{u}(0); \qquad (D.10)$$

that is, the limiting probability is independent of the initial probability mass vector.

Proof We write

$$\mathbf{u}(0) = \sum_{i=1}^{N} u_i(0)\mathbf{e}_i. \qquad (D.11)$$

Then

$$\overline{T}\mathbf{u}(0) = \overline{T}\left[\sum_{i=1}^{N} u_i(0)\mathbf{e}_i\right] = \sum_{i=1}^{N} u_i(0)\overline{T}\mathbf{e}_i = \sum_{i=1}^{N} u_i(0)\bar{\mathbf{u}} = \bar{\mathbf{u}}. \qquad (D.12)$$

□

Entropy and Mutual Information

The word *entropy* comes from the Greek word meaning "transformation." In the nineteenth century, the German physicist Rudolf Clausius introduced the term to describe the tendency for the world to move to a state of increasing disorder (the second law of thermodynamics). The concept was refined by Ludwig Boltzmann, who introduced the logarithmic mathematical model of the concept. In the thermodynamics context, entropy is a measure of the inability to convert energy into work (Prigogine, 1955; Georgescu-Roegen, 1971; Bailey, 1990).

In the mid-twentieth century, the engineer/mathematician Claude Shannon developed a mathematical model of information theory, and employed the concept of entropy as a measure of the degree of randomness associated with a phenomenon, such as a message transmitted through an imperfect medium (Shannon and Weaver, 1949). In this section we establish some of the central properties of entropy and the closely related concept of mutual information. Although the book employs these concepts in a praxeological context, in this appendix we present the discussion in the traditional probabilistic context. One of the premier references on the subject of information theory, which serves as the primary reference for the material presented in this appendix, is Cover and Thomas (2006).

Let $\{Y_1, \ldots, Y_n\}$ be a collective of discrete random variables taking values in a finite set $\mathcal{Y}$ with joint probability mass function $p_{1:n}: \mathcal{Y}^n \to [0,1]$, and let $p_i: \mathcal{Y} \to [0,1]$ denote the marginal probability mass function for Y_i, $i = 1, \ldots, n$.

Entropy

Definition E.1 The *entropy* $H(Y_i)$ is defined by

$$H(Y_i) = - \sum_y p_i(y) \log_2 p_i(y). \tag{E.1}$$

The *joint entropy* $H(Y_1, \ldots, Y_n)$ is defined by

$$H(Y_1, \ldots, Y_n) = -\sum_{y_1} \cdots \sum_{y_n} p_{1:n}(y_1, \ldots, y_n) \log p_{1:n}(y_1, \ldots, y_n).$$

(E.2)

□

Lemma 2 $H(Y_i) \geq 0$, $H(Y_1, \ldots, Y_n) \geq 0$.

Proof $0 \leq p_i(y) \leq 1$ implies that $\log p_i(y) < 0$, similarly for $p_{1:n}$. □

Definition E.2 The *conditional entropy* $H(Y_1|Y_2)$ is defined by

$$\begin{aligned} H(Y_1|Y_2) &= \sum_{y_2} p_2(y_2) H(Y_1|Y_2 = y_2) \\ &= \sum_{y_2} p_2(y_2) \sum_{y_1} p_{1|2}(y_1|y_2) \log p_{1|2}(y_1|y_2) \\ &= \sum_{y_2} \sum_{y_1} p_2(y_2) p_{1|2}(y_1|y_2) \log p_{1|2}(y_1|y_2) \\ &= -\sum_{y_1, y_2} p_{12}(y_1, y_2) \log p_{1|2}(y_1|y_2). \end{aligned}$$

(E.3)

□

Theorem E.7 The chain rule of entropy is as follows.

$$H(Y_1, Y_2) = H(Y_1) + H(Y_2|Y_1).$$

(E.4)

Proof

$$\begin{aligned} H(Y_1, Y_2) &= -\sum_{y_1, y_2} p_{12}(y_1, y_2) \log p_{12}(y_1, y_2) \\ &= -\sum_{y_1, y_2} p_{12}(y_1, y_2) \log p_1(y_1) p_{2|1}(y_2|y_1) \\ &= -\sum_{y_1, y_2} p_{12}(y_1, y_2) \log p_1(y_1) \\ &\quad - \sum_{y_1, y_2} p_{12}(y_1, y_2) \log p_{2|1}(y_2|y_1) \\ &= -\sum_{y_1} p_{12}(y_1) \log p_1(y_1) \end{aligned}$$

$$-\sum_{y_1,y_2} p_{12}(y_1,y_2)\log p_{2|1}(y_2|y_1)$$

$$= H(Y_1) + H(Y_2|Y_1). \tag{E.5}$$

□

Thus, $H(Y_1) \le H(Y_1, Y_2)$. By a similar argument, it follows that $H(Y_1, Y_2) \le H(Y_1, Y_2, Y_3)$ and so forth. By similar operations, it is also straightforward to show that

Corollary 3

$$H(Y_1, Y_2|Y_3) = H(Y_1|Y_3) + H(Y_2|Y_1, Y_3). \tag{E.6}$$

Proof The proof follows the same lines as the theorem.   □

Mutual Information

Definition E.3 The *mutual information* $I(Y_1, \ldots, Y_n)$ is defined by

$$I(Y_1, \ldots, Y_n) = \sum_{i=1}^{n} H(Y_i) - H(Y_1, \ldots, Y_n). \tag{E.7}$$

□

Theorem E.8 $I(Y_1, \ldots, Y_n) \ge 0.$

The proof follows from Jensen's inequality.

Lemma 3 Jensen's inequality. *Let f be a convex function and let $E[\cdot]$ denote mathematical expectation. Then*

$$E[f(Y)] \ge f(E[Y]). \tag{E.8}$$

Proof *Proof of Jensen's inequality.* Suppose Y is governed by a two-point probability mass function with $p(y_1) = 1 - p(y_2) = p$. Then

$$pf(y_1) + (1 - p)f(y_2) \ge f(py_1 + (1 - p)y_2), \tag{E.9}$$

which follows from the definition of convexity. The result is extended to the general case by mathematical induction.   □

Proof *Proof that mutual information is nonnegative.* Without loss of generality, let $n = 2$.

$$
\begin{aligned}
I(Y_1, Y_2) &= H(Y_1) + H(Y_2) - H(Y_1, Y_2) \\
&= -\sum_{y_1} p_1(y_i) \log p_1(y_1) - \sum_{y_2} p_2(y_2) \log p_2(y_2) \\
&\quad + \sum_{y_1, y_2} p_{12}(y_1, y_2) \log p_{12}(y_1, y_2) \\
&= -\sum_{y_1, y_2} p_{12}(y_1, y_2)[\log p_1(y_1) + \log p_2(y_2)] \\
&\quad + \sum_{y_1, y_2} p_{12}(y_1, y_2) \log p_{12}(y_1, y_2) \\
&= \sum_{y_1, y_2} p_{12}(y_1, y_2) \log \frac{p_1(y_1) p_2(y_2)}{p_{12}(y_1, y_2)} \\
&\geq \log \sum_{y_1, y_2} p_{12}(y_1, y_2) \frac{p_1(y_1) p_2(y_2)}{p_{12}(y_1, y_2)}
\end{aligned}
$$

(Jensen's inequality: logarithm is convex)

$$
\begin{aligned}
&= \log \sum_{y_1, y_2} p_1(y_1) p_2(y_2) \\
&= \log 1 \\
&= 0.
\end{aligned}
\tag{E.10}
$$

□

Theorem E.9

$$
I(Y_1, Y_2) = H(Y_1) - H(Y_1|Y_2).
\tag{E.11}
$$

Proof

$$
\begin{aligned}
I(Y_1, Y_2) &= H(Y_1) + H(Y_2) - H(Y_1, Y_2) \\
&= H(Y_1) + H(Y_2) + \sum_{y_1, y_2} p_{12}(y_1, y_2) \log p_{12}(y_1, y_2) \\
&= H(Y_1) + H(Y_2) + \sum_{y_1, y_2} p_{12}(y_1, y_2) \log p_{1|2}(y_1|y_2) p_2(y_2) \\
&= H(Y_1) + H(Y_2) + \sum_{y_1, y_2} p_{12}(y_1, y_2) \log p_2(y_2) \\
&\quad + \sum_{y_1, y_2} p_{12}(y_1, y_2) \log p_{12}(y_1, y_2)
\end{aligned}
$$

$$= H(Y_1) + H(Y_2) - H(Y_2)$$
$$+ \sum_{y_1, y_2} p_{12}(y_1, y_2) \log p_{1|2}(y_1 | y_2)$$
$$= H(Y_1) - H(Y_1 | Y_2). \tag{E.12}$$

□

Corollary 4

$$\begin{aligned} H(Y_1 | Y_2) &\leq H(Y_1) \\ H(Y_1, Y_2) &\leq H(Y_1) + H(Y_2) \end{aligned}. \tag{E.13}$$

Proof To establish (E.13),

$$0 \leq I(Y_1, Y_2) = H(Y_1) - H(Y_1 | Y_2), \tag{E.14}$$

from which the result follows. Also, from (E.4),

$$H(Y_1, Y_2) = H(Y_1) + H(Y_2 | Y_1) \leq H(Y_1) + H(Y_2). \tag{E.15}$$

□

Dispersion

Definition E.4 The *dispersion function* $d(Y_1, Y_2)$ is defined by

$$d(Y_1, Y_2) = H(Y_1, Y_2) - I(Y_1, Y_2). \tag{E.16}$$

□

It is straightforward to see that

$$d(Y_1, Y_2) = H(Y_1 | Y_2) + H(Y_2 | Y_1) \tag{E.17}$$

and

$$d(Y_1, Y_2) = 2H(Y_1, Y_2) - H(Y_1) - H(Y_2) \tag{E.18}$$

are alternative expressions for (E.16).

Theorem E.10 *The dispersion function $d(Y_1, Y_2)$ satisfies the following conditions.*

$$d(Y_1, Y_2) = d(Y_2, Y_1) \text{ (symmetry)} \tag{E.19}$$
$$d(Y_1, Y_2) \geq 0 \text{ (non-negativity)} \tag{E.20}$$
$$d(Y_1, Y_2) = 0 \text{ if and only if } Y_1 \models Y_2 \text{(strict positivity)} \tag{E.21}$$
$$d(Y_1, Y_2) \leq d(Y_1, Y_3) + d(Y_3, Y_2) \text{ (triangle inequality)}, \tag{E.22}$$

and thus is a true metric. The expression $Y_1 \vDash Y_2$ *means that there exists a permutation* $\pi \colon \mathcal{Y} \to \mathcal{Y}$ *such that*

$$p_{2|1}(y_2|y_1) = \begin{cases} 0 & \text{if } y_2 \neq \pi(y_1) \\ 1 & \text{if } y_2 = \pi(y_1) \end{cases}.$$

Proof Symmetry and non-negativity are obvious from the definition. To ensure strict positivity, consider the conditional entropy

$$H(Y_2|Y_1) = \sum_{y_1} p_1(y_1) \sum_{y_2} p_{2|1}(y_2|y_1) \log p_{2|1}(y_2|y_1). \tag{E.23}$$

Given that $Y_2 \vDash Y_1$, the conditional probability $p_{2|1}$ places its entire mass on $\pi(y_1)$. Thus, $p_{2|1}[y_2|y_1] \log p_{2|1}(y_2|y_1)$ takes values of either $0 \log 0 = 0$ or $1 \log 1 = 0$.[1] It follows that $H(Y_2|Y_1) = 0$ when $Y_1 \vDash Y_2$. But if there exists no permutation, then $H(Y_2|Y_1) > 0$ and thus $d(Y_1, y_2) > 0$.

To establish the triangle inequality, we first note that, by the corollary to the chain rule of entropy,

$$H(Y_2|Y_3) + H(Y_1|Y_2, Y_3) = H(Y_1, Y_2|Y_3) \leq H(Y_1|Y_3) + H(Y_2|Y_3) \tag{E.24}$$

or, canceling common terms,

$$H(Y_1|Y_2, Y_3) \leq H(Y_1|Y_3). \tag{E.25}$$

Similarly,

$$H(Y_2|Y_1, Y_3) \leq H(Y_2|Y_3). \tag{E.26}$$

Thus,

$$\begin{aligned} H(Y_1|Y_2) + H(Y_2|Y_3) &\geq H(Y_1|Y_2, Y_3) + H(Y_2|Y_3) \\ &= H(Y_1, Y_2|Y_3) \\ &= H(Y_1|Y_3) + H(Y_2|Y_1, Y_3) \\ &\geq H(Y_1|Y_3) \end{aligned} \tag{E.27}$$

By a similar argument,

$$H(Y_2|Y_1) + H(Y_3|Y_2) \geq H(Y_3|Y_1). \tag{E.28}$$

---

[1] We use the fact that $\lim_{\epsilon \to 0} \epsilon \log \epsilon = 0$.

Finally,

$$
\begin{aligned}
d(Y_1, Y_2) + d(y_2, Y_3) &= H(Y_1|Y_2) + H(Y_2|Y_2) \\
&\quad + H(Y_2|Y_3) + H(Y_3|Y_2) \\
&= H(Y_1|Y_2) + H(Y_2|Y_3) \\
&\quad + H(Y_2|Y_1) + H(Y_3|Y_2) \\
&\geq H(Y_1|Y_3) + H(Y_3|Y_1) \\
&= d(Y_1, Y_3).
\end{aligned}
\tag{E.29}
$$

□

Definition E.5 The *relative dispersion* $\mathcal{D}(Y_1, Y_2)$ is defined by

$$
\mathcal{D}(Y_1, Y_2) = \frac{d(Y_1, Y_2)}{H(Y_1, Y_2)}.
\tag{E.30}
$$

□

Theorem E.11 $\mathcal{D}(Y_1, Y_2)$ *is a true metric with* $\mathcal{D}(Y_1, Y_2) \leq 1$ *for all pairs* (Y_1, Y_2).

Proof Symmetry, non-negativity, and strict positivity are obvious, but it remains to establish the triangle inequality.

$$
\mathcal{D}(Y_1, Y_2) = \frac{H(Y_1|Y_2)}{H(Y_1, Y_2)} + \frac{H(Y_2|Y_1)}{H(Y_2, Y_1)}.
\tag{E.31}
$$

To establish the triangle inequality we follow Kraskov et al. (2003); Li et al. (2001). It is sufficient to show that

$$
\frac{H(Y_1|Y_2)}{H(Y_1, Y_2)} \leq \frac{H(Y_1|Y_3)}{H(Y_1, Y_3)} \frac{H(Y_3|Y_2)}{H(Y_3, Y_2)}
\tag{E.32}
$$

and a similar inequality for the second term in (E.31). Using the properties of entropy, it follows that

$$
\begin{aligned}
\frac{H(Y_1|Y_2)}{H(Y_1, Y_2)} &= \frac{H(Y_1|Y_2)}{H(Y_2) + H(Y_1|Y_2)} \\
&\leq \frac{H(Y_1|Y_3) + H(Y_3|Y_2)}{H(Y_2) + H(Y_1|Y_3) + H(Y_3|Y_2)} \\
&= \frac{H(Y_1|Y_3) + H(Y_3|Y_2)}{H(Y_1|Y_3) + H(Y_2|Y_3)}
\end{aligned}
\tag{E.33}
$$

$$\leq \frac{H(Y_1|Y_3)}{H(Y_1|Y_3) + H(Y_3)} + \frac{H(Y_2|Y_2)}{H(Y_2, Y_3)}$$

$$= \frac{H(Y_2|Y_3)}{H(Y_1, Y_3)} + \frac{H(Y_3|Y_2)}{H(Y_3, Y_2)}.$$

Finally, when Y_1 and Y_2 are independent, then

$$\mathcal{D}(Y_1, Y_2) = \frac{H(Y_1) + H(Y_2)}{H(Y_1) + H(Y_2)} = 1. \tag{E.34}$$

□

Bibliography

Abbas, A. E. From bayes' nets to utility nets. *Proceedings of the 29th International Workshop on Bayesian Inference and Maximum Entropy Methods in Science and Engineering*, pp. 3–12, 2009.

Abbas, A. E. and Howard, R. A. Attribute dominance utility. *Decision Analysis*, 2(4):185–206, 2005.

Arrow, H., McGrath, J. E., and Berdahl, J. L. *Small Groups as Complex Systems*. Sage Publications, Inc., Thousand Oaks, CA, 2000.

Arrow, K. J. *Social Choice and Individual Values*. John Wiley & Sons, New York, 1951. 2nd edition, 1963.

Essays in the Theory of Risk Bearing. Markham Publishing Co., Chicago, IL, 1971.

The Limits of Organization. W. W. Norton & Company, New York, NY, 1974.

Rationality of self and others in an economic system. In R. M. Hogarth and M. W. Reder, editors, *Rational Choice*, pp. 25–40. University of Chicago Press, Chicago, 1986.

Axelrod, R. *The Evolution of Cooperation*. Basic Books, New York, 1984.

The Complexity of Cooperation. Princeton University Press, Princeton, NJ, 1997.

Bacharach, M. Interactive team reasoning: a contribution to the theory of cooperation. *Research in Economics*, 23:117–147, 1999.

Beyond Individual Choice: Teams and Frames in Game Theory. Princeton University Press, Princeton, NJ, 2006.

Bailey, K. *Social Entropy Theory*. State University of New York Press, Albany, NY, 1990.

Balinski, M. and Laraki, R. *Majority Judgment*. Cambridge University Press, Cambridge, UK, 2010.

Banzhaf, J. Weighted voting doesn't work: a mathematical analysis. *Rutgers Law Review*, 19:317–343, 1965.

Battigalli, P. and Dufwenberg, M. Dynamic psychological games. *Journal of Economic Theory*, 144:1–35, 2009.

Bendor, J. B., Kumar, S., and Siegel, D. A. Satisficing: a "pretty good" heuristic. *The B. E. Journal of Theoretical Economics*, 9(1):1–36, 2009.

Bentham J. *An Introduction to the Principles of Morals and Legislation (Dover Philosophical Classics)*. Dover Publications Inc., Mineola, NY, ISBN 978-0486454528, 2009.

Berhold, M. H. The use of distribution functions to represent utility functions. *Management Science*, 23:825–829, 1973.

Bicchieri, C. *Rationality and Coordination*. Cambridge University Press, Cambridge, UK, 1993.

Blackwell, D. and Girshick, M. A. *Theory of Games and Statistical Decisions*. Dover, New York, NY, 1979. Originally published in 1954 by John Wiley & Sons.

Bolton, G. E. and Ockenfels, A. A stress test of fairness measures in models of social utility. *Economic Theory*, 24(4):957–982, 2005.

Bossert, W., Qi, C. X., and Weymark, J. A. Measuring group fitness in a biological hierarchy: an axiomatic social choice approach. *Economics and Philosophy*, 29:301–323, 2012.

Burns, T. and Stalker, G. M. *The Management of Innovation*. Tavistock Publications, London, UK, 1961.

Byron, M., editor. *Satisficing and Maximizing*. Cambridge University Press, Cambridge, UK, 2004.

Camerer, C. *Behavioral Game Theory: Experiments in Strategic Interaction*. Princeton University Press, Princeton, NJ, 2003.

Camerer, C., Lowenstein, G., and Rabin, M., editors. *Advances in Behavorial Economics*. Princeton University Press, Princeton, NJ, 2004.

Cartwright, D. Influence, leadership, control. In J. G. March, editor, *Handbook of Organizations*, pp. 1–47. Rand-McNally, Chicago, IL, 1965.

Castagnoli, E. and LiCalzi, M. Expected utility without utility. *Theory and Decision*, 41:281–301, 1996.

Castellano, C., Fortunato, S., and Loreto, V. Statistical physics of social dynamics. *Reviews of Modern Physics*, May 2009. URL http://dx.doi.org/10.1103/RevModPhys.81.591.

Chen, W. and Sim, W. Goal driven optimization. *Operations Research*, 57: 342–357, 2009.

Christakis, N. A. and Fowler, J. H. *Connected: The Surprising Power of Our Social Networks and How They Shape Our Lives*. Little, Brown and Company, New York, 2009.

Cohen, J. Deliberation and democratic legitimacy. In A. Hamlin and P. Pettit, editors, *The Good Polity*, pp. 17–34. Basil Blackwell, Ltd., London, UK, 1994.

Colman, A. M. Cooperation, psychological game theory, and limitations of rationality in social interaction. *Behavioral and Brain Sciences*, 26: 139–198, 2003.

Condorcet, M. J. A. N. Essai sur l'application de l'analyse à la probabilitié des décisions rendues à la pluralité des voix. l'Imprimerie Royale, Paris, 1785. Translated in Mclean and Urken 1995, pp. 91–113.

Cooper, R. W. *Coordination Games*. Cambridge University Press, Cambridge, UK, 1999.

Coughlin, P. J. *Probabilistic Voting Theory*. Cambridge University Press, Cambridge, UK, 1992.

Cover, T. M. and Thomas, J. A. *Elements of Information Theory*. John Wiley & Sons, New York, 2nd edition, 2006.

Cowell, R. G., Dawid, A. P., Lauritzen, S. L., and Spiegelhalter, D. J. *Probabilistic Networks and Expert Systems*. Springer-Verlag, New York, NY, 1999.

de Finetti, B. La prévision: ses lois logiques, ses sources subjectives. *Annales de l'Institut Henri Poincaré*, 7:1–68, 1937. translated as Forsight. Its Logical Laws, Its Subjective Sources'. In H. E. Kyburg Jr. and H. E. Smokler, editors, *Studies in Subjective Probability*, pp. 93–158, John Wiley & Sons, New York, NY, 1964.

DeGroot, M. H. Reaching a consensus. *Journal of the American Statistical Association*, 69:118–121, 1974.

Dewey, J. *Logic: The Theory of Inquiry*. Henry Holt and Company, New York, NY, 1938.

Doob, J. L. *Stochastic Processes*. John Wiley & Sons, New York, NY, 1953.

Drèze, J. H. *Essays on Economic Decisions under Uncertainty*. Cambridge University Press, Cambridge, UK, 1987.

Dryzek, J. S. *Deliberative Democracy and Beyond: Liberals, Critics, Contestations*. Oxford University Press, Oxford, UK, 2000.

Dufwenberg, M. and Kirchsteiger, G. A theory of sequential reciprocity. *Games and Economic Behavior*, 47:268–298, 2004.

Dyer, J. S. and Sarin, R. K. Measurable multiattribute value functions. *Operations Research*, 27:810–822, 1979.

Easley, D. and Kleinbergm, J. *Networks, Crowds, and Markets: Reasoning about a Highly Connected World*. Cambridge University Press, Cambridge, 2010.

Edgeworth, F. Y. *Mathematical Psychics*. C. Kegan Paul & Co., London, UK, 1881.

Einstein, A. On the method of theoretical physics. *Philosophy of Science*, 1(2):163–169, 1934.

Elster, J., editor. *The Multiple Self*. Cambridge University Press, Cambridge, UK, 1985.

Rational Choice. Basil Blackwell, Oxford, UK, 1986.

Fefferman, N. H. and Ng, K. L. The role of individual choice in the evolution of social complexity. *Annales Zoologici Fennici*, 44:58–69, 2007.

Fehr, E. and Schmidt, K. A theory of fairness, competition, and cooperation. *Quarterly Journal of Economics*, 114:817–868, 1999.

Ferguson, T. S. *Mathematical Statistics*. Academic Press, New York, NY, 1967.

Fishburn, P. C. Lotteries and social choice. *Journal of Economic Theory*, 5:189–207, 1972.

   The Theory of Social Choice. Princeton University Press, Princeton, NJ, 1973.

   The axioms of subjective probability. *Statistical Science*, 1(3):335–358, 1986.

French, J. R. P. A formal theory of social power. *The Psychology Review*, 63:181–194, 1956.

Friedkin, N. E. A formal theory of social power. *Journal of Mathematical Sociology*, 12:103–136, 1986.

   A Structural Theory of Social Influence. Cambridge University Press, Cambridge, UK, 1998.

   Social networks in structural equation models. *Social Psychology Quarterly*, 53:316–328, 1990.

Friedkin, N. E. and Johnson, E. C. Social influence and opinions. *Journal of Mathematical Sociology*, 15:193–205, 1990.

   Social positions in influence networks. *Social Networks*, 19:209–222, 1997.

   Social Influence Network Theory. Cambridge University Press, Cambridge, UK, 2011.

Friedman, M. *Price Theory*. Aldine Press, Chicago, IL, 1962.

G. Frobenius. Ueber matrizen aus nicht negativen elementen. *Sitzungsber. KÃũnigl. Preuss. Akad. Wiss.*, pages 456–477, 1912.

Gaertner, W. *A Primer in Social Choice Theory*. Oxford University Press, Oxford, UK, 2006.

Galilei, G. Il saggiatore, 1623. English translation in: *Controversy on the comets of 1618*, ed. by C. D. O'Malley and S. Drake, University of Pennsylvania Press, Philadelphia, 1960.

Gantmacher, F. *Applications of the Theory of Matrices*. Chelsea Publishing, New York, 1959.

Geanakoplos, J., Pearce, D., and Stacchetti, E. Psychological games and sequential rationality. *Games and Economic Behavior*, 1:60–79, 1989.

Genesereth, M. R., Ginsberg, M. L., and Rosenschein, J. S. Cooperation without communication. In *Proceedings of the Fifth National Conference on Artificial Intelligence (AAAI-86)*, pp. 51–57, 1986.

Georgescu-Roegen, N. *The Entropy Law and the Economic Process*. Harvard University Press, Cambridge, MA, 1971.

Gibbard, A. Manipulation of voting schemes. *Econometrica*, 41:587–602, 1973.

A pareto-consistent libertarian claim. *Journal of Economic Theory*, 7: 388–410, 1974.

Gilboa, I. and Schmeidler, D. Information dependent games. *Economics Letters*, 27:215–221, 1988.

Goodin, R. E. Laundering preferences. In J. Elster and A. Hylland, editors, *Foundations of Social Choice Theory*, chapter 3, pp. 75–101. Cambridge University Press, Cambridge, UK, 1986.

Goyal, S. *Connections*. Princeton University Press, Princeton, NJ, 2007.

Grabisch, M. and Rusinowska, A. A model of influence in social networks. *Theory and Decision*, 69(1):69–96, 2010a.

Different approaches to influence based on social networks and simple games. In A. Van Deeman and A. Rusinowska, editors, *Collective Decision Making: Views from Social Choice and Game Theory*, pp. 185–209. Springer-Verlag, Berlin, 2010b.

Habermas, J. *The Theory of Communicative Action*, volume one. Beacon Press, Boston, MA, 1994.

Hansson, B. The independence condition on the theory of social choice. Working paper no. 2, The Mattias Fremling Society, Department of Philosophy, Lund, 1972.

Harsanyi, J. Cardinal welfare, individualistic ethics, and interpersonal comparisons of utility. *Journal of Political Economy*, 63:309–321, 1955.

Rational Behavior and Bargaining Equilibrium in Games and Social Situations. Cambridge University Press, Cambridge, UK, 1977.

Henrich, J., Boyd, R., Bowles, S., Camerer, C., Fehr, E., and Gintis, H., editors. *Foundations of Human Sociality: Economic Experiments and Ethnographic Evidence from Fifteen Small-scale Societies*. Oxford University Press, Oxford, UK, 2004.

Henrich, J., Boyd, R., Bowles, S., Camerer, C., Fehr, E., Gintis, H., McLlerath, R., Alvard, M., Barr, A., Ensminger, J., Henrich, N. S., Hill, K., Gil-White, F., Gurven, M., Marlowe, F. W., Pattern, J. Q., and Tracer, T. "Economic Man" in cross-culturative perspective: behavorial experiments in 15 small-scale societies. *Behavioral and Brain Sciences*, 28(6):815–855, 2005.

Hicks, J. R. Foundations of welfare economics. *Economic Journal*, 49(196):696–712, 1939.

Hoede, C. and Bakker, R. A theory of decisional power. *Journal of Mathematical Sociology*, 8:309–322, 1982.

Holmes, S. The secret history of self-interest. In J. J. Mansbridge, editor, *Beyond Self-Interest*, chapter 17. University of Chicago Press, Chicago, 1990.

Homans, G. C. *Social Behavior: Its Elementary Forms*. Harcourt Brace & World, New York, 1961.

Hu, X. and Shapley, L. S. On authority distributions in organizations: controls. *Games and Economic Behavior*, 45:153–170, 2003a.

On authority distributions in organizations: equilibrium. *Games and Economic Behavior*, 45:132–152, 2003b.

Intriligator, M. D. A probabilistic model of social choice. *Review of Economic Studies*, 40:553–560, 1973.

Itô, K., editor. *Encyclopedic Dictionary of Mathematics*, volume II.12 (311 E). MIT Press, Cambridge, MA, 1987.

Jackson, M. O. *Social and Economic Networks*. Princeton University Press, Princeton, NJ, 2008.

James, W. *The Will to Believe and Other Essays*. Dover, New York, 1956.

Jaynes, E. T. *Probability Theory: The Logic of Science*. Cambridge University Press, Cambridge, UK, 2003.

Jensen, F. V. *Bayesian Networks and Decision Graphs*. Springer-Verlag, New York, NY, 2001.

Johnson, P. E. *Social Choice: Theory and Research*. Sage Publications, Thousand Oaks, CA, 1998.

Johnson-Laird, P. N. *The Computer and the Mind: An Introduction to Cognitive Science*. Harvard University Press, Cambridge, MA, 1988.

José, O. G. *Mirabeau: An Essay on the Nature of Statesmanship*, 1975. Historical Conservation Society, Manila.

Kaldor, N. Welfare propositions of economic and interpersonal comparisons of utility. *Economic Journal*, 49(195):549–552, 1939.

Karni, E. *Decision Making Under Uncertainty*. Harvard University Press, 1985.

Karni, E. and Schmeidler, D. An expected utility theory for state-dependent preferences. Working paper 48–80, the Foerder Institute of Economic Research, Tel Aviv University, Tel Aviv, 1981.

Karni, E., Schmeidler, D., and Vind, K. On state-dependent preferences and subjective probabilities. *Econometrica*, 51:1021–1032, 1983.

Keeney, R. L. and Raiffa, H. *Decisions with Multiple Objectives*. Cambridge University Press, 1976.

Kemeny, J. Fair bets and inductive probabilities. *Journal of Symbolic Logic*, 20(1):263–273, 1955.

Kolmogorov, A. *Grundbegriffe der Warscheinlichkeitsrechnung*. Springer, Berlin, 1933.

Kraskov, A., Stöbauer, H., Andrzejak, R. G., and Grassberger, P. Hierarchical clustering based on mutual information. *ArXiv q-bio/0311039 (http://arxiv.org/abs/q-bio/0311039)*, 2003.

Kreps, D. M. *Notes on the Theory of Choice.* Westview Press, Boulder, CO, 1988.

Game Theory and Economic Modelling. Clarendon Press, Oxford, UK, 1990.

Lam, S. W., Ng, T. S., Sim, M., and Song, J. H. Multiple objective satisficing under uncertainty. *Operations Research*, 61:214–217, 2013.

Lauritzen, S. L. *Graphical Models.* Springer-Verlag, New York, NY, 1996.

Lehman, R. S. On conformation and rational betting. *Journal of Symbolic Logic*, 20(1):263–273, 1955.

Levi, I. *The Enterprise of Knowledge.* MIT Press, Cambridge, MA, 1980.

Decisions and Revisions. Cambridge University Press, Cambridge, UK, 1984.

Lewis, D. K. *Convention.* Harvard University Press, Cambridge, MA, 1969.

Li, M., Badger, J. H., Chen, X., Kwong, S., Kearney, P., and Zang, H. An information-based sequence distance and its application to whole mitochondrial genome phylogeny. *Bioinformatics*, 17(2):149–154, 2001.

Luce, R. D. and Raiffa, H. *Games and Decisions.* John Wiley & Sons, New York, 1957.

Luenberger, D. G. *Introduction to Dynamic Systems.* John Wiley & Sons, New York, 1979.

Mackie, G. *Democracy Defended.* Cambridge University Press, Cambridge, UK, 2003.

Malone, T. W., Crowston, K. G., and Herman, G. A., editors. *Organizing Business Knowledge.* MIT Press, Cambridge, MA, 2003.

Margolis, H. Dual utilities and rational choice. In J. J. Mansbridge, editor, *Beyond Self-Interest*, chapter 15. University of Chicago Press, Chicago, 1990.

Misyak, J. B., Melkonyan, T. A., Zeitoun, H., and Chater, N. Unwritten rules: virtual bargaining underpins social interaction, culture, and society. *Trends in Cognitive Sciences*, 18:512–519, 2014.

Murray, J. A. H., Bradley, H., Craigie, W. A., and Onions, C. T., editors. *The Compact Oxford English Dictionary*, The Oxford University Press, Oxford, UK, 1991.

Neveu, J. *Mathematical Foundations of the Calculus of Probability.* Holden Day, San Francisco, 1965.

Nisan, N., Roughgharden, T., Tardos, E., and Vazirani, V. V. *Algorithmic Game Theory.* Cambridge University Press, Cambridge, 2007.

Palmer, F. R. *Grammar.* Penguin, Harmondsworth, Middlesex, 1971.

Parsons, S. and Wooldridge, M. Game theory and decision theory in multi-agent systems. *Autonomous Agents and Multi-Agent Systems*, 5: 243–254, 2002.

Pazgal, A. Satisficing leads to cooperation in mutual interests games. *International Journal of Game Theory*, 26(4):439–453, 1997.

Pearl, J. *Probabilistic Reasoning in Intelligent Systems*. Morgan Kaufmann, San Mateo, CA, 1988.

Penrose, L. S. The elementary statistics of majority voting. *Journal of the Royal Statistical Society*, 109:53–57, 1946.

O. Perron. Zur theorie der matrices. *Mathematische Annalen*, 64(2): 248–263, 1907.

Polanyi, M. *Personal Knowledge*. University of Chicago Press, Chicago, 1962.

Polya, G. *Induction and Analogy in Mathematics*. Princeton University Press, Princeton, NJ, 1954.

Popper, K. R. *Conjectures and Refutations: The Growth of Scientific Knowledge*. Harper & Row, New York, 1963.

Prigogine, I. *Thermodynamics of Irreversible Processes*. Thomas Press, Springfield IL, 1955.

Ramsey, F. P. Truth and probability. In R. B. Braithwaite, editor, *The Foundations of Mathematics and Other Logical Essays*. The Humanities Press, New York, NY, 1950.

Rawls, J. B. *A Theory of Justice*. Harvard University Press, Cambridge, MA, 1971.

Regenwetter, M., Grofman, B., Marley, A., and Tsetlin, I. *Behavioral Social Choice*. Cambridge University Press, Cambridge, UK, 2006.

Russell, B. *Human Society in Ethics and Politics*. Allen and Unwin, London, 1954.

Russell, S. J. and Norvig, P. *Artificial Intelligence: A Modern Approach*. Prentice-Hall, Upper Saddle River, NJ, 2nd edition, 2003.

Sartorius, C. *An Evolutionary Approach to Social Welfare*. Routledge, London, UK, 2003.

Satterthwaite, M. A. Strategy-proofness and arrow's conditions: existence and correspondence theorems for voting procedures in social welfare functions. *Journal of Economic Theory*, 10:187–217, 1975.

Savage, L. J. *The Foundations of Statistics*. John Wiley & Sons, New York, NY, 1954. Second revised edition published by Dover in 1972.

Schelling, T. C. *The Strategy of Conflict*. Harvard University Press, Cambridge, MA, 1960.

Scitovsky, T. A note on welfare propositions in economics. *Review of Economic Studies*, 9(1):77–88, 1941.

Sen, A. K. Rational fools: a critique of the behavioral foundations of economic theory. *Philosophy & Public Affairs*, 6(4):317–344, 1977.

Collective Choice and Social Welfare. Elsevier Science Publishers, B. V., Amsterdam, The Netherlands, 1979.

Shamma, J. S., editor. *Cooperative Control of Distributed Multi-Agent Systems*. John Wiley & Sons, Chichester, UK, 2007.

Shannon, C. E. A mathematical theory of communication. *Bell System Technical Journal*, 27:379–423,623–656, 1948. This paper was printed in two parts.

Shannon, C. E. and Weaver, W. *The Mathematical Study of Communication*. University of Illinois Press, Urbana, IL, 1949.

Shoham, Y. and Leyton-Brown, K. *Multiagent Systems*. Cambridge University Press, Cambridge, UK, 2009.

Shubik, M. *Game Theory in the Social Sciences*. MIT Press, Cambridge, MA, 1982.

Game theory and operations research: some musings 50 years later. Yale School of Management Working Paper No. ES-14, 2001.

Simon, H. A. A behavioral model of rational choice. *Quarterly Journal of Economics*, 59:99–118, 1955.

The role of expectations in an adaptive or behavioristic model. In *Models of Bounded Rationality*, volume 2, pp. 380–399. MIT Press, Cambridge, MA, 1982.

Rationality in psychology and economics. In R. M. Hogarth and M. W. Reder, editors, *Rational Choice*. University of Chicago Press, Chicago, 1986.

Sober, E. and Wilson, D. S. *Unto Others: The Evolution and Psychology of Unselfish Behavior*. Harvard University Press, Cambridge, MA, 1998.

Steedman, I. and Krause, U. Goethe's *Faust*, Arrow's Possibility Theorem and the individual decision maker. In J. Elster, editor, *The Multiple Self*, chapter 8, pp. 197–231. Cambridge University Press, Cambridge, UK, 1985.

Stirling, W. C. *Satisficing Games and Decision Making With Applications to Engineering and Computer Science*. Cambridge University Press, Cambridge, UK, 2003.

Theory of Conditional Games. Cambridge University Press, Cambridge, UK, 2012.

Sugden, R. Thinking as a team: towards an explanation of nonselfish behavior. *Social Philosophy and Policy*, 10:69–89, 1993.

Team preferences. *Economics and Philosophy*, 16:175–204, 2000.

The logic of team reasoning. *Philosophical Explorations*, 6:165–181, 2003.

Tversky, A. and Kahenman, D. Rational choice and the framing of decisions. In R. M. Hogarth and M. W. Reder, editors, *Rational Choice*, pp. 67–94. University of Chicago Press, Chicago, IL, 1986.

Unger, P. *Ignorance: A Case for Skepticism*. Oxford University Press, Oxford, UK, 1975.

van Mill, D. *Deliberation, Social Choice and Absolute Democracy*. Routledge, New York, NY, 2006.

von Hayek, F. A. The use of knowledge in society. *American Economic Review*, 35:519–530, 1945.

Vlassis, N., editor. *A Concise Introduction to Multiagent Systems and Distributed Artificial Intelligence*. Morgan & Claypool Publishers, San Rafael, CA, 2007.

von Neumann, J. and Morgenstern, O. *The Theory of Games and Economic Behavior*. Princeton University Press, Princeton, NJ, 1944. (2nd edition 1947).

Weick, K. E. *Sensemaking in organizations*. Sage Publications, Thousand Oaks, CA, 1995.

Weiss, G., editor. *Multiagent Systems*. MIT Press, Cambridge, MA, 1999.

Whitehead, A. N. *Adventures in Ideas*. Macmillan, London, 1937.

Williams, J. R G. Generalized probabilism: Dutch books and accuracy domination. *Journal of Philosophical Logic*, 41:811–840, 2012.

Yanovskaya, E. B. A probabilistic model of social choice. In *Russian Contributions to Game Theory and Equilibrium Theory*, chapter 2. Springer-Verlag, Berlin, 2006.

Young, H. P. Social choice scoring functions. *SIAM Journal of Applied Mathematics*, 28:824–838, 1975.

Zadeh, L. A. What is optimal? *IRE Transactions on Information Theory*, 4 (1):3, 1958.

Zeckhauser, R. Majority rule with lotteries on alternatives. *Quarterly Journal of Economics*, 83:696–703, 1969.

Authors

Abbas, A. E. 53, 73
Andrzejak, R. G. 184
Arrow, H. 29
Arrow, K. J. 2, 5, 6, 8, 11, 12, 19, 33, 40, 99
Axelrod, R. 10, 30, 37, 96

Bacharach, M. 30, 82, 97
Badger, J. H. 184
Bailey, K. 178
Bakker, R. 29
Balinski, M. 30
Banzhaf, J. 29
Battigalli, P. 29
Bendor, J. B. 136
Bentham, J. 25
Berdahl, J. L. 29
Berhold, M. H. 53
Bicchieri, C. 30, 96, 97
Blackwell, D. 124
Bolton, G. E. 29
Bossert, W. 30
Burns, T. 56

Camerer, C. 29
Cartwright, D. 37
Castagnoli, E. 53
Castellano, C. 20
Chen, W. 135
Chen, X. 184
Christakis, N. A. 20
Cohen, J. 75
Colman, A. M. 29
Condorcet, M. J. A. N. 5
Cooper, R. W. 96
Coughlin, P. J. 72
Cover, T. M. 178
Cowell, R. G. 59

Dawid, A. P. 59
de Finetti, B. 46

DeGroot, M. H. 29
Dewey, J. 9
Doob, J. L. 81, 174
Drèze, J. H. 19
Dryzek, J. S. 75
Dufwenberg, M. 29
Dyer, J. S. 144

Easley, D. 4, 96
Edgeworth, F. Y. 14
Einstein, A. 20

Fefferman, N. H. 30
Fehr, E. 12, 29
Ferguson, T. S. 124
Fishburn, P. C. 42, 50, 72
Fortunato, S. 20
Fowler, J. H. 20
French, J. R. P. 29
Friedkin, N. 29
Friedkin, N. E. 29
Friedman, M. 7, 8, 10

Gaertner, W. 62
Galilei, G. 1
Gantmacher, F. 174
Geanakoplos, J. 29
Genesereth, M. R. 4
Georgescu-Roegen, N. 178
Gibbard, A. 22, 24, 33, 43, 69, 88
Gilboa, I. 29
Ginsberg, M. L. 4
Girshick, M. A. 124
Goodin, R. E. 11
Goyal, S. 4, 96
Grabisch, M. 29
Grassberger, P. 184
Grofman, B. 30

Habermas, J. 75
Hansson, B. 42

Harsanyi, J. 51, 103, 134, 148
Hayek, F. A. von 10
Henrich, J. 29
Hicks, J. R. 150
Hoede, C. 29
Holmes, S. 21
Homans, G. C. 10
Howard, R. A. 53, 73
Hu, X. 29

Intriligator, M. D. 72

Jackson, M. O. 4, 96
James, W. 139
Jaynes, E. T. 55, 73
Jensen, F. V. 59
Johnson, E. C. 29
Johnson-Laird, P. N. 140
Johnson, P. E. 7

Kahenman, D. 2, 133
Kaldor, N. 150
Karni, E. 19, 29
Kearney, P. 184
Keeney, R. L. 144
Kemeny, J. 46
Kirchsteiger, G. 29
Kleinberg, J. 4, 96
Kolmogorov, A. 52
Kraskov, A. 184
Krause, U. 148
Kreps, D. M. 124, 135
Kumar, S. 136
Kwong, S. 184

Lam, S. W. 144
Laraki, R. 30
Lauritzen, S. L. 59
Lehman, R. S. 46
Levi, I. 139
Lewis, D. K. 96, 97
Leyton-Brown, K. 4, 96
Li, M. 184
LiCalzi, M. 53
Loreto, V. 20
Luce, R. D. 6
Luenberger, D. G. 174

Mackie, G. 75
Margolis, H. 148
Marley, A. 30

McGrath, J. E. 29
Morgenstern, O. 122, 124

Neveu, J. 173
Ng, K. L. 30
Ng, T. S. 144
Nisan, N. 4
Norvig, P. 4

Ockenfels, A. 29

Palmer, F. R. 21
Parsons, S. 4
Pazgal, A. 136
Pearce, D. 29
Pearl, J. 55, 59
Penrose, L. S. 29
Polya, G. 133
Popper, K. R. 141
Prigogine, I. 178

Qi, C. X. 30

Raiffa, H. 6, 144
Ramsey, F. P. 46
Rawls, J. B. 25, 37, 63, 134
Regenwetter, M. 30
Rosenschein, J. S. 4
Roughgharden, T. 4
Rusinowska, A. 29
Russell, B. 134
Russell, S. J. 4

Sarin, R. K. 144
Sartorius, C. 30
Satterthwaite, M. A. 33, 43
Savage, L. J. 71
Schelling, T. C. 83, 96, 97
Schmeidler, D. 19, 29
Schmidt, K. 12, 29
Scitovsky, T. 150
Sen, A. K. 7, 13, 14, 33, 148
Shannon, C. E. 99, 178
Shapley, L. S. 29
Shoham, Y. 4, 96
Shubik, M. 5, 8, 12
Siegel, D. A. 136
Sim, M. 144
Sim, W. 135
Simon, H. A. 38, 135
Sober, E. 8

Song, J. H. 144
Spiegelhalter, D. J. 59
Stacchetti, E. 29
Stalker, G. M. 56
Steedman, I. 148
Stirling, W. C. xvii, xxii, 145
Stöbauer, H. 184
Sugden, R. 30, 82, 97

Tardos, E. 4
Thomas, J. A. 178
Tsetlin, I. 30
Tversky, A. 2, 133

Unger, P. 137

van Mill, D. 75
Vazirani, V. V. 4

Vind, K. 19
von Neumann, J. 122, 124

Weaver, W. 178
Weick, K. E. 29
Weymark, J. A. 30
Whitehead, A. N. 141
Williams, J. R G. 158
Wilson, D. S. 8
Wooldridge, M. 4

Yanovskaya, E. B. 72
Young, H. P. 35

Zadeh, L. A. 133
Zang, H. 184
Zeckhauser, R. 72

Index

abstraction, 1, 4, 8, 27
acyclicity, 54, 56
affine transformations, 51
aggregation, xxi, 1, 28, 32
  Arrovian, 5, 11, 32, 33
  classical, 33
  coherent, 57
  coordinated, 37
  endogenous, 88
  exogenous, 88
aggregation theorem, 59
agreement, 49
alternative set, 5
altruism, 8, 9, 12
atoms, 148

Bayes rule, 61, 172
Bayesian network, xxi, xxiii, 58–60,
    76, 163
  acyclic, 76
  dynamic, 76
binary digits, 100
bivariate ordering, 49
boldness index, 147
Boolean algebra, 140, 145, 169

channel capacity, 101
collaboration, 82
commitment, 14, 16
communication theory, 99
comparisons
  binary, 2
  inter-alternative, 143
  intra-alternative, 144
  ordinal, 2
compromise, 9
Condorcet paradox, 1, 84
congruency, 51
conjecture, xxi, 18
  conditioning, 18

  rejecting, 151
  selecting, 151
  stochastic, 117
conjecture lottery, 124
conjecture profile, 18, 38
cooperation, 9
coordinatability, 108
coordination, xvii, xxii, 9
  conflictive, 98
  cooperative, 98
  definition, 28, 37, 97
  deliberative, 82
  endogenous, 39, 60, 97
  exogenous, 38, 97
  satisficing, 156
  stochastic, 117
coordination function
  deterministic, 118
  expected, 124
  rejecting, 152
  selecting, 152
  steady-state, 94
coordination index, 111
coordination ordering, 38, 62
cost-benefit analysis, 150
cycles
  k-cycle, 77
  embedded, 91
  non-root, 92
  non-simple, 89
  root, 92
  simple, 77
  subcycles, 89

degrees of comparison, 136
deliberation, xx, xxii, 74, 75
democracy, 1, 40, 75
  deliberative, 82
  operational, 45
  pure, 40

dialogue, xxii, 74, 75
dictator, 41
dispersion, 110, 182
    relative, 110, 184
dispersion measure, 111
dispositional modes, 149
Dutch book, 158
Dutch book theorem, xxi, xxiii,
    46, 158

ecological fitness, 28, 37
effectiveness, 144
egoism, 3, 8
eigenvalue, 81
eigenvector, 81
Einstein's razor, 20
emergence, 32, 37, 38, 40, 60, 62,
    72, 98, 114
entropy, 101, 104, 178
    chain rule, 179
    conditional, 179
    joint, 106
epistemic utility theory, 139
epistemology, 51
error avoidance, 138, 139
expected utility, 123
    conditional, 124
    coordination, 119, 124
    marginal, 125, 130

failure avoidance, 142
fairness, 12
Frobeneiius–Perron theorem, 174

game theory
    behavioral, 29
    psychological, 29
graph theory
    d-separation, 167
    acyclic, 17
    blocked vertex, 165
    child, 18
    closed path, 17
    connections
        converging, 165
        diverging, 165
        serial, 163
    descendants, 18
    directed, 17
    edges, 17

parent, 18
vertices, 17

hypothetical proposition, 18, 19,
    44, 52
    antecedent, 19, 52
    consequent, 19, 52

impossibility theorem, 5, 6, 9, 26,
    33, 48
independence
    conditional, 77, 163
    random variables, 172
    social, 61
    statistical, 170
inefficiency, 144
information, 101
    definition, 104
    mutual, 101, 107
    self, 104
informational value of rejection, 139
interpersonal comparability, 51
invariance, 54, 56, 57
inverse image, 171
isomorphism, 47
    order, 44
    sure gain, subversion, 46
    sure loss, subjugation, 46

Jensen's inequality, 180

linear ordering, 3
    conditional, 18
    social, 5
lottery, 47

majority judgment, 30
marginalization, 60
Markov chain, 176
Markov convergence theorem, 80, 174
Markov process, 77
material benefit, 13
mixed strategies, xxii
mixed strategy, 122
multiple selves, 148
mutual information, 101, 106,
    114, 180

negotiation sets, 63
network, 3
    acyclic, 59, 60

Bayesian, 58
dynamic, 77
stable, 76
stationary, 76
stochastic, 117
trivial, 3, 17

Occam's razor, 20
opportunity cost, 103
optimization, 133, 134, 136
  constrained, 134

positive matrices, 174
praxeology, 51, 53
preference
  conditional, xxi
  cyclic, xxii, 83
preference profile, 5, 11,
    26, 33
  conditional, 20
preferences
  ex ante, xix, 6, 37
  categorical, 6, 9, 16, 37
  conditional, 18, 26
  coordination, 60
  cyclic, 74, 85
  randomized, 122
  stationary, 76
price system, 10
probability mass function, 171
  conditional, 172
  joint, 171
  marginal, 172
probability mass vector, 176
  steady-state, 177
  transition, 176
probability measure, 169, 170
  conditonal, 170
probability space, 170
probability theory, 72
  axioms, 48, 160
  chain rule, 54, 59, 170
  frequentist, 52
  subjective, 52
profile
  conditional, 20
  conjecture, 18
  stochastic, 117

random variable, 116, 117,
    121, 171
randomization, xxii
rationality
  expanded, 9
  group, 1, 5
  individual, 1–3, 6, 7
  operational definition, 2–4
  satisficing, 149
  social, 5, 6
Rawlesianism, 25, 37, 63,
    135
reactive behavior, 11
reframing, 69
resource conservation, 143
responsive behavior, 13

sample space, 121, 169, 173
satisficing, xxii
  neo, 137
  Simonian, 135, 136
satisficing set, 147
  compromise, 153
  individual, 153
  network, 152
scoring rule, 35
  Borda rank-order rule, 36
  plurality rule, 35
self-interest, 2, 3, 8, 9, 15
Shannon information theory,
    xxii, 99
singleton set, 34, 142, 147, 170
small groups, 29
social benefit, 13
social choice function, 34, 62
  Arrovian, 40
  Borda, 36
  plurality, 35
  rejecting, 152
  selecting, 152
  social justice, 37
  utilitarian, 36
social choice model
  dynamic, 76
  stable, 76
social choice rule, 33
  consistent, 34
  symmetry, 34
    anonymity, 34
    neurality, 34

social choice theory
  Arrovian, 33
  behavioral, 30
  coordinated, xx
  deliberative, 75, 82
  deterministic, 132
  randomized, 115
  satisficing, 151
  stochastic, 116
social coherence, 39, 42, 43, 45, 46, 48
social evolution, 30
social framework
  anarchy, 10
  collective, 10, 11
  network, 20
social influence, xix, xx, 12, 17, 20,
      28, 37, 38, 106, 108, 111, 115
  cyclic, 76
  dynamic, 76
social influence propagation, xxi, 17,
      76, 83
social model, 4, 24, 28, 38
  endogenous, 4, 27, 60, 72
  exogenous, 4, 27
social welfare function, 5, 33
solution concept, 34, 40, 62
  compromise, 63
  coordination, 62
  satisficing, 133
subjugation, 42, 44, 46
subordination function, 103
subversion, 41, 44
suppression, 42

sure loss, 46, 47
sure win, 48
surprise function, 102
sympathy, 14, 16

team reasoning, 30, 82, 97
transition mass function, 116, 117
transition matrix, 176
  closed-loop, 79
  regular, 80, 176
  state-to-state, 78
transition probability measure, 172

unanimity principle, 42
utilitarianism, 25, 36
utility
  ex ante, 61
  ex post, 61
  categorical, 60
  conditional, 60, 62
  satisficing, 147
  steady-state, 81
utility density function, 125
utility mass function
  ex post marginals, 61
  categorical, 50
  conditional, 50
  rejecting, 148
  selecting, 148
utility mass vector, 78

von Neumann–Morgenstern theorem,
      123

Printed in the United States
By Bookmasters